Interpretation from A to Z

Philip McShane

M.Sc., Lic. Phil., S.T.L., D. Phil. Oxon.

AXIAL PUBLISHING
Vancouver

COPYRIGHT © 2020 by Philip McShane
All rights reserved. No part of this publication may be reproduced, stored in a retrieval system, or transmitted, in any form or by any means, photocopying, electronic, mechanical, recording, or otherwise, without prior permission of the copyright holders.

Axial Publishing
2-675 Victoria Drive
Vancouver, British Columbia
V5L 4E3 Canada
www.axialpublishing.com

Canadian Cataloguing in Publication Data
McShane, Philip, 1932–
Interpretation from A to Z

ISBN   978-1-988457-06-2
1. Methodology   2. Philosophy   3. Religious Studies   I. Title

Text layout and cover:
James Duffy

For my collaborator

James Duffy,

who shares my dreams and screams

Table of Contents

Preface i
Introduction ix
A ~ An Adventure: Interpretation from A to Z 1
B ~ {Assembling (Interpretations)³ }⁴ 9
C ~ Interpreting "The Divine Missions" 15
D ~ Canons of Engineering 19
E ~ *Cantower* XIV 27
F ~ The Full Problem of Development 55
G ~ *Insight*'s Search for Genetic Control 59
H ~ A Potential Totality 63
I ~ Self-Assembly: The I of the Storm 71
J ~ Inventing Techniques 75
K ~ A Universal Language 83
L ~ Bridges 89
M ~ 60910 93
N ~ Abstruse Principals 99
O ~ Understanding the Object 107
P ~ Understanding the Words 113
Q ~ Understanding the Author 119
R ~ Understanding Oneself 127
S ~ Correct Enclosing 131
T ~ A Clarification 137
U ~ Stating the Meaning of the Text 141
V ~ "Do you know His Kingdom?" 145
W ~ *Insight* Chapter 17 in a Geohistorical Engineering Context 151
X ~ The Truth 161
Y ~ Stalking Jesus 165
Z ~ *The Future* as Life Stile: From Mild Mess to Wild Bliss 171
Epilogue: The Fallen Flower 175
Method Going Mainstreet: Deliberated Backfiring 183

I'll so offend to make offense a skill,
Redeeming time when men think least I will.

—Shakespeare, *Henry the Fourth*, Part One, I.ii.209–10

PREFACE

The demands of "a statistically effective form for the new cycle of human action"[1] within Lonergan studies pushes me into writing this brief blunt preface.

This little book is offensive in a very full sense. It is an attack on conventional reading or interpretation reaching to those who aspire to get scientifically beyond common sense, particularly those involved with writing or teaching in Lonergan studies. But it also is offensive in a sense nicely spoken of in the Shakespeare of my Frontispiece: "I'll so offend to make offense a skill / redeeming time when men think least I will."[2] In my 89th year I may not be expected to attack three or four generations of Lonergan students: not them all of course: indeed, if you are poised to read this book seriously, with a Dionysian bent,[3] you are probably not one of them. The attack is indirect, since the book is addressed to present young people interested in what Lonergan points to in his writings. Why is it not directly addressed to the few generations of Lonergan between me and them? Because I am sadly of the opinion that those generations are psychically cut off from what I am writing about here. Further, their writings and teachings and theses-directings "increase the confusion and accelerate the doom,"[4] and this "at a rather critical moment in the historical process."[5]

---

[1] "Essay in Fundamental Sociology," *Lonergan's Early Economic Research*, edited with commentary by Michael Shute, University of Toronto Press, 2010, 20. I refer to this Essay throughout the book as *Essay in Fundamental Sociology*.

[2] The end of the Prince's speech and the conclusion of Act 1 scene ii of *Henry the Fourth, Part 1*. The full speech is a relevant reading. Try J-Wrapping it! See below, Essay P, notes 17 and 18, 116.

[3] *CWL* 10, *Topics in Education*, 40, line 1 puts it nicely. "Man insisting on the good of order is Apollonian; but as ready to tear it all down is Dionysian." The issue is to tear it down creatively, to meet climate issues, to lift us to the positive Anthropocene. The present stale poise in Lonergan studies is just not in that ballpark. For light on this see my Helsinki Climate Change Paper of 2019, available as *Æcornomics 5*: "Structuring the Reach towards the Future" (http://www.philipmcshane.org/ecornomics). A context is the previous essay there, *Æcornomics 3*: A Common Quest Manifesto." On the Dionysian, see further note 23 of Essay S below, p. 134.

[4] *CWL* 18, *Phenomenology and Logic*, 308.

[5] *Ibid.*, 300.

INTERPRETATION FROM A TO Z

My problem in getting this book effectively "out" is getting it past that opposition. For instance, for decades I have nudged those colleagues of mine to take seriously Lonergan's compact and brilliant non-functional challenge of the turn-of-the-page paragraph *Insight* 609–10.[6] They remain fixed in the mythology of lines 3–8 of *Insight* 604. This book certainly will not be read or recommended by them. Are you a student that might cunningly annoy them? Cunningly? I recall Lonergan writing to me in 1968 about handling my work in Oxford: "Give the guy what he wants. It's only a union card." You may not even have a scientific bent, but still you sniff the settled rot, and you may be inclined to "out" the need. Perhaps do it cautiously. On the other hand, you could take a leaf out of Greta Thunberg's gallant book.

But let me take a practical turn now. This little book moves along with many twists and turns, but it is also a straightforward help to begin to read properly the two main treatments by Lonergan of the topic of Interpretation: Section 3 of chapter 17 of *Insight*, and chapter 7 of *Method in Theology*. You might find it useful to read my text here first without venturing into the notes. Indeed, rambling round the alphabet sections can be an enlightening venture.

Chapter 7 of *Method in Theology* is a good starting point. You have read it or been led to read it by experts. The leading and the reading were, I suspect, in some way that tied the effort to present conventions. Lonergan's intention was quite other: as we'll see better in our alphabet ramble, his intentions were to start a revolution in the strategies of interpretation. Thinking of seeing thus better in our ramble is our problem here, yours and mine. I ask for patience and a strange poise of—perhaps I can say repetitively—Dionysian expectation. What do I mean by that? Well, there is your first brush with the problem of patience. As I move along through the alphabet I shall return regularly but colorfully to topics like this "Dionysian expectation." For the moment there is Lonergan's pointing, already quoted in note 3. "Man as insisting on the good of order is Apollonian; but as ready to tear it down he is Dionysian."[7]

I am ready to tear up Lonergan studies, and of course wish you to join me. Tearing up: thinking of Archimedes screwing up water![8] I have been trying to

---

[6] But what have I myself done in the zone of interpretation? Little beyond puttering along, since 1956, trying to glimpse and promote Lonergan's shocking shake-up of philosophy and theology. I am just a mathematician that strayed into methodology.

[7] *CWL* 10, *Topics in Education*, 40, top lines.

[8] See the diagram on page 19 below, at the beginning of Essay D.

Preface

screw up Lonergan studies since 1961[9]: I have failed. I think of Samuel Beckett: "Try again; fail again; fail better."[10] But, no, that is not good enough for me in this, my last shot. This shot I intend to be a success—well, ho ho in the very long run!

But now I am distracted helpfully by my memory of one of my shots at screwing up. It occurred during the Montreal Concordia Conference on Interpretation that gave rise to the volume *Lonergan's Hermeneutics. Its Development and Application*.[11] The morning that I was to reply to a paper by Fr. Bob Doran, I had a leap of imagination which gave me what is now a centerpiece of my grip on future effective intervention in human progress: but here think of it as simply rocking the boat at the conference. I have written about the failure of the gathering and the volume,[12] and this little book will give you, as it does me, a better perspective on it. Briefly, we moved along cozily in that meeting without venturing into either of the topics functional collaboration or the canons of hermeneutics. Instead of sharing my published comments on Bob Doran's paper during my presentation I risked sketching my entire leap on the blackboard, a sketch you find on the page iv.

There were a few bright questions, but in the main it screwed nothing up, nor has it since. Let us see, or let you see, if you get a laugh and a nudge out of my mad presentation. And I note that a grip on your spontaneous response is important. Diagrams generally frighten people, put people off. So, try a little

---

[9] "The Contemporary Thomism of Bernard Lonergan," *Philosophical Studies*, Ireland, 1962. The article is available as *Published Article* no. 2, (http://www.philipmcshane.org/published-articles). I sing along with Robin Gibbs on the failed effort in *Æcornomics 6*: "I Started a Joke." The *Æcornomics* series is available at: http://www.philipmcshane.org/ecornomics.

[10] I think, too, of Lonergan marking with approval, as he read Beckett's remark quoted on p. 67 of my 1976 book *Lonergan's Challenge to the University and the Economy*. (His marked copy, photocopied, is available at: http://www.philipmcshane.org/published-books). "Here is direct expression—pages and pages of it. And if you don't understand it, Ladies and Gentlemen, it is because you are too decadent to receive it. You are not satisfied unless form is so strictly divorced from content that you can comprehend the one almost without bothering to read the other. This rapid skimming and absorption of the scant cream of sense is made possible by what I may call a continuous process of copious intellectual salivation. The form that is an arbitrary and independent phenomenon can fulfill no higher function that that of a stimulus for a tertiary or quartary conditioned reflex of dribbling comprehension." (Beckett, "Dante … Bruno. Vico … Joyce," *Our Exagmination Round His Factification For Incamination of Work in Progress*. A New Direction Book, New York, 1972, 13.

[11] Edited by Sean E. McEvenue and Ben F. Meyer, The Catholic University of America, 1989.

[12] I commented, in *Cantower 9, Positions, Poisitions, Protopossession* (available at: http://www.philipmcshane.org/cantowers), pp. 21–24, on this volume, with fair tolerance. But it is, I see more clearly now, a dismal failure.

humor here. It is of serious consequence in our efforts to listen "with sincere respect to the Stoic description of the Wise Man, and then request an introduction."[13]

My normative description of the wise men and women of the future needs to draw on the "possible functions of satire and humor," but now think of the joke being on you, in you, in my tossing before you the diagram that I eventually identified as W_3. Take seriously Lonergan's final pointer in that strange section of chapter 18 of *Insight*. "Humor can aid him to the discovery of the complex problem of grasping and holding the nettle of a restricted effective freedom."[14] And now perhaps the aid I provide can have a response more like you lying on your back awaiting a cataract removal. So here you have it, so easily passed by, aye. Pause please and look it in the eye, the I, the possible Aye. How does it strike you?

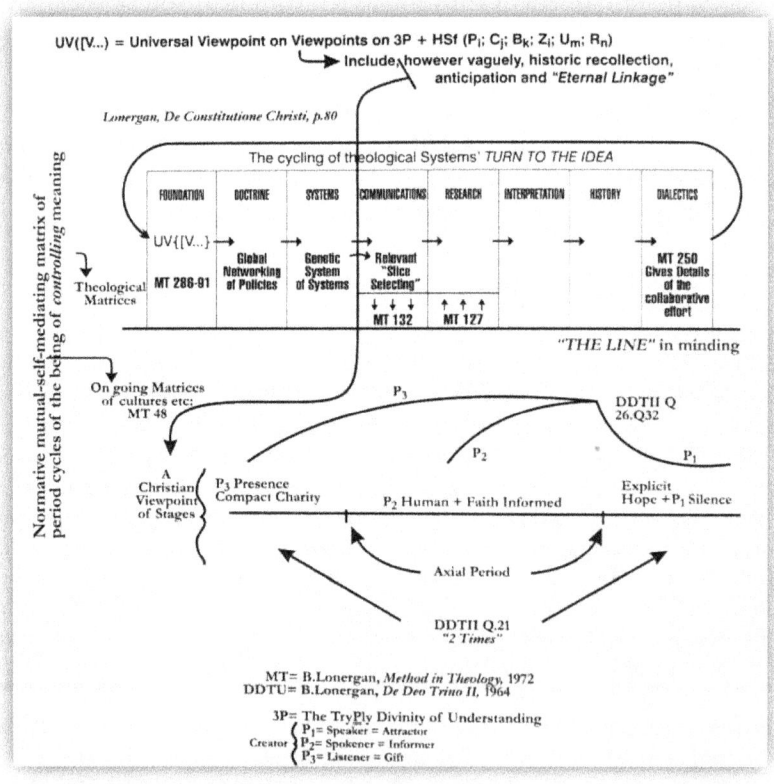

---

[13] *CWL* 3, *Insight*, 649.
[14] *Ibid.*, final lines.

Preface

The diagram surely strikes you as horridly complicated, certainly way too much to "take in" even at a very long glance. But then you are not expected to take it in even at a week of glancings and dancings round its bits and pieces. If you did school chemistry you would recall the periodic table, sometimes even placed at the beginning, the inside cover, of a grade 12 book. Taking it in: well, that is a matter of going beyond a first degree in chemistry. But at any stage, even an initial stage, it helps you hold the stuff together as you climb. Does that idea brighten your gaze at W_3? You are heading into, say, London, not Lonergan: a map is useful. W_3 is my suggestion of a map.

That Montreal conference was my first effort to rock the "interpretation boat" with W_3. It rocked nothing, then or since. But let us move back to my present effort to rock the boat in a manner that can help you to move into its odd alphabetic challenge. Then think of my effort as one that might rock the boat of the conventional readings of chapter seven of *Method in Theology*. So, after this Preface you might well go directly to that rocking in the Essays O, P, Q, R, S, T, U, which parallel the seven sections 2, 3, 4, 5, 6, 7, 8, of that seventh chapter. The key problem emerges—might I say gently and obviously emerges?—in Essay O: the problem of acknowledging the need for a genetic grip of the knowing of the object.[15] What sort of a genetic grip? Well, that is the puzzle of this entire book, about which I wish to say no more here.

Might you venture into reading the entire book after this smaller venture into seven of its sections? I leave that decision to you, but I do suggest that you might sadistically enjoy the lift to your reading of those sections that you get by turning over in your minding the suggestion of Essay J, that there are two possible types of reading of those sections, indeed of anything. That distinguishing is key to a massive lift of all of Lonergan studies. But no more about that here: nor do I wish to get into further pointings about the subtle pedagogical mishmash of topics in the alphabet soup.

The pedagogical effort led me to some strange jugglings. Obviously, relevant to the effort was my own long climb these past sixty-four years: my notes focus on that, and I avoid references to others, even if they agree, since this book might be thought of as a non-apology *pro vita mea*. I have written elsewhere about the norms of such a climb and its strange accelerating character.[16] The normative

---

[15] That brings you to share my problem posed at note 6 above. Might it bring us to slowly rocking the boat and the related boaters?

[16] See e.g. my final pages of *Lack in the Beingstalk*, Axial Publishing, 2006; also the beginning of chapter 2 of *Process: Introducing Themselves to (Young) Christian Minder* (http://www.philipmcshane.org/website-books). The accelerating character is to be a

pattern, when decently attained, leaves you a stranger to yourself of the same date last month. Thus, I am massively strange to you who may well be sixty years younger than me. Can that strangeness be conveyed? Oh la la that is a question for a mature distant science of interpretation. But I was led to give you a definite illustration of a month's climb by my initial attempt at Essay E, where I wished to sketch my long climb towards the meaning of Lonergan's canons of hermeneutics: the sketching just was not working. So it dawned on me that a month of my climb in that searching presented to you even as printed in my series of *Cantowers* would work better—a statistical business. Thus, Essay E became just a presentation of my April climb of 2005, part of which month I spent moving around New York, thinking of its engineering needs. Pause to imagine the day of those days that I spent going by public transport from the Bronx to Coney Island—to walk there on its beach and in its waters—and back, musing, as I would put it now, on the educative engineering of the future of Manhattan. This is not your climb, but there is the possibility of some parallel madness of sanity, as I suggested in another essay after a week of walking round my native Dublin, "The Dialectic of My Town, *Ma Vlast.*"[17]

The deeper problem of reading Essay E is to sense the gap[18] between the writing of the younger me—I was only 71—from my more advanced grip 18 years later. Does that help in facing the challenge of detecting the advanced grip Lonergan had on interpretation when he wrote of it in *Method in Theology* 16 years after his 1953 effort?

My concluding puzzle in this Preface, for you and me, is, what can help us students of Lonergan escape from the shambles of present Lonergan studies?" I think of Fred Crowe writing 56 years ago. "This is rather blunt, I am afraid, but is there not room for a measure of bluntness at this stage?"[19]

And here you come to my second boat-rocking illustration of this Preface.

Read again part of Crowe's comment: "is there not room for a measure of bluntness at this stage?" Has it become more suggestive? Not yet. Think now of

---

norm in the positive Anthropocene. At present there is the ethos that had Maslow writing of less than 1% of adults growing.

[17] The title of *Quodlibet 8*, written after living through the disastrous gathering—LOL: a paper every thirty minutes!—in Regis College Toronto, commemorating Lonergan's 100th birthday.

[18] The gap and this sensing is to become increasingly normative as we enter the positive Anthropocene age.

[19] "The Exigent Mind," p. 27 of the word edited by Crowe, *Spirit as Inquiry. Studies in Honor of Bernard Lonergan, S.J.*, Herder and Herder, New York, 1964.

Preface

Lonergan battling towards a fresh effective *nomos* of bluntness as he worked on a new meaning of dialectic. What is that new meaning? It is, here, the topic of Essay I, a shocking challenge to the community of "I"s that face the effective detection of progress. Do I not thus leave you nicely in suspense as we come to the end—the *finis*, which is to bring you to suspense and self-suspicions—of the Preface?[20]

---

[20] I have pretty well completed the book, but pause now over it and its effect, and write this final footnote. Frankly, I am not optimistic. Our culture of reading is such that you can float over the words in the mood and ethos of one who pretty-well understands. Think of how you happily read words like *light* or *electricity*, with no sense of the "quite beyond me" even of the partial meaning of Maxwell's Equations. If you have never done any serious physics, then that is your crippling poise, and it would take a miracle of Graceful belief to get you moving, thinking, climbing otherwise. I return once again to Lonergan's brutal statements of *CWL* 6, *Philosophical and Theological Papers 1958–1964*, both from 1963, (page 121 of "Time and Meaning" and page 155 of Exegesis and Dogma), both lectures to audiences that I know were quite entrenched in the ethos of commonsense competence, "never bitten by theory" (155) "lost in some no man's land between the world of theory and the world of common sense" (121). So back to my final question: "Do I not thus leave you nicely in suspense as we come to the end—the *finis*, which is to bring you to suspense and self-suspicions—of the Preface?" Perhaps my added footnote tilts a few readers towards the cultural shock and the effective YES that anticipates the breakthrough to the positive Anthropocene age. But the vast majority float on in brutal destructiveness, as they have floated past Lonergan's familiar voice and words for sixty years.

INTRODUCTION

We make a beginning on this odd book that seems to purport some full treatment of the topic of Interpretation by suggesting a ramble convenient for your own interests round meanings of interpretations. You may be someone who regularly interprets poets to a grade 12 class; you may be someone interpreting biology for a university-level class. Think of your successes and failures. The successes, of course, are cheerier topics, remembrances of good things past. I think now of two of my successes in teaching areas that lead me right into my topic. First, a grade 12 boys' class to which I was just a visitor, and one of my topics was catching on, in the mental sense, when playing soccer football. In particular, I was talking about the goalkeeper for a penalty shot catching on, cutely, to the subtle run-up moves of the penalty-taker. But I wrote on the board at one stage, "What is a schoolboy" and paused. One bright boy remarked, "Sir, you forgot the question mark." Had I? So, we settled down to interpret the four words "what is a schoolboy." Might you notice here a lucky road to self-discovery for the lads?

The other illustration that I cherish was my teaching a second-year university course on engineering mathematics. I was in the middle of handling, on the blackboard, a machine rotation problem, when it dawned on me that I was, so to speak, handling it alone with my weaving around integrals and differentiations. I turned to the class—a group of over 400 students staring down at that instant at me, paused in their note-taking—and asked "how many of you know what this differentiation and integration stuff is about?" A great deal of head-shaking led to suggest that we break off for a couple of days and try to make sense of the process: which we did.[1]

My illustrations are certainly just that but they are more. "What is an Interpreter." Is that not a lead in to our topic? And then there is the problem of each of us engineering our way through classes, as teachers or students, but thus probably engineering our way in a conventional manner that leaves something out, or should I say leaves something to be desired? But desired by whom? "The neglected subject does not know himself. The truncated subject not only does not know himself but is unaware of his ignorance and so, in one way or another,

---

[1] A presentation in line with my effort then is given by Terrance Quinn, "The Calculus Campaign," *Journal of Macrodynamic Analysis*, volume 2 (2002).

concludes that what he does not know does not exist."[2] That quiet claim of Bernard Lonergan goes on to weave comments around "daytime somnambulism," ending the paragraph with realistic "pragmatists would divert our attention to action and results." But how early in human history did the diverting occur? Certainly it haunts Pāṇini's truncated grammar. It cripples modern grammar. Does it haunt the grammar of your interpretations?

So I invite you to spread your interest over history, perhaps like Voegelin, perhaps like Burckhardt, looking for a broader optimistic view of "the eternal stream of human beings, of the strivings of the human spirit."[3] We have recently found a classification for our effect on the evolutionary stream of our human twists in and of that stream: the name of our times is *The Anthropocene Age*. It helps us focus attention on climate change and destructive elements of humanity's striving. But might not we rise to a long-term optimism by thinking of a not-yet positive Anthropocene age, so that we find Lonergan's quiet identification of truncation as grounding a division of the prior negative Anthropocene age into an early neglected subjectivity, wandering higher animals gifted with a W-enzyme,[4] moving into a block-headed stage, the truncated Anthropocene, so blockheaded as to think of itself, Toynbee-style, as generating a series of decent civilizations? You may well pause here over such blockheadedness as 'normal' colonialism, but my aim is your optimism, very long-term optimism about all varieties of colonialism.

Think, then—as I suggested briefly but differently in the Preface—in what I might call wild Dionysian fantasy, of, very literally, a new heading of humanity, reading itself from childhood as a fullness of what. Then what is to be interpreting what to what in a global cycle of what-cherishing that is quite beyond our present fancy. It is to become, by the tenth millennium, a nanochemistry of "dancing on the ceiling"[5] where *nano* means, yes, every little detail of substructural success, but

---

[2] Lonergan, "The Subject," *A Second Collection*, Darton, Longman and Todd, 1974, 73.

[3] Herman Hesse, *The Journey to the East*, London, 1970, 12.

[4] The heuristic notion of W-enzyme was introduced by me on page 2 of the book referenced in the following note. It points to an integral compacting of the layers of human desires, a compacting that is relevant to Lonergan's search for an integral theology. See below, note 4 of Essay L, 90. (Greek: *en-*, in + *zyme*, leaven: a catalyst, initiating, boosting, or speeding reactions.)

[5] I am recalling Lionel Richie's song about "dancing on the ceiling" but also pointing to that dancing achievement—a methodological Gecko business—as it is envisaged in the final chapter of my *The Future: Core Precepts in Supramolecular Chemistry and Nanochemistry* (Axial Publishing, 2019). That oddly titled book is my answer, after 54

Introduction

also an ethos of glocal unity, of **N**ot **A**lone **N**ot **O**paque. The seeding and the stalking of this what-engineering will not be easy. The Latin, *abstrudere*, "to thrust away," gives us the word *abstruse*, and a savoring of the poise of "thrust away" can lift us to a sense of a blockheaded globe whose psyche is busily inert in "the arrogance of omnicompetent common sense."[6] What is being thrust away? What is being thrust away.

How are we to savor that, when we are presently blockheaded from birth, cartooned into toys or us? We become interpreters, warped truncated characters handing on, *"cor ad cor loquitur,"*[7] engineering forward, "the vacant, the empty, the vapid, the insipid, the dull."[8]

I have been writing us towards the mood of thinking of interpretation in the broadest manner, but the vacancy that this little book rambles around is a precise vacancy regarding the climb to "abstruse principles" that are at the heart, in the enzyme-heart, of the human matter. The vacancy is in the sub-population of those who make a life out of interpretation in the normal restricted academic sense. The name *Lonergan* has been mentioned already more than once, and those who know my writings are not surprised at that, but now I home in on my little effort here of interpretation, and it is the interpretation of two sections of the work of Lonergan. The two sections, pretty obviously, are the sections of his work explicitly focused on Interpretation: the third section of his seventeenth chapter in *Insight*, the seventh chapter of his later book, *Method in Theology*.

There are the pointers in the Preface to that homing in, but now I wish to place that pointing, and the pointing of the Introduction so far, in the disturbing context that was touched briefly in the Preface: the context of Essay I in this series, with its odd title, "Self-Assembly: The I of the Storm."

Recall, then, the beginning of the Preface and its end. Both point to the challenge of rocking the boat and boaters effectively. To the general blunt offensive pointing of the second paragraph of the Preface was added the possibility of a definite experience of it in the concluding shifting of the meaning of Fred Crowe's apparently simple commonsense question, "is there not room for

---

years, to Lonergan's questions to me, in 1966, about how to go about writing *Method in Theology*.

[6] *CWL* 17, *Philosophical and Theological Papers*, "Questionnaire on Philosophy: Response," 370.

[7] *Method in Theology* 73[70].

[8] *Ibid.*

a measure of bluntness at this stage?"[9] I can presume that you read it thus if you did read that key article of 1964. But what if it was Lonergan's question of that decade, part of the questioning he shared with me in the summer of 1966? His questions then were about effectively sharing the measure, the *nomos* of theology. In 1962, 31 months before his leap of discovery regarding the cycle of collaboration he had been talking about "The Genetic Circle"[10]: "That circle does not occur just once. It occurs over and over again in a self-correcting process of learning."[11] It was, in his mind, a more subtle version of the circle he had written of in his 30th year.[12] The fuller subtle circle was there after the February leap of 1965, but had he at that stage the measure of bluntness that would be effective? Decades later I began using the quaint title, "A Rolling Stone Gathers *Nomos*,"[13] but I still had not realized how refined his final twist of that measure, that *nomos*, was. Did you?

That question puts you right into the twist. The question is posed in a fulsome context in the chapter that follows that so-titled chapter of *A Brief History of Tongue*, and climbs there to a section 4.3, titled *mos* and *nomos*. The Latin and the Greek help to hint that the effective rolling stone succeeds in "providing a statistically effective form for the next cycle of human action."[14] But my treatment there falls short of pinning down such an effective form, just as Lonergan's treatment of 1969 also does. The failure in Lonergan can be glimpsed from a single paragraph of that essay.

> Now the study of these viewpoints takes one beyond the fact to the reasons for conflict. Comparing them will bring to light just what differences are irreducible, where they are complementary and could be brought together

---

[9] "The Exigent Mind," p. 27 of the word edited by Crowe, *Spirit as Inquiry. Studies in Honor of Bernard Lonergan, S.J.*, Herder and Herder, New York, 1964.

[10] *CWL* 22, *Early Works in Theological Method I*, "Knowing, Believing, and Theology," (July 16, 1962), p. 140.

[11] *Ibid.*

[12] "A fresh intellectual synthesis understanding the new situation created by the old intellectual form and providing a statistically effective form for the next cycle of human action." *Essay in Fundamental Sociology*, 20 (see note 1 of the Preface).

[13] The title is used as a chapter heading both in *A Brief History of Tongue. From Big Bang to Coloured Wholes* (Axial Publishing, 1998) and in *Economics for Everyone. Das Jus Kapital* (Amazon, 3rd edition, 2019).

[14] See note 12.

Introduction

within a larger whole, where finally they can be regarded as successive stages in a single process of development.[15]

Did you get the point, the pointing? If you did, then you are poised to be on my side in this struggle for a science of cyclic interpretation. So, in the words of that text, *Comparing* and *irreducible*, one brightly and cheerily sees and seizes an edging towards the *Comparison* and *Reduction* of section 5 of the tenth chapter of *Method in Theology*.

> *Comparison* examines the completed assembly to seek out affinities and oppositions. *Reduction* finds the same affinity and the same opposition manifested in a number of different manners; from the many manifestations it moves to the underlying root.[16]

Lonergan, you have now noted, was pushing for a refinement of his outline of 1969, a statistically effective refinement. The refinement does not come for him in his division of the process of sifting the past into the "six italicized" processes, *Assembly, Completion, Comparison, Reduction, Classification, Selection*. The leap comes afterwards, and perhaps one can sense its glittering in his eye, his I, as he types "Now" at the beginning of the final paragraph of that section 5, "Dialectic the Structure." He has, indeed, hit on a brilliant structure, a heuristic rescuing of people like Plank, a heuristic grounding of a Kuhnian shift of scientific heuristics. But the heuristic grounding is elusive, a de-truncation process that will elude the truncated, perhaps for centuries. But it can, and does, elude his disciples, claiming to be a culture of "the self-scrutinizing self." Does it elude you, this challenge of the final paragraph of section 5?

I steal here, with twisted meaning, from Lonergan's "A Clarification" of the chapter in *Method in Theology* on Interpretation. The scientific shift "is arduous and time consuming: it leads into the impasse of scrutinizing the self-scrutinizing self and leads into the oddity of the author who writes about himself writing: such authors are rare."[17]

"Scrutinizing the self-scrutinizing self" is a slogan that I shall repeat often in this book, but here I wish you to pause thus over the first of the six italicized words: *Assembly*. Round it there is to be, in this decade, a sub-strategy that could seed the full strategy anticipated by Lonergan. There are problems with the other

---

[15] *Method in Theology*, end of 129[125, mid-page].
[16] *Ibid.*, 250[235].
[17] *Ibid.*, 167[158].

italicized words, especially the key word *Comparison*,[18] that block immediate ventures into the full dialectic method that he advocates. But the process of that last paragraph can be applied in the small domain of suggestions of contributions to progress. Small interested groups—I am not thinking of expert dialectic specialists—can pick any such suggestion and agree to face the exercise of the three objectifications that belong to the task of that final paragraph.[19] For instance, this Introduction could be the object of the exercise. You are asked to brood out your position on it, to brood further towards stating where that positioning leads to in practice, then to circulate the brooding among the group. The first two are two tough tasks, tasks that reveal one's position on a heuristics of progress. But the real trouble is the third objectification. The scrutinizing of the self-scrutinizing subject is pushed to be normatively communal. It becomes a brutal "embarrassing"[20] business of being "at pains not to conceal his tracks but to lay all his cards on the table."[21] Think concretely of the group writing to each other, even being round the table with the cards on it. "You are really way off on the topic," "this is a quite silly view," "you are totally out of date," "you missed Lonergan's point entirely." Whatever.

Have I missed Lonergan's point entirely? Has Lonergan missed out in this paragraph I focus on? Is that why the entire Lonergan tradition —from my point of view, disgustingly—does nothing about this paragraph's brilliant heuristics? "That is rather bluntly said, I am afraid, but it there not room for a measure of bluntness at this stage?"[22] There is need for a measure of bluntness about this measure, this *nomos*, of bluntness, so clearly proposed by the genius you apparently admire.

---

[18] Its meaning is the focus of my recent little book, *The Road to Religious Reality*, Axial Publishing, 2012.

[19] The exercises are, in fact, being organized by James Duffy, and he anticipates publishing the efforts in the *Journal of Macrodynamic Analysis*. He may be contacted at humanistasmorelia@gmail.com.

[20] *Method in Theology*, 299[279]. "Doctrines that are embarrassing will not be mentioned in polite company." The doctrine of this final paragraph of section 5, chapter 10, of *Method of Theology*, is certainly embarrassing, dodged as it has been for 48 years. And I have no inclination to be polite in the matter in 2020.

[21] *Ibid.*, 193[180].

[22] The reference is worth repeating. "The Exigent Mind," p. 27 of the word edited by Crowe, *Spirit as Inquiry. Studies in Honor of Bernard Lonergan, S.J.*, Herder and Herder, New York, 1964.

A ~ An Adventure: Interpretation from A to Z

My beginning of this adventure is really the second musing here. The first was Essay B, which I felt, after a few days' pause, was way too heavy a start on this adventure in and around that shocking third section of chapter 17 of *Insight*. I still find that section shocking, despite my reading it and rereading it for, yes, sixty years. Even the title, "The Truth of Interpretation" shocks me freshly this morning. But let's not go there yet.

What am I trying to do here, in this series of 26 musings about the section? I am having a last shot at getting the Lonergan community to read effectively this shockingly practical piece of writing of Lonergan's odd summer of 1953. I sense the move towards that effectiveness lies initially in a shot at reading the first sentence of the section referentially—should I add, reverentially? At this stage in his mad climb to finish[1] the solitary leaping of four years, Lonergan writes out of his life's hidden world of illustrations thus:

"The problem of interpretation can best be introduced by distinguishing between expression, simple interpretation, and reflective interpretation."[2]

I ask you to pause with me over this sentence in the initial stumbling fashion of a beginner. We really don't know the problem too well if at all. It is, after all, the problem to which Lonergan got the core of a solution eleven and a half years later. But let's start with fixing an initial meaning of *expression* and *simple interpretation*.

I came up with three zones of my own experience that help me, that could help you in sharing this adventurous searching: a zone of my learning and a zone of my teaching: learning from N.T. Wright in the past decade; teaching a course in mathematical physics during the academic year 1959–60;[3] reaching for the meaning of the sixth section of *The Triune God: Systematics*.[4] My previous two footnotes indicate that I am going to stay here with N.T. Wright and Christian Scriptures. So, we have a first opportunity to putter round the problem of the

---

[1] He was pressured to finish *Insight* by the requirement to begin teaching in the Gregorian University Rome in the autumn of 1953.

[2] *Insight*, 585.

[3] That will be a topic in the second Essay, B.

[4] This topic will occupy us in the third Essay, C.

meshing of the seventh chapter of *Method in Theology* with the dense stuff of the third section of *Insight*'s seventeenth chapter.

You certainly have some experience that parallels the first zone: reading scripture and its interpretations. The thing about Wright is that he illustrates magnificently Lonergan's meaning of *expression* and *simple interpretation* by two stages in his career. There is the learned stuff of his early scholarly work; there is the effort "addressed to a different audience" of his later years perhaps neatly symbolized by the work *Simply Jesus*.

Here I ask you to go back and read the paragraph on *Insight* 579 that begins (line 22) with the sentence, "By way of illustration let us suppose that a writer proposed to communicate some insight A to the reader." Can we pin down vaguely some such A in Wright's efforts? I think of Wright's poise before his two audiences in an illuminating (for you, I hope) manner by recalling Lonergan's question of 1934, "Do you know His Kingdom?" Indeed, the first sentence of Wright's chapter "Jesus: The Ruler of the World" weaves brightly for me round a plea from an apparently quite different world in Lonergan. From Wright we have "What on earth does it mean today, to say that Jesus is king, that he is Lord of the world?"[5] Lonergan writes to a superior in 1935, I would say in vain, "What on earth is to be done? I have done all that I can in spare time and without special opportunities …." Lonergan's frustrated life-struggle was towards interpreting his sniff of the Kingdom's Cosmopolis.

How did you find the reading of that last occurrence of the word "interpreting"? Did it not ring oddly? What on earth are Wright and Lonergan really doing? Are they not trying to engineer the Kingdom? What, then, do we properly mean, are we to properly mean, by *interpretation*? A question worth raising now, even though its adequate answer belongs to a future effort.[6]

---

[5] *Simply Jesus. A New Vision of Who He Was, What He Did, and Why He Matters* (Harper Collins, 2011), 207. For Wright's reach to the other audience, see the index, under *Kingdom of God*, of *The New Testament and the People of God*, Fortress Press, 1992. I return to Wright and his work throughout this book (see note 13, p. 5, note 19, p. 18, note 5, p. 101, note 15, p. 128, note 12, p. 168) because I have struggled with his excellent work over the years in my effort to detect the needed shifts in theologies grounded in scriptures in any religion. A nudge regarding the direction they might take may be had from my essays *Disputing Quests* 4, 5 and 8, "Turn Wright" I, II, and III (available at: http://www.philipmcshane.org/disputing-quests). See also *Disputing Quests* 9, "Interpretation Wright Turn, Right Turn" and *Disputing Quests* 10, "Paul's Epistles and Functional Systematics."

[6] Throw in the delightfully odd title of chapter 14 of Wright's *Simply Jesus*: "Under New Management: Easter and Beyond."

An Adventure: Interpretation from A to Z

That last sentence is surely question-raising? Suppose I had written, "A question worth raising now, even though its adequate answer belongs to a past effort"?

My double-taking, double-talking, throws me back, in my nudge to get you to come back with me, to conversations I had with Bernard Lonergan in the summer of 1966. He paced his room, up against the problem of interpreting interpretation in its fullest seeding seething possibilities. We focused on the problem of a first chapter, on how he might start his venture. The problem stayed with him, relatively unsolved, haunting his days and his years as he battled unsatisfactorily with the challenge until one evening in the winter of 1970–71 he strolled into the recreation area of the old Bayview Regis College and announced to his colleague Sean McEvenue that he was finished, although, alas, he still had to write an Introduction. Sean replied, "Well, write a page!" Lonergan took the bright suggestion back to his room and wrote, well, two pages.[7]

I add this context to bring you to read the first two words of his chapter "Interpretation" in *Method in Theology* freshly: "Our concern." Lonergan with his conventional plural, bent to type his way forward in his dodgy presentation. Dodgy?[8] He was dodging the inflicting on his present theological readers of his past semi-successful effort, in *Insight*, of presenting his concern.[9]

---

[7] *Method in Theology*, xi–xii[3–4].

[8] The dodginess frames his talk throughout the book. Read, e.g., the last sentence of the first note in this chapter on Interpretation: "For instance, what there is termed a universal viewpoint, here is realized by advocating a distinct functional specialty named dialectic." The present book hovers round the future forms—in genetic sequence—of the process. At note 3 of Essay W (p. 151) I write of the process as a 9-fold care, and I think of a fuller meaning of *interpretation* that covers all specialties and their exchanges, including exchanges with global cultures. The subjects, the characters, in the 8-fold Tower of functional recycling are to interpret sequentially to the next in the cycle. The cultural ethos is to involve a subjectivity that is a solution to the problem of the chasm identified earlier by Lonergan (see note 9, p. 90) I would note that the word *chasm* does not appear in either edition of *Method in Theology* or their indices. This was part of Lonergan's problem in facing into writing his short tired book.

[9] Semi-successful, obviously, because it needed the refinement of functional divisions. Think, for example of the ending of *Thirdly*, of his *Sketch* of his achievement on *Insight* 602. "In either case they are pure formulations if they proceed from an interpreter that grasps the universal viewpoint and if they are addressed to an audience that similarly grasps the universal viewpoint." The later leap of genius splits the audience into a cycle of differentiated audiences and puts the purification of pure formulations into the task of dialectic.

INTERPRETATION FROM A TO Z

I am quite aware that I am pointing, certainly in the previous footnote 9, to deeper issues than belong to beginnings on the topic, but the pointing is useful to our struggle. It connects obviously to Lonergan's own struggle, his pressured thinking and typing. Might I suggest that it would help you, at this stage—but feel free about such a suggestion—to go to section Q of my present effort, beginning that section by a cursory reading of the three paragraphs of section 4, "Understanding the Author" of *Method in Theology* chapter 7? Focus on the final sentence of the second paragraph. "This is, however, the enormous labor of becoming a scholar." That gives you a clue to Lonergan's poise of concern in the adventure of this chapter. Might you not easily weave the run of these three paragraphs around your effort to read profitably N.T. Wright in either of the two periods of his writing and, in the second case, writing and pod-casting? There is a sense in which, for his texts, "the meaning of a text is plain"[10] yet sometimes problematic in the ways that Lonergan goes on to write about here. N.T. Wright is dealing mainly with the context of understanding "a first century Christian" like Paul.[11] You have comfortably read Paul, but are you tuned into Wright's meaning of Paul? Supposing you were conversant with the scholarly work of his early days, might you be able to say to Tom Wright about his later writings and presentations, "this stuff is 'just like you'"?[12]

I have been writing here to float you into impressions rather than to present coherence. But note that my pause over Tom Wright's work seems to fit the approach that Lonergan takes in this chapter on Interpretation. Think of his puzzling in the summer of 1966: he was at a loss regarding his possible expression, or simple interpretation or reflective interpretation of interpretation. He settled for a weaving of shades and shadows of his view round standard exegesis. Let's pick up on a twist of the question that ended the previous paragraph. Supposing you were conversant with the scholarly work of his early days, might you be able to say to Bernard Lonergan about his later writings and presentations, "this stuff is 'just like you'?"

I could go on with an enlightening paralleling of Wright and Lonergan, round the three periods of their work. The middle period? Wright became a busy bishop; Lonergan became a busy teacher at the Gregorian University. The third period for both seems to be a popular turn, though Lonergan's podcasts are to the inner community of serious interpretation, not just to the interested public.

---

[10] The first line of section 4, "Understanding the Author," *Method in Theology* 160[151].

[11] *Ibid.*, 161[152].

[12] I quote from the center paragraph of section 4, *Ibid.*, 160[152].

An Adventure: Interpretation from A to Z

But I must leave Wright behind now, pointing to my other writings about Wright's challenge to "Turn Wright,"[13] a challenge he is too old to take.[14] We home in, then, on Lonergan's simple expression of chapter 7 of *Method in Theology*. Haunting it, certainly, is the mood of reflective interpretation that he shared with me in 1966. But that effort of reflective interpretation led to his best effort in the book of somehow mixing a non-terrifying introduction to his new view with enough indications of his long-term reach.[15] One must add to that notion a perspective on his sickness and weariness throughout those years. The best effort of "a far larger"[16] venture than *Insight* envisaged by the forty-nine-year-old Lonergan was out of the question.

Detecting the mixings in this seventh chapter of *Method in Theology* is extremely tricky and quite beyond my intention. Lonergan holds remarkably to the context of the various flows associated with scriptural interpretation. Indeed, he seems to back away from a poise that haunts the book, the haunting pressure towards theory.[17] See that in page 170[160–61] where he writes about the

---

[13] See Essays 4, 5, 8, 9, and 10, of my series *Disputing Quests*, available at: http://www.philipmcshane.org/disputing-quests.

[14] The tradition of scripture studies in all religions is solidly locked in a poise to which this book is a shocking challenge: it is a challenge to the embedded molecularity of an axial superego. See my essay *Humus 2*: "*Vis Cogitativa*: Contemporary Defective Patterns of Anticipation," http://www.philipmcshane.org/humus.

[15] This, of course, is central to the effort of this book and its predecessor, *The Future: Core Precepts in Supramolecular Method and Nanochemistry*. A context of the effort is summarily indicated in note 16, p. 66 below. A suggested approach to up-reading Lonergan's strategy in writing *Method in Theology* is given in the essay 13, "*Method in Theology* ASAFACT" (available at: http://www.philipmcshane.org/website-articles). There is a larger up-reading that was and is quite beyond my present effort: it is hinted at, pointed to, here and there in the essay; it is implicit in the repeated request for "a resolute and effective intervention in this historical process," (*CWL* 18, *Phenomenology and Logic*, 306), but that effectiveness as structured into the forward functional specialties is a massive task for those committed to engineering the future.

[16] *Insight*, 754.

[17] I recall Lonergan's remark, "in the Greek patristic tradition *theoria* became the name of contemplative prayer," ("Mission and the Spirit," *A Third Collection*, Paulist Press, 1983, 27). I urge theologians to take seriously a sublation of that tradition. The urging comes in various essays titled *The Interior Lighthouse*. Best give a broad pointer to them, borrowing footnote 41 of my "The Coming Convergence of World Responsiveness," (*Divyadaan: Journal of Philosophy and Education* vol. 30, no. 1, [2019]): *HOW* 13, "The Interior Lighthouse" (http://www.philipmcshane.org/how) introduced the topic, *Interior Lighthouse*, under that title. *Disputing Quests* 12, "The Interior Lighthouse

properly-conducted seminar being "an exhilarating experience for students"[18] but one in which there may hover the odd suggestion of earlier in the page, effective perhaps in such a seminar, "I conceive the coming to know himself, not as part of the job of the exegete, but as an event of a higher order, an event in his own personal development."[19] What, one may ask, of his mature view of generalized empirical method and its pedagogical demands? That is subtle question that I prefer to leave dangling. But I would note a broader point regarding context-adherence in this chapter. The word *theory* occurs with amazing regularity throughout the book, but in this chapter he seems to avoid it. It occurs three times in a single sentence in a way that restricts its large meaning in this the context. "Our present concern is theory, and, indeed, not the general learning theory that regards students, but the special learning theory that regards exegesis."[20] It occurs twice elsewhere in a side acknowledgment of cognitional theory.[21] One might scarcely notice the two nudges towards its fuller relevance in the comments there:

II" continued the reflection, as did *Disputing Quests* 13, "The Interior Lighthouse Zero" (available at: http://www. philipmcshane.org/disputing-quests). Those essays were followed by *Interpretation* 4, "The Interior Lighthouse III," *Interpretation* 16, "The Interior Lighthouse IV: Twenty Seventh Lea," and *Interpretation* 17, "The Interior Lighthouse V: Interpreting *God*" (available at: http://www.philipmcshane.org/interpretation). The topic, however, goes back to *Process: Introducing Themselves to Young (Christian) Minders* (1989)(available at: http://www.philipmcshane.org/website-books) and the broad challenge is made explicit in the five essays, *Prehumous* 4–8, on "Foundational Prayer" (available at: http://www.philipmcshane.org/prehumous). It is the heart of the matter in my recent book, *The Allure of the Compelling Genius of History*. The drive of that series was towards an appreciation of the need for a contemplative ingestion of *Insight* if we are to arrive at a sub-population competent "Tower-wise" "to be a resolute and effective intervention in the historical process" (*Phenomenology and Logic* 306).

[18] *Method in Theology*, 170[161]

[19] *Ibid.*, 170[160]. This poise is sublated by the norm of generalized empirical method articulated in *A Third Collection* (Paulist Press, 1978, top of page 141). Might you read it with a shocked freshness? "Generalized empirical method operates on a combination of both the data of sense and the data of consciousness: it does not treat of objects without taking into account the corresponding operations of the subject; it does not treat of the subject's operations without taking into account the corresponding objects." See, further, note 28 below. Think of my normative slogan for future teaching: "Teaching children geometry is teaching children children." The slogan simply applies the poise of generalized empirical method to a particular zone of communication.

[20] *Ibid.*, 156[149].

[21] *Ibid*, 161, line 1[152, line 26], 165, line 1[156, line 4–5].

"something quite different from commonsense understanding,"[22] "what is needed is not mere description but explanation."[23]

But what is, what was, wanted here, here and now?

I hope that my treatment of the topic of interpretation in this Essay A, and indeed, throughout this book, is seen as neither just description nor a shot at explanation. Yes, it is the product of a hidden reflective interpretation that lurks behind an expression that is strategic, pedagogic, shadowing the eighth functional specialty in devices and deviances and techniques, especially techniques of repetition.[24] It draws attention to two existential gaps, one immediate and ontic, the other distant and phyletic.[25]

Here I appeal, in both gap-cases, to aspects of my teaching of a course in honors mathematical physics exactly sixty years ago.[26] The ethos of the class, when it shrunk sufficiently, was that of a respect for theory and the detailed[27] and arduous climb to decent mastery. Occasionally difficult forward-looking questions were raised by some member of the class, and my suggestive answers were received in a recognition of what they were: glimpses, guidances, postponements to graduate work. This is not normally the case in present theology and

---

[22] *Ibid.*, 168[159].

[23] *Ibid.*, 172[162].

[24] Essay J focuses on a particular technique that would ground exercises. But it is of very serious grounding significance: without its habituation in students and guides the following of Lonergan is a matter of bluffing along in initial meaning. Essay J will push you to start again. It parallels, curiously, Lonergan point: "from such a broadened basis one can go on," (*Method in Theology*, 287, line 19[269, line 9]) go back, indeed, to reread and rewrite either book. See also note 27(p.8) below.

[25] I regularly appeal to the last two chapters of *CWL* 18, *Phenomenology and Logic*. The appeal of the 13th chapter is mainly to the subject, to an ontic repentance; the appeal of the 14th chapter is for a long-term group collaboration that is to change history.

[26] Curiously, the only notes I have from my career as teacher as the notes for the lectures in this course. The notes were written prior to the classes but not used in them: the presentation was a free-flowing exchange, with exercises tagged on for between classes (see the next note). I made the notes available as *Website Articles* 7 and 8: http://www.philipmcshane.org/website-articles). I appeal to the example of this course in, e.g., *Vignette* 5, "Going on to Intervene": http://www.philipmcshane.org/217-vignettes-2018-33) where I talk of a nun in that class who was sharp in detecting the demands of the climb; the later *Vignette* 20, "The None's Story" points to the failure to thus detect in theological studies, indeed in most other zones.

[27] I am thinking of the importance of exercises in the process of instruction. This is not usual in the world of philosophy or theology. Imagine *Insight* with a bundle of exercises built in at the end of each chapter.

philosophy, or indeed in the humanities. Has it the possibility, the potential, to become the norm, the *nomos*? This book raised that question, I would hope effectively. It did so for me in a startling fashion that, as I point out in the Epilogue, startled me into a fresh answer as I grappled with those final pointings. I did not allow that final leap to shake up the text I had written from a more elementary and self-climbing perspective.[28] But I would note that the goal I now have in my heuristic minding is symbolized nicely but discomfortingly[29] by the title of the essay to follow.[30]

---

[28] Bear in mind the slogan that haunts my book: "Scrutinizing the self-scrutinizing self" (*Method in Theology*, 167[158]). It is "a process of self-constitution, a *Selbstvollzug*" (*ibid*, 363[334]) that is to start with some few ontic crazies and slowly become a norm, "a process of self-constitution occurring within a worldwide society," town and gown, Tower and plane plain meaning, but in differentiated ways.

[29] I pause here over the discomfort, the leaving in suspense, the repetitions, the incompletnesses. The "alphabet essays" were not written in sequence, and there was a deal of juggling going on through the months of creating proper invitations and openness. Part of the inviting involved judicious omissions, repetition, etc., something expressed very nicely in the quotation from a previous book, itself repeated here on page 95, note 10 and on page 106. In that quotation there is a nudge to the deeper meaning of repetition. In my final meshing together of the essays I refrained from eliminating such oddities. Think, for example: repetitions are never repetitions. Heraclitus would agree, and you surely more and more, that one never steps into the same quotation or diagram twice. To come to bear that in mind, a context of one's reading and one's life, is the seed of bearing it ever better in mind: a Proustian lift to your pilgrimage. I think, too, of Rilke: "Love consists in this, that two solitudes guard and bind and greet each other."

[30] I add here the first of eleven (pp. 8, 62, 70, 74, 87, 92, 118, 140, 141, 150, 169) boldfaced notes that point to a distant meaning of the full text and, of course, of the meaning of the paragraph ending Essay B, p. 13, the road to that of the end of Essay K, p. 87. My key statement regarding those eleven notes is that "Integral W-enzyme Growth is Normatively Concave Upwards." This is a statement for *Assembly* at the end of your reading: asking you privately for your three objectifications about the eleven notes. I avoid a precise geometry or equations of growth-meaning: the statement refers uncomplicatedly to you and my normative view of your growing mindful. It is minimalist: I am suggesting a growth-curve of $y = x^{1+n}$, where n is greater than zero. Might the real norm not be closer to $= e^x$? Massive shifts of culture in the positive Anthropocene lurk here. On you go to note 23, on page 62, at the end of Essay G.

B ~ {ASSEMBLING (INTERPRETATIONS)³ }⁴

"If interpretation is a science then it has to discover some method."[1] That ongoing discovery "here is realized by advocating a distinct functional specialty dialectic."[2]

Am I quite daft, at a doddering 88, to now have a shot at giving a popular sniff of the answer that Lonergan gave to the question, "Is interpretation scientific"? He had a very respectable answer in his head as he paced before me in his little room on the sixth floor of the Bayview Avenue Regis College, asking me rhetorically and really, about tackling its presentation in a book he was struggling to begin. It was the summer of 1966. Early after my arrival that summer I sat face to face with him in his room and he flexed his two matching four-fingers before me and gave me a popular sniff of his answer, beginning his flight with the words, "Well it's easy: you just double the structure." There was a sense in which, yes, it was easy for us two then. I had been puttering towards the answer since 1956, when I shifted from graduate studies of mathematics and physics that included such works as the classic *Space-Time Structure* by Erwin Schrödinger. I moved then towards *Insight*'s appearance in 1957 through a first venture into what was talked of then as the *Verbum Articles*. Next there came the shock, as I began a first reading of *Insight*, of finding that Schrödinger's great book, sweated over in details of tensor scribbles during the year 1955–56, left me quite inadequately prepared for *Insight*'s fifth chapter on *Space and Time*.

That sense of inadequacy is key to what I am about to attempt here.[3] Likely you do not have it, in relation to the topic of, the naming of, *interpretation*. Please shelve offense here, with humor and patience.[4] I am, yes, going to get to popular twistings towards glimpsing the wild Dionysian fantasy of Lonergan at 30, when he posed for himself the question "What is progress?," and bubbled up his molecular patterns into the enzyme notion of cycles of "fresh intellectual synthesis

---

[1] *Insight*, 586.

[2] *Method in Theology*, the end of the first footnote in the chapter on Interpretation.

[3] Perhaps it would be helpful for you to locate my first push here with a hovering over lines 24–25 of *Insight* page 559. May I call you Sal for this moment of intimacy? "Sal: most of all what is lacking is knowledge of all that is lacking, and only gradually is that knowledge acquired."

[4] Yes, I am thinking at the moment of that great sub-section of *Insight*'s "The Problem of Liberation" (Section 3: 643–56: in five sub-sections).

understanding the new situation created by the old intellectual form and providing a statistically effective form for the next cycle of human action."

But let us drop down from this Dionysian Daftness to sniff personally, in whatever way you find helpful, around this vague notion of inadequacy. The sniffing is the long-term ontic and phyletic problem[5]: how do we sniff it into our neuromolecules, into redeeming us from our present tongue-lashings?[6]

Our present tongue-lashing is a global business of layerings of shrunken and regularly immoral *haute vulgarization*s, but let us not go there now, in this effort to be helpful towards the emergence of global tongue tidings of great joy. Let us go to a nice positive example of such joy, such smooth smooch talk. Back I go then to thinking about my experience of teaching a first year honors-level mathematical physics in University College Dublin, 1959–60. Pause to share my musings, musings that go far beyond my thinking at the time of teaching, musings that identify significantly a cultural ethos that is still with us, though regularly battered by professors, teachers, *Scientific American*.

My class was small and keen. The chair of the department met me in the corridor in the first week or so asking how it was going. When I told him of all going well, he told me, "Lecture over their heads for a couple of weeks and clean out the group: then you'll have a great year." So, my class became a hard-working dozen. But I wish us to pause over what I might call the molecular meaning of that "hard-working." The ethos I mentioned in the previous paragraph was in their attunement to our exchanges. They knew enough about physics and math to know that they were beginners.

There are two ways for me to go here, two questions for you to entertain, or rather to strain over. Do you know enough about physics and math to know you are only beginners? Do you know enough about interpretation to know you are only beginners? Your answer to the first question could be yes, but only for a

---

[5] I hesitate about footnoting as I go along. Think of most of them as simply leads to helpful pointers for perhaps later musings. Here I refer you to those two final chapters of Lonergan's lectures on existentialism, *CWL* 18, *Phenomenology and Logic*, chapters 12, "Subject and Horizon" and 13, "Horizon, History, Philosophy." They poise us brilliantly in 2020 in "a summons to decisiveness at a rather critical moment in the historical process." *Ibid.*, 300.

[6] I think again (recall p. xii) back now to my younger (I was only 65) effort of *A Brief History of Tongue. From Big Bang to Coloured Wholes* (Axial Publishing, 1998), especially the two sections "Tongue Tide" (4.2) and "*Mos* and *Nomos*" 9(4.3). I have now an altogether more refined scientific grip on the meaning of the previous chapter three's title, "A Rolling Stone Gathers *Nomos*." Can I help you towards sniffing the wind of that grip? The text above goes on to what I think is a key helpful analogy.

{Assembling (Interpretations)³ }⁴

minority. In a normal group of students of philosophy or theology there are rarely more than a few who have a decent competence in physics. The second question however has, for me, a clear answer to be normatively expected from you, to be actually not expected from you. "I do not know enough about interpretation to say Yes." Think, honestly, of your reading of the previous Essay A; think, indeed, of previous readings of chapter seven of *Method in Theology*. Were not both readings relatively comfortable? Interpretation is what you have been doing, perhaps for decades: you as an individual, you as a community. Check out the journals; check out—as I do on a daily basis—*academic.edu*. Think of the flow of classes given or received. In my fuller sense of interpretation as having nine divisions, there is the interpretation of the pulpit and the zone of religious instruction. All these areas and flows are, well, you might claim, alive and reasonably well.

They are not: but how am I to win you over effectively to this negative view "at a rather critical moment in the historical process."[7] Yes, I am trying to make "a resolute and effective intervention in this historical process," something Lonergan did not manage to do in those final lectures on Existentialism in July of 1957. My comfort is that there is, in this year, a significant little shift in the statistics of success.[8] That shift is an effective shift in the process that begins with *Assembly*, a process that gives precision to the critical role of dialectic: but that is a topic dealt with elsewhere, and in this book particularly in Essay I.[9]

But a simpler existential help came to mind as I struggled here, the help of adding a third question to the two above re physics and re interpretation. The question—in the same format as the previous two—is, Do you know enough about botany to know you are only beginners? The startling aspect of that question is that the you includes present botanists.[10] And it includes the possibility of those botanists admitting that, wow, "we are not there yet."[11] That possibility shifts to

---

[7] *CWL* 18, *Phenomenology and Logic*, 300.

[8] Mesh the indication of the 1934 *Essay in Fundamental Sociology*, 20, lines 19 and 22, with *Insight*, 144, lines 1–3.

[9] Essay I, "Self-Assembly: The I of the Storm" brings us to focus on the identification of dialectic achieved by Lonergan, the topic of chapter three, "Self-Assembly" of my *The Future: Core Precepts in Supramolecular Chemistry and Nanochemistry*

[10] For brevity sake I keep this to a footnote here. Pause over *Insight* 489–91 and muse over present botany's gross failure to tackle the problem of some sort of logic of development. The question haunts the two pages 490–1. "What is the operator?" Indeed. The road to asking that effectively requires that the myths of gene codes and information theory have to be effectively identified as such.

[11] *CWL* 21, *For a New Political Economy*, 20. The phrase is the start of a brilliant paragraph that runs over a page, well worth pausing over in this 'beginning' context.

the context of slim probabilities, like a Poisson distribution, in so far as you find in your W-enzyme[12] a teetering towards the poise of resonating with "all that is lacking."[13] This century's idiocies of both politics and economics will gradually nudge us towards that slim statistics.

However, here we are at the beginning of the alphabet soup that I hope is to be an effective component in that nudging. So, let's cut short reflection on these large reachings by going to the symbolization of them that was presented in the Preface under the title W_3. I am tempted to repeat it here, but just glimpse back at page iv. And then poise over my other version of that cyclic venture, the simple diagram below:[14]

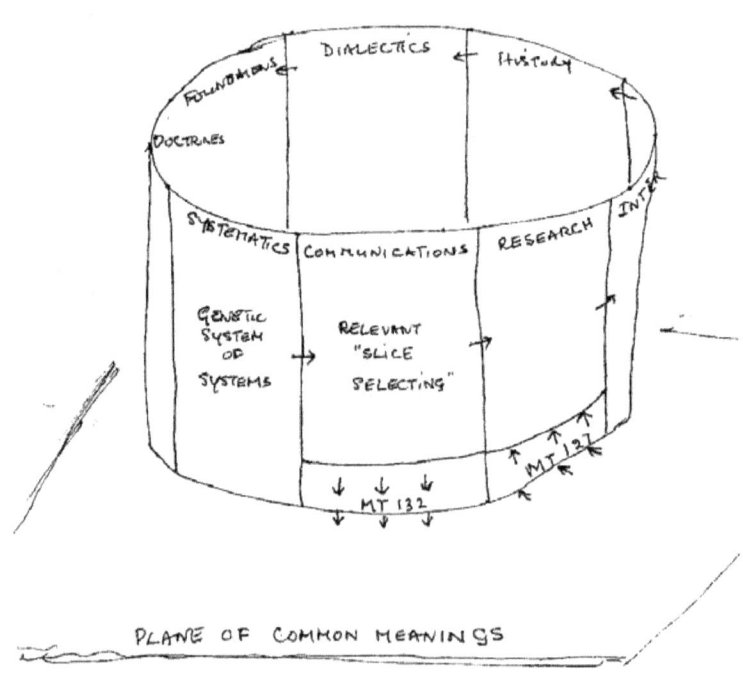

Society "must lift its eyes": that is the "redeeming time" stance of the "offense," attack-poise, of my Frontispiece. The issue is to patiently seed the positive Anthropocene.

[12] See note 4 of the Introduction, p. x.

[13] *Insight*, 559, line 24. I would wish you to pause freshly sometime soon over lines 14–24. Add the context of my musing with Eric Voegelin: See note 17 on page 61.

[14] There is a helpful discussion of details of the tower diagram on pp. 70–76 of *The Future: Core Precepts in Supramolecular Method and Nanochemistry*. See further, note 17 below.

{Assembling (Interpretations)³}⁴

Your glimpse back to W_3 shows you no sign of my present pointing towards a lack of genetic analysis, and that absence of sign has nudged me over decades to change the UV of that complex image to something like GEN:[15] but I refrain from messing with "W_3," the sublation of these shots at images and symbolization I leave to the future science of Futurology. However, see and seize and size up, in my tower, the word *Genetic* in the zone of systematics. That genetics has all the heuristic characteristics described in *Insight* 587–91 under the title "The Notion of a Universal Viewpoint." But there is further work to be done to deal with the genetics of that genetics.

Best halt at this stage, directing now your attention to the image that I presented as the title of this essay: $\{\text{Assembling (Interpretations)}^3\}^4$. The climb to its meaning involves facing the tough climb such as is described in my article "Method in Theology: From $[1 + 1/n]^{nx}$ to $\{M(W_3)^{\theta\Phi T}\}^{4''}$[16] It seems to me best to leave the topic and the diagram thus there with you, but to be held by you as a problematic presentation. Might it grow in legitimacy over these next centuries? Think of Lonergan's reply to a question posed to him at a Lonergan Workshop in the late 1970s: how much physics should a theologian know?" Lonergan: "Well, he should be able to read Lindsay and Margenau." Will the Tower of Able Community be able to read front-line reaches in some strangely symbolized genetic logic?[17]

---

[15] In my own pedagogical efforts over the years I find that "The Universal Viewpoint" is off-putting. I focus rather on the genetic heuristics, giving hope and help by musing over the sunflower. Lonergan gives help with his musings on the control of progress in mathematics (see below, page 58).

[16] *Journal of Macrodynamic Analysis*, Volume 10, 105–135.

[17] This is the key door being opened in this book, but only if my repetitions and diagrams (see note 20 on page viii) lead you to non-linear readings. Why do I keep repeating diagrams, or even just repeating my pointing to conversing with Lonergan in the summer of 1966? There is a shocking genetic shift radiating from that summer talking. I talk to you in spring of 2020 about reading the word *Genetic* in the Tower diagram. Might there be a shocking start for you, for us, towards an effective and optimistic reading of *Genetic* in the mess of this messy millennium's beginning? Will the Tower look different the next time you meet it in this book?

C ~ Interpreting "The Divine Missions"

The project of this little essay puzzled me greatly in the final months of 2019. How to keep brief an invitation to tackle the future task of a fully-contexualized explanatory presentation of the sixth section of *CWL* 12, *The Triune God: Systematics*?

By then I had outlined the full venture from A to Z, and even fully written various later sections. The problem of brevity, of course, haunts this entire effort, and in a few of the sections I went well beyond what was my initial norm: keep the sections of my nudging to around 1000 words. At one stage in my musing it seemed to me that I had best use my Trinitarian reflections, with their autobiographical context, from the Epilogue to *Seeding Global Collaboration*.[1] Eventually I leaped to the notion of a simplified autobiographical approach that yet would be a first nudge for your fresh pausing over the tough beginning of Lonergan's section 3 of *Insight* chapter 17.

The beginning of Lonergan's effort comes in fact before he tackles "The Problem" formally on page 585: it is there for us to read now, on lines 22–38 of page 579. A "writer proposed to communicate some insight A to a reader," and in the process he twirls around towards[2] various candidates for the role of the "practical insight F" so as to overcome "relevant deficiencies E of the anticipated reader."

My first shot at interpreting thus Lonergan's Trinitarian theology was in a month of the summer of 1961. My audience was to be the readers of *Theological Studies*. Fr. John Courtney Murray had read my dense article "The Contemporary Thomism of Bernard Lonergan"[3] and requested me to tackle an article that would

---

[1] "Embracing Luminously and Toweringly the Symphony of Cauling" the Epilogue of *Seeding Global Collaboration* edited by Patrick Brown and James Duffy, Axial Publishing, 2016.

[2] Recall my slogan of note 28, p.8, one that raised the problem of your present advancing stance as pushing the self-scrutinizing of a self-scrutinizing subject: how luminously are you poised in the "twirl around" mention. The mention is made explicit in later references to it: See note 25, p. 140, note 1, p. 165.

[3] *Philosophical Studies* (Ireland), vol. 11, 1962: the article is available as *Published Article* no. 2: http://www.philipmcshane.org/published-articles.

present to theologians the core of the five *Verbum* articles.[4] What I actually did—as you may check in the published article on the website[5]—was to dodge the complexities of those articles by focusing my attention on the second chapter of Lonergan's Latin text of the time: *Divinarum Personarum Conceptio Analogica*.[6] It was a high-level pedagogical piece still useful in a teaching context. But it made no attempt to get into the topics of the sixth chapter of the book.

My next audience was a strange mixed audience of nuns and reformed prostitutes. I was preaching, I suspect, on Trinity Sunday, in a convent in Dublin dedicated to such rescuing and as I vested before the service a possible communication, in terms of four questions, bubbled up in Supermolecule[7] me.[8] I later gave a compact indication of my effort in *Music That is Soundless*. Best patch the relevant paragraph in here, including the footnotes added at the time.

"The basic question to raise is, *when did I last[9] have a real conversation*? That question must be asked in an authentic personal memory-search, and its answer is

---

[4] I was finishing a terrible first year of theology at the time, a common sense run round the meaning of the Church and of Eschatology. Much later, with a grin, Fred Crowe informed me that had the editor known I was only a beginner he would not have asked for the contribution. When I reached fourth year theology I was "invited" to move to the English Jesuit House of theology: I suspect the professor dealing with the course on the Trinity that year was uncomfortable with the possibility of me being in the class.

[5] "The Hypothesis of Intelligible Emanations in God" is available as article no. 1 of *Published Articles*: http://www.philipmcshane.org/published-articles.

[6] Gregorian Press, Rome 1957, 52–91. See *CWL* 12, 124–229.

[7] The drive of this book and the previous one, *The Future: Core Precepts in Supramolecular Chemistry and Nanochemistry*, is towards an integral explanatory self-heuristic that will historically—I think of the positive Anthropocene—solve the problem Lonergan raised in "Understanding and Method," his 1959 seminar. See note 9, p. 90.

[8] The bubbling up, of course, was a broad lift, a lift towards the generalized empirical method that is popularized in the principle mentioned in note 19 (p. 6). But there are to be refined bubblings as we move into the positive Anthropocene and guide it to maturity. Broad bubblings ferment in small breakthroughs. The end comment in this essay points to a higher broad breakthrough to explanation, a breakthrough that is left dangling at the end of Lonergan's considerations of the Divine Missions. Smaller lifts are involved in de-dangling, lifts altogether obscure to the present generation. As an illustration of such obscurity, exercise your contemplative talent in perusing Lonergan's shifts in the 1964 edition from his thinking in the 1956 version, a version given in *CWL* 12, Appendix 4, pages 742–91. There are no simple ways round such advances. In Essay Y the point is to be repeated regarding the higher plane of geohistorical genetics.

[9] The word *last* here might seem superfluous. Its use is related both to the strategy of attention to a concrete particular (See *Insight*, 369, 461) and to the rhythm of the

aided by its threefold specification: *When was I last understanding, understood? When did I last speak? When did I last listen?* The process is an effort to locate personal data—and one may honestly find that one has little or no data. Some people pay their psychiatrist $100 an hour to attempt conversation—no one should assume that they achieve it every day. Contemporarily, for instance, real conversation rarely occurs in an institutional context: if this seems an exaggeration it is no worse than the psychologist Maslow's contention than less one percent of adults grow. In so far as one has had some experience of real conversation—indeed even if the question raised produces nothing more than a glimpse of its absence,[10] one has data for the understanding of conversation. But only data, only a beginning—as the Epilogue reiterates."[11]

The presentation given, be it in homily or in classroom, quite obviously is more conversational. It rises, as I later identified it, to being dominated by what I call *The Childout Principle*, put popularly thus: "when teaching children geometry one is teaching children children." But note also—self-seed[12]—that there is a seeding there of the venture that was and is my focus in this skimpy essay. There is the seed of a self-seeding of the explanatory intussusception of The Divine Missions.

I am raising here a hierarchy of questions that haunt this entire little book. They are questions of contemplative self-seeding that I return to briefly in Z, where I quote *The Prison Meditation of Father Delp*,[13] and point to the challenge of turning the Tower of Theology towards being a community at home in the apokataphatic poise of The Interior Lighthouse.[14] We cannot go there now but perhaps there is a helpful nudge in contemplating the first sentence of Thomas

---

question ("This rhythm of language is a mysterious trait that probably bespeaks biological unities of thought and feeling which are entirely unexplored as yet." S. Langer, *Feeling and Form*, Scribners, New York, 1953).

[10] This parallels Lonergan's point in "Christ as Subject," *CWL 4, Collection*, 174: "If anyone cares for clarity on this issue, he can begin from the statement, 'non si riesce a compredre' (one fails to understand). He can contrast that experience of not understanding with other experiences in which he felt he understood. Then he can turn his attention to understanding and not understanding."

[11] Philip McShane, *Music That Is Soundless. A Fine Tuning for the Lonely Bud A*, 1968, third edition, Axial Publishing, 2005, 7–8.

[12] Again, think in terms of my slogan, "Scrutinizing the self-scrutinizing subject."

[13] Herder and Herder, New York, 1963. Fr. Alfred Delp was hanged by the Nazi regime, February 2nd 1945. In his last prison letter he wrote, "The actual reason for my condemnation was that I happened to be and chose to remain a Jesuit" (*Op. cit.*, ix)

[14] See note 17, p. 5.

Merton's Introduction to the Delp book. "Those who are used to the normal run of spiritual books and meditations will have to adjust themselves, here, to a new and perhaps disturbing outlook."[15]

Interpreting the Trinity is in that zone, and the destiny of humanity is to be in that zone,[16] and I am inviting you to anticipate that zone in a fantasy that sniffs the positive Anthropocene, that opens you to the wildness of a "Yes I said yes I will yes"[17] to the question, "Do you view humanity as possibly maturing—in some serious way—or just messing along between good and evil, whatever you think they are?"[18] But the invitation here is limited to asking you to contemplate the oddity of the shift to explanation that would leave quite behind the abundance of scripture references that Lonergan gives in the final pages[19] of his consideration of the *Divine Missions*.[20]

---

[15] *Ibid.*, vii.

[16] This is a hugely difficult topic and involves a massive reorientation of the poise of contemplation. It is the world of what I call *The Interior Lighthouse*, but now lifted forward to face what Lonergan calls *the chasm*. See the index to *CWL* 23, *Early Works on Theological Method 2* under *Chasm*. The lifting forward is related to the existential turn of thinking of yourself, Supermolecule, as containing, and being contained by, the integrating dynamic that I write of as your W-enzyme. That dynamic has to face a challenge of inventiveness regarding the failure pointed to in note 15, p. 5.

[17] The final words of James Joyce's book, *Ulysses*, spoken by Molly Bloom.

[18] This existential question blossomed for me perhaps six years ago out of contemplating the pointing of the conclusion of Lonergan's 1934 *Essay on Fundamental Sociology* regarding *Isaiah* 2:2–4.

[19] Pause very seriously over page 501 in *CWL* 12. *The Triune God: Systematics*. Contemplate those two magnificent final paragraphs both with and without the added venture into the scripture referred to in the notes. Might you suspect that there are to be other sets of notes developed that lift the venture of understanding the operations of the Trinity, somewhat as the operations of electricity are lifted to luminosity by Maxwell's Equations? This is a world quite distant from the World of N.T. Wright.

[20] A final point worth making is about the benefit of having the original Latin available on the opposite page. One thus gets nudges, even with weak Latin, of revisions regarding minding both divine and human conversations. So, the top line of page 521 is properly translated and read, "that by believing the Word we might speak true inner words and understand." Is this important? One needs a luminous inner grip on the vectors of the electricity of God weaving round our heart-strings. That weaving is the task I touch on occasionally as we move along: the problem of the chasm within, the need for an integral radiance of you W-enzyme.

D ~ Canons of Engineering

We can begin our flight of fancy with two diagrams:

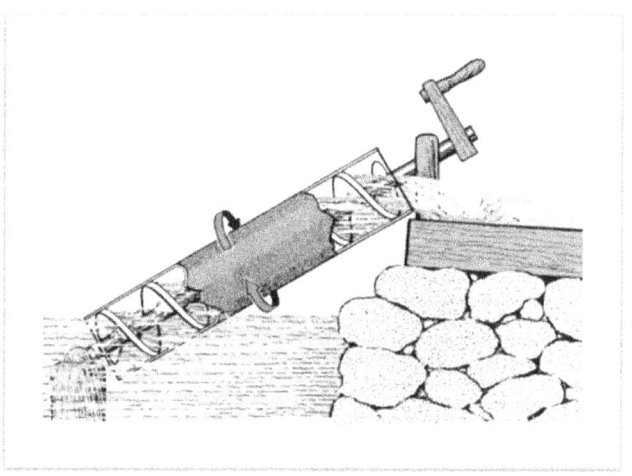

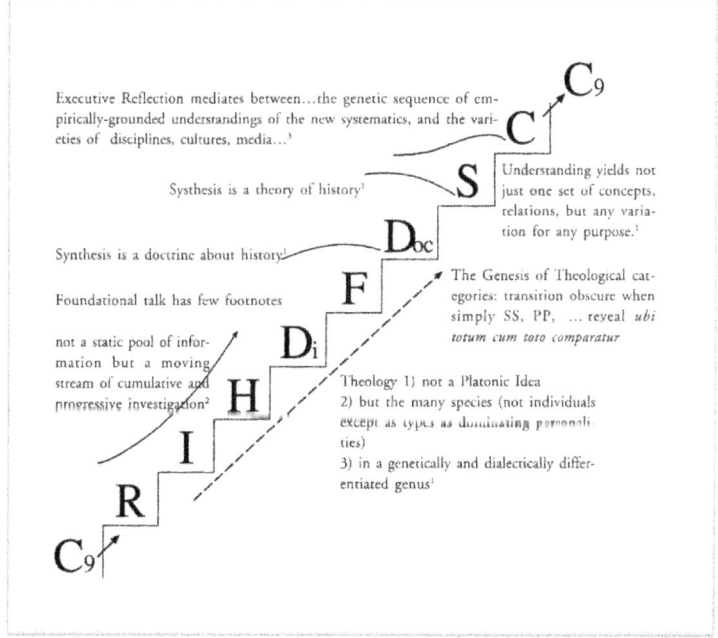

The first diagram images the invention by Archimedes of his Screw-structure designed to raise water. The second diagram images Lonergan's invention of a cyclic process calculated to raise culture.

At this stage in my venture to nudge us to think further about engineering the future, I paused over the difficulty and novelty of you beginning to think thus. I could turn back to the second paragraph of *Method in Theology* and invite you to muse over the meaning of "bolder spirits," leading you to slowly come to suspect that we have been misled by Aristotle and his followers, who boldly identify science with, well, with the three steps R, I, H, of the second of the above diagrams. That misleading haunts the flaw mentioned in note 15 of Essay A, p. 5: the failure in theology to turn to the future with effective explanatory structures. It is better to come at that failure with apparent indirectness by getting you to think positively of the needed moves in the context of the present global crisis of climate, economics, culture. So it seemed good to give you the flavor of my effort to lift climate studies to an effective heuristic dynamic. The following, then, gives you that flavor: it is the beginning of my paper for the Helsinki Conference of 2019 on those problems. I halt abruptly at the beginning of Part One of the paper, and that abrupt halting leaves you conveniently poised over the issue of "redeeming time" that I raised in the Frontispiece. This Essay D is followed, obviously, by Essay E: but, as I noted in the Preface, I found it of strategic value to replace early efforts at telling my story of "redeeming time" with a single month's effort of doing so: *Cantower 14*, which fermented forward from April Fool's day of 2003 towards its Mayday, m'aider, appearance.

Structuring the Reach towards the Future

> To see things as comprehensively
> As if afar they took their point of sight,
> And distant things as intimately deep
> As if they touched them. Let us strive for this.[1]

Prologue

The focus of my paper is on the topic structuring or rather on re-structuring, since there are already structures and structurings and structuring-efforts among us regarding the reach that concerns us here. It seems to be vital as well as bright to structure my talk within the novel structure I have in mind, yet at the same time

---

[1] Elizabeth Barrett Browning, *Aurora Leigh*, Book 5, lines 185–8. [I leave the footnotes, with their references forward, as they are in the text].

show its roots in present and past structure. That bright shift leads me to split this paper in two. What is central and needing our attention is the topic of Part One: "An Effective Structuring of Peaceful Coexistence." Part Two, "Remembrance of Times Past and Future," deals, at least sketchily but in proleptic poise, with previous efforts to structure our existence, efforts that obviously range across a spectrum of what I loosely call *progress*.[2]

To be strict in my division I introduce, not in Part One, but in the Prologue, the key pedagogical nudge that I indicated in my original sketch of a paper: the nudge given by Archimedes' invention of the apparatus that lifts water from a lower to a higher level. There is a range of lessons to be learned from that venture, that creative deliberation. The first lesson comes to the heart and hearts of our gathering: it is the lesson precisely of the need for creative deliberation and for luminosity regarding its own characteristics: to this I return in the Epilogue. The need for the activity is illustrated by a simple pause over Archimedes' leap of inventiveness; the need for characterizing it can be sniffed out slowly by simply pausing over the shabby attention "deliberation" has received in the intellectual traditions of humanity.[3]

Such a characterization cannot be a priori. It is an empirical business of attending to creative deliberations as they occur in more and more sophisticated forms precisely because of scientific progress and—may I use the phrase loosely

---

[2] I have used the words *effective*, *existence*, and *progress* here. Looseness of meaning is the name of the game here, though you may well think of our present meshed with the concern expressed by the existentialist movement of the twentieth century. I go on in the text to use the word *deliberation* and it shares the same looseness. Part Two will tackle the issue of the road to effective precisions of meaning. Finally, I would note that the center of our concern is a meaning of *effective* that is effective, shifting towards and beyond a Poisson statistics of success in out century to the Bell Curve of future millennia. Our present crisis is one of "effective shifting towards."

[3] Here you meet a central problem of my paper. Might I symbolize it by pointing to the gap between Aristotle (384–322 BC) and the crippled thinking of Peter Drucker (AD 1909–2005) both—note their dates—axial males? (On *axial*, see notes 69 and 71 below.) Suffice it to see that deliberation has not been seriously deliberated upon even if puttered skillfully round by a tradition that includes Aristotle, Nemesius, Damascene, and Aquinas. The paradigm represented by our first diagram of the screw has not had the deliberate attention it needs as symbolizing deliberation, and this cripples the movement for sustainability and peaceful coexistence. You may later follow my struggle here through notes 6, 17, 20, 22, 33, 45, 56. Then do the Hamlet (see the text around note 25) or Hal (see the text at note 59) thing, or the lady Sands thing of note 55: whatbore into your core.

for the moment—the engineering that blossoms from it.[4] The weeds of axial engineering, however, are a dominant reality.[5] Our gathering here is in the context of the present destructive sophistications, and, further still, that we are pressured by time. We have a Canadian television program, running since 2009, titled *Chopped*. The challenge there is to move from mess to meal in 30 minutes. I do not think that Archimedes was pressured in his deliberations, but we are. Have we thirty years to lift global living from present swamp waters to some sort of beginning of a sane waterworld? Let us pause, with this question, over an image of Archimedes' achievement.

How are we to raise the cultural waters so as to rescue and freshen the waters and bloodstreams of nature? Might I suggest extravagantly that we oppose the poise of Archimedes on science to Aristotle's poise?[6] But that is a teasing leap into and beyond Part 2 of the paper. Let me just note that primitive humanity needed primitive science to work. It did not have a bourgeois interest in art or science for its own sake. A decent pause over how humanity got by in a pre-bourgeois non-ecumenic world[7] would gradually show that science is not a neat little academic three-step going to the moon but a ten-step collaborative global cherishing of earthlings and their cosmic home. That gradual showing is part of our larger task.

---

[4] Engineering is to blossom only in the luminous boring of that core that asks, what-bright, "what might be, what might this be?" It requires a present subtle dismantling, a new mantle, a taking root of the long road of the new mantling of the diagram on the next page. See further, on mantling, notes 16 and 49 of "Structuring the Reach towards the Future," presented at The 3rd Peaceful Coexistence Colloquium," Helsinki Finland, June 13, 2019 (available as *Æcornomics* 5 at: http://www.philipmcshane.org/ecornomics).

[5] The meaning of *axial* is a topic, too, of the Epilogue. Perhaps it stirs the imagination a little to say that is it an evolutionary period that covers the Holocene age and the negative part of the Anthropocene.

[6] I pick up from note #3 Aristotle's "bourgeois" poise (see notes 43 ad 69 below) that locked science into a three-fold way of verifying theory in data. Deliberating over Archimedes' deliberation is to push us towards a radical effective shift in our view of the disorientations of industrial humanity. On the bourgeois poise in the history of economics, see Geoff Mann, *In the Long Run We are All Dead: Keynesianism, Political Economy and Revolution*, Verso, N.Y. 2017. On the core of the road to economic science and sanity, see P. McShane, *Economics for Everyone: Das Jus Kapital*.

[7] I am thinking now of the fourth volume, titled *The Ecumenic Age*, of Eric Voegelin's *Order and History*. It ends in early China but does it not empirically live on in megacorporations?

Part One: An Effective Structuring of Peaceful Coexistence

It seems best to begin with a diagram that encourages us, gives hope that we really can do this. Even though the beginnings of "this" are to involve messy skirmishing,[8] the strategy is to blossom through the next seven millennia into a global ethos of care.[9] So, here you are: a diagram of a cultural apparatus resembling Archimedes' screw for, in various good senses, screwing up civilization.

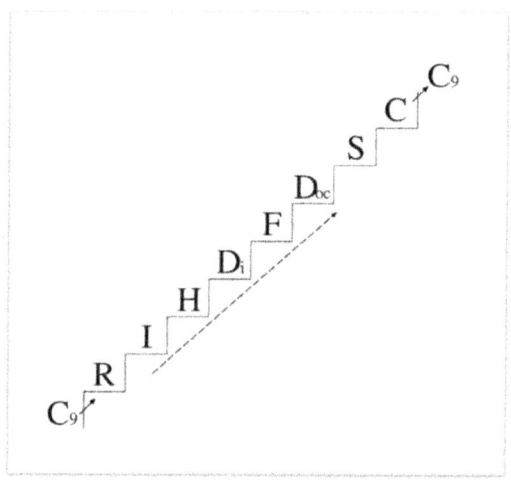

---

[8] Immediately I think of Todd LeVasseur's article "It's Getting Better and Better, Worse and Worse, Faster and Faster: The Human Animal in the Anthropocene," *Sustainability and Peaceful Coexistence for the Anthropocene* (ed. Pasi Heikkurinen [New York: Routledge, 2017]) and the varieties of resistance he presents, such as DGR (deep green resistance) and DEW (decisive ecological warfare). *Sustainability and Peaceful Coexistence* also has essays that address the varieties of human ecological displacements that are likely to lead to more than skirmishing. I think of that idiot slogan in the low-grade film, *Independence Day*, "We will not go quietly into the night." So, yes, "worse and worse," but somehow the global plague poises an increasing number to take seriously the push of Bernard Lonergan, "insofar as there is to be a resolute and effective intervention in this historical process, one has to postulate that the existential gap must be closed" (*Phenomenology and Logic*, Collected Works of Bernard Lonergan 18, ed. Philip McShane [Toronto: University of Toronto Press, 2001], 306). Ruuska's *Reproduction Revisited: Capitalism, Higher Education and Ecological Crisis* (MayFly Books, 2018) [hereafter *Ruuska*] points vigorously to the gap. My effort here is to specify an effective dynamics of closing the gap. In the short term, we face agonies, such as those described in David Wallace-Wells book, *The Uninhabitable Earth* (New York: Tim Duggan Books, 2019), a book that will seed a little positive fright. And there is the larger positive that I draw attention to in note 32. I comment at length on LeVasseur's essay in "Better and Better, Worse and Worse," available at: http://www.anthropositivecene.org.

[9] See note 56 below. Add the fuller context of the Epilogue.

My presentational effort here is foundational, in a sense sought by Arne Naess forty years ago,[10] but it is steered by me here into a foundational pedagogy. To give a glimpse of that in another diagram helps us move forward pedagogically, even though it seems altogether too early for such a complexification. My conversation here is, in the letters of the above diagram, **FC**$_9$, and in the diagram below C$_{59}$. ***F*** points to Foundations, eventually to become a dominant social group, outwitting, in a cyclic collaborative dynamic, the remnants of the present "dominant fundamental group"[11] in its national and transnational varieties. ***C*$_9$** points to the global community in its full historical concreteness, and if you like a cute image of what the reach in this conversation is, fancy the slave-built pyramids inverted to grant a munificent global microautonomy.

On the final page of this Essay D, page 26, you find, then, my next pedagogical diagram. Think of the spread there as a new periodic table, but now the elements are human groups collaborating towards "redeeming time."[12] This diagram locates the previous step diagram as an inner community, an inner circle matrix, committed to a science of cosmic care which I have named *Futurology*.[13] But now we must ask together: What is this identification of the diagonal, the axis, **C**$_{ii}$ of the full collaboration, **C**$_{ij}$, that is to deliberate cyclically, spirally, a vortex[14]

---

[10] In 1989, as I struggled in a sabbatical in Oxford to brood forward towards *Process: A Paideiad*, a detecting, leaning into India, of history's effort to educate us, I was astonished to find his detecting of a parallel structure of cosmic deliberation. My book was thus titled in its promise at the end of *Wealth of Self and Wealth of Nations* (1975), but its final title is *Process: Introducing Themselves to Young (Christian) Minders* (1990). These two books seed the present essay. They are both available at http://www.philipmcshane.org. For more on Naess, see note 58 below.

[11] I am referring here to Gramsci's view of guiding ethos. "The spontaneous consent given by the great masses of the population to the general direction imposed on social life by the dominant fundamental group; this consent is 'historically' caused by the prestige (and consequent confidence) which the dominant group enjoys because of its position and function in the world of production."

[12] Shakespeare, *Henry IV*, 1.ii.210. The full line is "redeeming time when men least think I will," a suitable slogan for anyone who takes a stand on sustainability and peaceful coexistence. In the Epilogue I return to the full soliloquy of the prince (lines 188–210) which ends thus.

[13] *Futurology Express* (Axial Publishing, 2013) is the title of my recent popular presentation of this future poise. At present the train is in the ramshackle station.

[14] Yes, another image here, helpful, hopefilled. It comes from the eccentric Ezra Pound of a century ago. Pound wrote "if you clap a strong magnet beneath a plateful of iron filings, the energies of the magnet will proceed to organize form . . . the design in

of redeeming time from the mad destructive greed of the "civilized"[15] majority of the present global population?

---

the magnetized iron filings expresses a confluence of energy." ("Affirmations, Vorticism," *The New Age*, xvi, 11, Jan, 1915, 277.)

[15] Lurking in my essay there is a sense that we are no more civilized in this millennium than a sunflower is after a week's weed-pressed growth. Since Marx wrote, the masses have ascended into apparent financial comfort, but real enslavement. I nudge for a longer view and hope of "Arriving in Cosmopolis" (see note 55 below) and recall in that article a note worth repeating here. "There is an obvious reference here to Ortega y Gasset's *The Revolt of the Masses*. But I would note that Ortega's notion of the masses was quite complex. Chapters 6 and 8 of the book are directly on the topic, but also chapter 12 on "The Barbarism of Specialization." Saul Bellow, in his Foreword to the translation, neatly sums up Ortega and also the problem of the changes in the meaning of mass man since Ortega's time. "Ortega when he speaks of the mass man does not refer to the proletariat: he does not mean us to think of any social class whatever. To him the mass man is an altogether new human type. Lawyers in the courtroom, judges on the bench, surgeons bending over anaesthetized patients, international bankers, men of science, millionaires.... differ in no important respect from TV repair men, clerks in Army-Navy stores, municipal fire inspectors, or bartenders. It is Ortega's view that we in the West live under a dictatorship of the common place." (*The Revolt of the Masses*, translated by Anthony Kerrigan, edited by Kenneth Moore, with a Foreword by Saul Bellow, University of Notre Dame Press, 1985, p. ix.)

INTERPRETATION FROM A TO Z

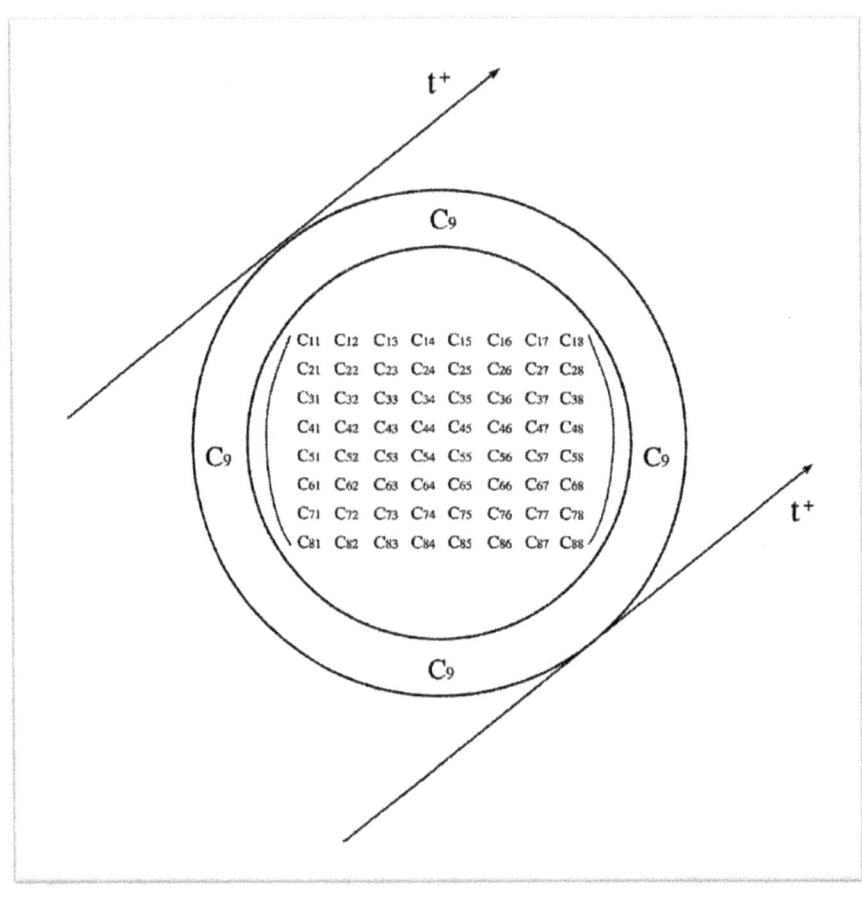

E ~ *Cantower* XIV

Communications and Ever-ready Founders
May 1st 2003

This *Cantower* is peculiar in that the first section was not written for the series. Indeed, it was written in 1986, as the sixth chapter of a projected book which never saw the light of day. The title of that book was "The Foundations of Communications": I would now drop the 'the' because it is evident, if you are with me so far, that while foundations as subjects are core-invariant, and while the thematic of foundations may be pretty stable during a significant period—think of the parallel I drew with the Calculus of Variations[1]—still, the slope of the tower-reaching promises enrichments beyond present fantasy and understanding. Thematic and expressed foundations are no more fixed, awaiting a few decimal-place corrections, than physics was rounded off in 1903, a century ago. Indeed, as you may well know, regularly I find dates suggestive: the periodic table emerged a century before Lonergan's hodic table. With a little luck the year 2004, Bloomsday centennial, Lonergan birth-centennial, will produce some shake-ups in our perspective. This *Cantower* points towards that possibility, probability. It is a two-part invention on the same theme, with a bridge section. Part 1 is the afore-mentioned 1986 effort; part 2, in section 3, is my present effort to identify heuristically the full task of communications; the bridge, section 2, invites you to place the reading of this fourteenth *Cantower* in the context of two other fourteens: chapter fourteen of both *Insight* and *Method in Theology*.

There are, of course, many other contexts that could be, need to be, brought into present and proximate efforts to reach a conception and affirmation and implementation of the eighth functional specialty. This *Cantower* is just a nudge, added to previous nudges such as "Systematics, Communications, Actual Contexts."[2]

There is the large nudge of the previous *Cantowers* and of *Lack in the Beingstalk*. Depending on how much those nudges are heart-held by you, the third section here may lift you—as it does me—to a startling freshening of view regarding the manner in which "the antecedent willingness of hope has to advance from a generic reinforcement of the pure desire to an adapted and specialized auxiliary

---

[1] In chapter four of *Lack in the Beingstalk*.
[2] *Lonergan Workshop*, (7)1987, edited by Fred Lawrence, Scholars Press, 143–174.

ever ready to offset every interference"³ with the pilgrim poise and progress of streets and states. You will notice in the quotation the source of the words "ever ready" in my title. The measure of that readiness is to be the measure of the beauty and unity of culture in humanity come-of-age.

14.1 Foundations of Communications[4]

The focus of this chapter is the structure, genesis and implementation of the heuristic named 'the universal viewpoint'. Lonergan is moved to conceive of this complex heuristic by his thematization of the difficulties of the precise communication of meanings between authors and audiences by an interpreter.[5] Against a broad indication of what is meant by such a viewpoint, he proceeds to sketch its operation and, against the background of an additional discussion of the resistance to such a heuristic that can spring from the normal opposition to an enlarged change of perspective and from the deeper opposition of erroneous philosophic stances, he specifies further his notion of the operation of the heuristic through an outline of canons of hermeneutics. His discussion throughout is dense and exclusive of illustrations and it might well be remarked, in his own words, that "there are many different states and patterns of consciousness and it would take volumes to give a tolerably adequate description of any one of them."[6] Moreover, to that problem of condensed treatment there is added the further problem of differentiations of consciousness that postdate in Lonergan, existentially and thematically, the treatment of *Insight*. We refer here particularly to the fundamental set of differentiations that come under the name of functional specialization. It is to this set that Lonergan refers when he remarks, at the beginning of his treatment of the specialty Interpretation, "observe how ideas presented there (in *Insight*, 562–594[585–617]), recur here in quite different specialties. For instance, what there is termed a universal viewpoint, here is realized by advocating a distinct specialty named dialectic."[7]

The present chapter, then, tackles a variety of related fundamental issues. It takes off, first, from the discussion of chapter three {a missing chapter!} to pose more fully the problem an interpreter faces when he attempts to mediate the meaning of an author to a community. This problem will engage us through the first two sections on the universal viewpoint and the canons of hermeneutics. The

---

[3] *Insight*, 727[747].

[4] The original title of the chapter was "Towards a Transposition of Hermeneutics."

[5] *Insight*, 562–4[585–587].

[6] Lonergan, *The Road to Nicea*, 9–10 [C. O'Donovan's translation of part of *CWL* 11].

[7] *Method in Theology*, 153, n.1.

third section of the chapter indicates the need to broaden the discussion towards an anticipation of the transposition of elements of Lonergan's sketch of hermeneutics into a genetically structured eightfold vortex of academic collaboration in the human control of human meaning.

14.1.1 The Universal Viewpoint

As was noted already, Lonergan's treatment of the universal viewpoint and its emergence is unadorned either by illustrations or by developed analogies. It should help, then, to begin with an extended analogy that gives some parallel to the procedural innovation constituted by the heuristic conception and implementation of the universal viewpoint, a context for ongoing collaboration in the field of interpretation. The analogy comes from the history of chemistry and its methods, its centrepiece being the emergence and implementation of the conception of the periodic table: but, needless to say, what is sketched here in broad strokes requires personal involvement in detail for its intellectual intussusception.[8]

The chemical analogue is, of course, altogether simpler than the complex heuristics of the higher sciences. While the history of chemistry is both genetic and dialectic, the object of the science itself can be considered as a case of static system—not however in the sense opposed to dynamics in mathematical physics, but in a sense that includes chemical and thermal dynamics, and so not requiring intrinsically genetic methodologies. On the other hand, the object of hermeneutical inquiry is "not a static system, nor some dynamic system, but a variable manifold of dynamic systems. For, the successive systems that express the development of human understanding are systems that regard the universe of being in all its departments.... Only the broadest possible set of concepts can provide the initial basis and the field of differences that will be adequate to dealing with a variable set of moving systems that regard the universe of being."[9]

So, more concretely, one may contrast the relatively invariant modern systematics of the periodic table with the vast genetico-dialectic array of interpretations of Christianity running through Mark, John, Tertullian, Origen, all the way through and beyond Hegel. Nevertheless, however different the two heuristics and the historical tasks are, the parallel is worth dwelling on as showing

---

[8] Lonergan used the analogy from chemistry at the beginning of his lectures on Method in 1962. A solid background here would be J.R. Partington, *A History of Chemistry*, MacMillan, London, 1961, vols 2–4.

[9] *Insight*, 508[532].

the dimensions of the transition called for by Lonergan, who can thus write of a significant resistance to his heuristic:

> The introduction into physics of tensor fields and eigenfunctions raised a barrier between the theoretical physicists that grasped the mathematics but possessed no great skill in handling laboratory equipment and, on the other hand, the experts in experimental work for whom the recondite mathematics was sheer mystery. In similar fashion one may expect the diligent authors of highly specialized monographs to be somewhat bewildered and dismayed when they find that instead of simply following the bent of their genius, their aptitudes, and their acquired skills, they are to collaborate in the light of common but abstract principles and to have their individual results checked by general requirements that envisage simultaneously the totality of results.[10]

In this chapter we are pushing for an initial glimpse, especially through analogies with physics and chemistry, of the common but abstruse table or plateau of transposed hermeneutics. In the following chapter {never written!} we will avail of more complex analogies from the study of plant and animal development to further specify that future collaborative task of human studies.

In reaching for the analogy in chemistry for such a collaboration one must consider, not just simple innovations, such as is represented by the achievement of Lavoisier regarding oxygen,[11] but a fuller sweep such as that which includes the first serious formulation, within an incipiently theoretic context, of the phlogiston hypothesis by George Stahl (1660–1734), through Lavoisier's successful challenge to that hypothesis and beyond to the relative maturation of chemistry brought about by the work of Mayer and Mendeleev around the year 1868. Moreover, it is well to bear in mind the deeper roots of the blind search for chemical system in Chinese and Arabic chemistry: one may expect to find a parallel, more subtle, alchemy, in the field of interpretation.

The transition represented by the period indicated is a transition from a largely descriptive chemistry having an overlay of methodological confusions and imaginative differentiations to the conception of the realities of chemistry within a relatively[12] clear explanatory pattern of terms and relations represented by the

---

[10] *Insight*, 581[603–4].

[11] H. Butterfield, *The Origins of Modern Science*, Bell and Sons, London, 1965, chapter 11, considers the work of Lavoisier as marking the maturing of chemistry as a science. The broader perspective indicated above seems preferable.

[12] On the state of present chemistry and its methodology see W. Danaher, *Strategies of Chemistry*, University Press of America, 1986.

periodic table. Now it is this total transition that serves as a parallel to Lonergan's structuring of the task of hermeneutics. A great deal of present discussion of the problem of interpretation, of which Gadamer's classic *Truth and Method*[13] might be taken as summative and representative, bogs down in descriptive meanings, mythic aspirations, and a failure to suspect or envisage the radical leap to a full explanatory context that results from Lonergan's formulation of the universal viewpoint with its concomitant implementable canons. So, for example, one moves from the naive hope of some fulsome transfer into a reader of a past author's meaning through a sympathetic open reaching of that reader, to a sober limited explanatory perspective that offers a precise control of descriptive meanings. The chemical parallel is helpful in that it is otherwise extremely difficult to come to grips with the large discontinuity represented by Lonergan's achievement. We must now, however, envisage that achievement in step by step fashion, not in some summary way that would express briefly what Lonergan expresses at some length in chapter seventeen of *Insight*, but in a manner that complements that treatment and seeks to make it more plausible.

One might say that Lonergan's take-off point for a methodical hermeneutics is the parallel between common sense and historical sense. Just as common sense can hit on a correct, if limited, set of insights that describe a particular situation—one may recall shifts from alchemy to early chemistry—so an interpreter with a relatively sound historical sense can reach successfully such an appreciation of the common sense of another time as to permit precise indications of behavior and speech of that time to his or her scholarly contemporaries. Now in the chemical search there is the hope, and the drive within humans and circumstances, to move beyond the limitations of commonsense orientations by the discomforting leap from description to explanation that lifts the account of chemical reality beyond the relativity and confusions of particular groups' perspectives. Description still remains a "tweezers"[14] but the central scientific content is culturally invariant. What is needed, then, in hermeneutics is something that will lift the historical sense towards a thematic anticipation of some parallel cultural invariance: "if interpretation is to be scientific, then it has to discover some method of conceiving and determining the habitual development of all audiences and it has to invent some technique by which its expression escapes relativity to particular

---

[13] Seabury Press, New York, 1975.
[14] *Insight*, 291[316].

and incidental audiences."[15] The key lies in the jump to the scientific perspective[16] that embraces all viewpoints in an ordered pattern much as the periodic table orders the totality of chemical elements and compounds. We may note here that a parallel from biology adds a further dimension. "Study of the organism begins from the thing-for-us, from the organism as exhibited to our senses,"[17] but from the heuristic perspective of genetic method the organism is envisaged in terms of a sequence of increasingly complex operators and integrators,[18] a problem we reserve to the next chapter {never written: but we'll get to it in *Cantower LXIX*!}.

A simple image may help here. Lonergan's solution to the problem of the relativity and descriptiveness of interpretations may be diagramed as a 'right-angle shift' akin to a similar shift in ordinary science from description to explanation:

SCIENCE	INTERPRETATION
thing-to-thing ……. Explanatory	
O_1---O_2---O_3	X_1---X_2---X_3 …. explanatory interpretation
thing relative to scientist	interpreting interpreter

Just as the scientist shifts from description, for example, of 'push', 'size', to correlations like $PV = C$ or of acids and salts to reaction equations, so the interpreter moves out of relativity to self and self's culture by the jump that contextualizes heuristically, for example, the interpretation of X_2 in the culturally-invariant explanatory framework that meshes the interpretation into a genetico-dialectic set of relations with previous and posterior authors, including the interpreter as author.

Lonergan at this stage of his analysis goes into some detail regarding the notion of the universal viewpoint, related levels and sequences of expression, and limitations that are inherent in any reach towards system.[19] Rather than including what would necessarily be a summary indication of that general analysis, it seems better to move to a sketch of the actual dynamics of interpretation that makes

---

[15] *Insight*, 564[587].

[16] In a fuller treatment of interpretation a discussion of perspectivism would be required. See *Method in Theology*, 216–18.

[17] *Insight*, 464[489].

[18] *Insight*, 465ff[490ff].

[19] *Insight*, 573–7[595–600].

that dynamics proleptically plausible through a parallel with the dynamics of inquiry in the lower sciences.

14.1.2 Canons of Inquiry

The present section continues and broadens the discussion of analogies of inquiries by extending that discussion to the treatment of the two sets of canons of inquiry summarized in *Insight*.[20] These two sets of canons should be viewed as related, on the one hand, more to the debates on research methods and their history associated with people like Kuhn and Lakatos [21] rather than older philosophies of science, and on the other hand to discussions of possible strategies of exegesis rather than to general philosophic comments on hermeneutics.[22] Since the canons of *Insight* have so far received scant attention in the literature, the present brief treatment can only point up the need for lengthier empirically-based inquiry.

In discussing the structure of interpretation Lonergan remarks, "let us begin by recalling the structure of classical empirical method"[23] and goes on first to give general indications of parallels between the two methods, then to give canons of hermeneutics[24] that resemble the previous set of canons of chapter three of *Insight*. We will begin by indicating the relations and differences between the two sets of canons, reaching through that indication complementing illumination of the empirical operation of the potential universal viewpoint.

A listing of the two sets of canons bringing them into loose isomorphism helps towards more detailed discussion.

---

[20] *Insight*, 70–102[99–125]; 586–94[608–16].

[21] On must note, however, that the efforts of these groups are crippled by truncation. See *Lonergan's Challenge to the University and the Economy*, chapter 1. The canons are best appreciated when related to actual innovative scientific practice.

[22] One may note how Lonergan's treatment of interpretation in *Method in Theology*, which fits into a transposition of the *Insight* treatment, focuses on strategy.

[23] *Insight*, 577[609].

[24] *Insight*, 586–94[608–16].

Interpretation from A to Z

Canons of Empirical Method	Canons of Hermeneutics
Canon of	Canon of
1. Selection	3. Successive approximations: principles of criticism: (a) demand for UV (b) conditions of extrapolation {self-knowledge: schol. differences}
2. Operations	(c) perspective of sequences of meaning and lags of expression (d) the goal, a hypothesis with evidence within (a), (b), (c)
3. Relevance	1. Relevance
4. Parsimony	4. Parsimony
5. Complete explanation	2. Explanation
6. Statistical residues	5. Residues

First, let us note some particular points regarding the listings.

The last three canons on each of the lists require little comment. The canons of parsimony and explanation correspond fairly well to the general descriptive requirement of a necessary and sufficient account of any phenomenon. The addition of 'complete' to the fifth canon of empirical method serves to emphasize the point, made at length in chapter 5 of *Insight*, that physicists, and consequently chemists, are regularly tempted—and thus plunged into paradoxes in their field— to let extensions and durations slip out of the net of explanation.

In the case of the final canon of both listings one may note that the canon of hermeneutics is more generic: residues are not only statistical. "An unverifiable host of accidents can enter into the decision"[25] leading to the production and survival of manuscripts. Furthermore, the interpreter reaching for a particular hypothesis does so in a way that differs from the natural scientist's reaching for a general hypothesis and from it to particular situations through boundary conditions contextualized by statistical laws.

The first two canons of empirical method are paralleled by a single canon of hermeneutics. Instead of operations on the selected data of sense, there occurs in interpretation no selection—since interpretation reaches both data of sense and

---

[25] *Insight*, 593[616].

data of consciousness—by a cycling towards ever-improving approximations to the history of the meaning of meanings. Lonergan's view here reaches for a sublation of August Boeckh's idea of philosophy as "the interpretative reconstruction of the constructions of the human spirit."[26] Lonergan's view indeed goes on to transpose that of Droysen. As Lonergan remarks, "What Boeckh did for philology, Droysen would do for history. He moved the notion of understanding from a context of aesthetics and psychology to the broader context of history by (1) assigning expression as the object of understanding and (2) noting that not only individuals but also such groups as families, peoples, states, religions, express themselves."[27] How Lonergan effects this transposition into a perspectivist universal heuristic requires precise discussion but first some more particular comments need to be made regarding the first three canons on each list.

The canons of selection and relevance aim at determining the limited type of understanding sought by empirical science: an understanding of the forms of the actually seen etc.[28] In contrast, the hermeneutic canon of relevance and the first principle of criticism both assert the openness of hermeneutics in the demand for the universal viewpoint. The universal viewpoint has limits set only by the notion of being and indeed is open to a full theological transformation.[29]

One final comment before moving to the ground of the universal viewpoint in the notion of being regards the second principle of criticism. It points up two conditions of adequate extrapolation. In the later Lonergan these emerge as two precise differentiations of consciousness, that of explanatory interiority and that of scholarship.[30] However, an accurate reading of the context of the discussion of the demands for the universal viewpoint leads one to the conclusion that the full conditions of extrapolation require the fullness of the fivefold differentiated consciousness specified by Lonergan in *Method in Theology*.[31] Without that full differentiation, "the full range of possible combinations"[32] of experiences, insights, judgments and orientations would escape the interpreter. The interpreter could be faced with an object of inquiry "quite beyond the horizon of ancient Greece and Medieval Europe."[33]

---

[26] Quoted in *Method in Theology*, 210.
[27] *Ibid.*
[28] *Insight* 76[100].
[29] *Insight*, 740[762]; *Method in Theology*, 23.
[30] *Method in Theology*, 274.
[31] *Method in Theology*, 272.
[32] *Insight*, 567[590].
[33] *Method in Theology*, 317.

The achievement of an adequately differentiated consciousness is of prime importance in coming to grips with the uniqueness and clarity of Lonergan's solution to the fundamental modern problem of hermeneutics, and to bring out elements of that importance and clarity a further context needs to be added, supplied by the doctorate work of Professor Frederick Lawrence, summarily presented in a paper at the Florida Conference of 1970.[34]

Lawrence treats of the long and not entirely successful struggle of the German tradition of hermeneutics to escape various facets of Cartesianism. The fundamental aspect of that perspective is expressed in the question "how can subjectivity dwelling within itself (*res cogitans*) know objects existing outside (*res extensa*) itself? This posing of the problem is objectivist in so far as it implies the ultimacy and the primordiality of the subject-object dichotomy; and within that set-up a distorted primacy of the subject who, in isolation from the world, instrumentally disposes of ideas and representations (*Vorstellungen*) by means of a reflection thought of only as technical, and who has therefore the problem of deciding whether or not these immanent creations have any transcendent reference to the 'real out there'. And as a final irony, the subject of this relationship ultimately knows itself as object distinguished from other objects only be being present in an immediately evident way."[35]

Gadamer's struggle with this perspective as it pervades the tradition is discussed in detail by Lawrence, who acknowledges "that Gadamer has made his important contribution to the shift of the hermeneutic tradition from an epistemology of interpretation to an ontology of understanding."[36] But Gadamer, according to Lawrence, fails to reach an adequate viewpoint clearly beyond the tradition, to some extent because "anti-Cartesianism causes him to shy away from confronting the procedures and norms incarnate in authentic scientific inquiry."[37] And it is precisely by not shying away from such a confrontation—or intussusception—that Lonergan comes to his own clarification of subjectivity's orientation to being. The basis of that clarification may best be summed up for present purposes in Lonergan's comment on the problem of transcendence:

> The principal notion of objectivity solves the problem of transcendence. How does the knower get beyond himself to a known? The question is, we suggest, misleading. It supposes the knower to know himself and asks how

---

[34] F. Lawrence, "Self-knowledge in History in Gadamer and Lonergan," *Language, Truth and Meaning*, Gill and Macmillan, 1972, ed. P. McShane, 167–217.
[35] *Ibid*, 168-9.
[36] *Ibid.*, 175.
[37] *Ibid.*, 201.

he can know anything else .... we place transcendence, not in going beyond a known knower, but in heading for being within which there are positive differences and, among such differences, the difference between subject and object.[38]

Our digression on the basic modern problem of hermeneutics brings us closer to the value of drawing together the canons of empirical method and those of interpretation as illuminative of the heuristic, the universal viewpoint. Both sets of canons are heuristic structures, the first strongly, the second incipiently growing out of strategies of investigation that enlarge and precise the protean heuristic notion of being. That notion must be taken, however, in the full subtlety given by the context of the first 388 pages of *Insight* (1957). A proximate context certainly is the seventy pages prior to the statement of invulnerable performative assumptions of page 388, but the first part of *Insight* is a contemporary existential necessity. The escape from Cartesianism and the root liberation of the human mind are achievements "that modern science has made possible."[39]

Let us come closer, then, to specifying the limited assertion that is implicit in the advocacy of the universal viewpoint by enlarging the core heuristic operation of the two sets of canons.

First it should be noted that both sets of canons are remote yet concrete and the fruit of the illumination of subjectivity possible only through the strategy of generalized empirical method as formulated in the later Lonergan.[40] This distinguishes clearly the canons both from the German tradition already discussed and from the range of subjectivity-opaque contemporary efforts in the methodology of the sciences. Both sets of canons, then, are heuristic specifications of the notion of being as it is existentially and explanatorily contextualized by a positional stand on what is real. Just as the canons of empirical method find that context in its full richness in the developed heuristic of emergent probability, so the canons of hermeneutics share the richness of that heuristic but enormously enlarged—the difference is between system and source of systems— by the heuristic that is the universal viewpoint. Just as the first set of canons reaches towards genera and species of beings within the four lower sciences, so the second set of canons reach towards genera and species of intentional[41] beings,

---

[38] *Insight*, 377[401].

[39] *Insight*, 487[511].

[40] *A Third Collection*, 141.

[41] The meaning of 'intentional' must be gleaned from the context of Aquinas' thinking.

viewpoints that provide, by mediation and muddling, central components of the sequence of cultures of the human group.

This parallel should help to make the various properties of the universal viewpoint listed by Lonergan[42] more intelligible, more plausible, more acceptable. The universal viewpoint is potential just as the heuristic of generalized emergent probability is potential. It no more determines the genera and species and varieties of viewpoints than does emergent probability determine the emergent species of particles, chemicals, plants and animals. Yet it is, like the more elementary heuristic, ordered, total, ready to advance on, and with, the discovery, genesis, criticism, survival of genera and species and varieties of viewpoints. Unlike the heuristics of the nonspiritual[43] evolution, however, the heuristics offered by Lonergan under the blanket name of 'universal viewpoint' is novel, unappropriated, untried, and hampered in its acceptability by the present culture of interpretation.

> The core of meaning is the notion of being and that notion is protean .... in the measure that one grasps the structure of this protean notion of being, one possesses the base and ground from which one can proceed to the content and the context of every meaning. In the measure that one explores human experience, human insights, human reflection, and human polymorphic consciousness, one becomes capable, when provided with the appropriate data, of approximating to the content and context of the meaning of any given expression.[44]

But what is lacking in present culture—and one should continually recall the structure of community in the natural sciences—is a community of interpreters adequately controlled by, and in control of, the structure of the heuristic notion of being of viewpoints.

So it is that the key canon of hermeneutics of present scholarship must be the third canon, the canon of successive approximation, with its four principles of criticism. What Lonergan foresees here is the cumulative labour of generations of interpreters. In the first principle of criticism he emphasizes the demand for the universal viewpoint, which a critic can make of a contributor, as a contributor can make of himself or herself, in order to lift a contribution into the context of a scientific program analogous to that controlled demand imposed by the canons of emergent probability in physics, chemistry, botany and zoology. The second

---

[42] *Insight*, 564–8[587–91].
[43] For an initial meaning of the word 'spiritual' see *Insight*, 516–20[539–543].
[44] *Insight*, 567[590].

principle of criticism pins down the basic condition of such progress in the need for adequate self-knowledge as ground of the possibility of adequate knowledge of the other.

What we have, then, is a program and a heuristic for generations of scholarly collaboration that calls for detailed empirical, slow, honest initiation. Moreover, it is a program that survives, with refinements of specification, the transposition of hermeneutics into the further differentiation of functional specialization. While this transposition is the concern of the following chapter {another unwritten chapter!}, some further points may be added here to indicate the focus and dimensions of that transposition.

14.1.3 Towards a Remote Complex Transposition

What Lonergan sketches so briefly in *Insight*[45] becomes in *Method in Theology* a finely tuned historic enterprise in mutual self-mediation[46] within the third stage of meaning. It becomes an invariant change in the control of meaning, and "if social and cultural changes are, at root, changes in the meanings grasped and accepted, changes in the control of meaning mark off the great epochs in human history."[47]

The sketch referred to is brief and stark, and can best be illuminated in its anticipation of functional specialization by relating it to a short section of the Epilogue of *Insight* which merits full quotation:

"The discussion of interpretation envisaged
(1) initial statements addressed to particular audiences,
(2) their successive recasting for sequences of their particular audiences,
(3) the ascent to a universal viewpoint to express the initial statements in a form accessible to any sufficiently cultured audience, and
(4) the explanatory unification from the universal viewpoint of the initial statements and all their subsequent re-expressions.

But isomorphic with this interpretative process, there is the Catholic fact of
(1) an initial divine revelation,
(2) the work of teachers and preachers communicating and applying the initial message to a succession of different audiences,
(3) the work of the speculative theologian revealing the doctrinal identity in the verbal and conceptual differences in (1), (2), and (3)."[48]

---

[45] *Insight*, 579–581[602–3].
[46] See Lonergan, "The Mediation of Christ in Prayer," *Method*, (2) 1984.
[47] Lonergan, "Dimensions of Meaning," *Collection*, conclusion.
[48] *Insight*, 739–40[761].

In the sketch one can recognize the canons of hermeneutics in compact form. Lonergan twice draws a parallel between this sketch and the general statement that physics is a metathematization of sensible data. The sketch and the parallel provide a clear lead to the goal of hermeneutic inquiry—a goal which will become highly differentiated through the mediation of functional specialization. For one may note that, just as an explanatory physics reaches for a set of invariants that go beyond particular observers and particular boundary conditions,[49] so the search in scientific hermeneutics must be for like invariants, which Lonergan calls 'pure formulations'.

Just as the invariants of physics are contextualized by some heuristic of world geometry,[50] so the pure formulations are contextualized by the world heuristic of meanings which is the universal viewpoint. Just as the physics invariants lead to expressions of possible concrete and verifiable equations through integration and the addition of boundary values so the pure formulations can lead, through the inclusion of concrete conditions and contexts, to hypothetical expressions that approximate expressions in particular cultures.

Among the tasks of the following chapter {!} is the investigation of this parallel in its full suggestiveness within the context provided by the transposition to functional specialization. Here, however, I add some points connecting the text quoted from the Epilogue of *Insight* with the problem of that enlargement of perspective.

A first approximation of correspondence between the task sketched in *Insight* 579–81[602–3], 739–40[761] and functional specialization would relate pure formulations to systematics, "(3) the work of the speculative theologian seeking a universal formulation of the truths of faith," and hypothetical expression with the effort associated with historical and doctrinal theology requiring that the totality of verified hypothetical expressions stand in some one-to-one correspondence with the totality of documents.

But there is the larger task of interpretation that leads to a second approximation. That second approximation would see pure formulations as the bridge of systematics linking doctrinal expression with the hypothetical expressions of the functional specialty communications. Here, secular analogies are helpful. Descriptive agricultural doctrines such as 'spare the hedges' in some particular temperate zones or 'do not clear stones from soil' in some particular arid zones have systematic ecological explanations that permit their refined

---

[49] In the analogy being developed here, I pass over complexities related to quantum theory, as well as considerations of secondary determinations of relations.

[50] *Insight*, 510[533–4].

transfer to other like zones. Again, in literature there are descriptive doctrinal characterizations of the human significance of particular culture-bound epics and lyrics which, through purification and enrichment[51] can mediate perspectives on contemporary and future symbol and narrative. Again, there are descriptive doctrines of tranquility in such oriental tradition as Taoism which can have explanatory systematizations in biochemistry, reflexology and human zoology in general that make them relevant and available to any culture in stress. And so on.

Yet however rich these approximations may seem to be they are liable to suffer from major and minor deficiencies. The major deficiency is that which Lonergan characterizes as "post- ..."[52]: post-systematic, post-theoretic, etc. The functional specialties represent a differentiated academic shift that can be lost in a nominalist identification of parts of the old wine of theologies and other disciplines with the new bottles of a sophisticated focusing of consciousness, in two modes, on each of four elusive levels. The major deficiency is a permanent feature of human culture: general bias and commonsense eclecticism.[53]

The minor deficiency has to do with the need, not for approximations, but for a total transposition, and so it will dissolve in the full identification of the total set of tasks[54] of hermeneutics defined by functional specialization. Then the first and second approximations will be seen as calling for approximations of other orders, all to be transposed through differentiation and richer procedural analogues. The further orders spring from reaching back to the primary, secondary and tertiary documents [55] (and one must widen 'documents' to broader expressions of meaning) to display a spectrum of interlocking schemes of collaborative recurrence spanning the first four functional specialties, generating a set of movements[56] towards approximations to pure formulations circling round the demand for personal foundational expression on the part of the dialectician,[57] and so seeding the permanent academic demand for the universal viewpoint.[58] The reaching back is proleptically oriented beyond foundations towards a

---

[51] One may think of the transposition of the work of such as Fry, Levi-Strauss, Progoff, Durand.

[52] *Method in Theology*, 304–5.

[53] *Insight*, 225–42[250–67], 416–21[441–48].

[54] The context is the scheme of the human good of *Method in Theology*, 48, 184, 359.

[55] *Insight*, 579[602].

[56] One's heuristic perspective should reach out to the concrete actualities of scientific practice: departments, libraries, conventions, etc.

[57] *Method in Theology*, 250.

[58] See *Method in Theology* 153, n.1.

sublating transposition of the first and second approximations geared, within emergent probability, towards the flowering of human history and destiny.

Among the enriched procedural analogues the central place is occupied by the meta-analysis of development, including the development of the understanding of development. The relevance of that analogue is clearly indicated by Lonergan in the context of the quotation form the Epilogue of *Insight* given above. Lonergan speaks of the relevance of "our analysis of development"[59] and notes that "if the parallel with the interpretative process emphasizes identity and continuity, there also is development though its complexity can be no more than sketched in an epilogue."

Lonergan's own long struggle with the problem of a full inclusion of metadevelopmental reflection in the transposition of theology is evident mainly in his unpublished works. There is a grappling with the relation between history and system in *De Intellectu et Methodo* (1959); there is the incipient effort to lace system into the history of system in his late economic writings; there is the earlier heuristic, which surely coloured these efforts, specifying logic as a genetically-structured system of system.[60] What would result from that century-slow full inclusion is a matter of fantasy: "a process of self-constitution, a *Selbstvollzug*"[61], mediated by luminous foundational subjectivity, mediating, through the vortex of specializations, a new radiance of poet, prophet, priest.

14.2 Method in Metaphysics and Theology

I have already, in the introductory comments to this *Cantower*, drawn attention to the need to contextualize your effort here at reading as best you can. Chapter six of *Process. Introducing Themselves to Young (Christian) Minders* was an earlier (1989) attempt to push the advantage of explicit contextualization.[62] There I paralleled the sections 6.1, .6.2, 6.3, 6.4 with two sequences in *Insight*: A sequence of complexifications mounting from chapter 15 of *Insight* through *Method in Theology*; a sequence of neglected prerequisites that noted a parallel between the four sections 6.1, 6.2, 6.3, 6.4 and the four chapters 4,3,2,1 of *Insight*. While that final chapter of *Process* contains, certainly for me, its own enriching lift of

---

[59] *Insight*, 740[762].

[60] See *Searching for Cultural Foundations*, edited by P. McShane, University Press of America, 1984, xix–xxi, 126–7, 193 n.96.

[61] *Method in Theology*, 363.

[62] It was there, also, that I first brought out (see pp. 150–1) the need to parallel the two sets of canons, a task key to handling the popular Kuhnian thinking of the past fifty years. I will have more to say on this in *Cantower XVI*.

perspective, it can be seen to be at least an effort to invite a serious re-reading of Lonergan's works.

And the same comment applies to the present section, to the present *Cantower*, to the *Cantowers* of this year. Certainly, the few pointers of the next paragraphs cannot be mistaken for adequate reference, essential contextualization. While they may have for me the significance of a startling re-reading after forty years with *Insight*, they are just a nudge for you to read the two chapters referred to with a new verve, a fresh seriousness. And the same may be said even more about the final section with its focus on New York. Even a single serious reading may well light up the concrete problem of "the reorientation of common sense"[63] and the reality of that reorientation's challenge in which "in each case ends have to be selected and priorities determined. Resources have to be surveyed ... Conditions need to be investigated ... Plans have to be drawn up ... and coordinated."[64] There you have a meshing of quotations and references to the two chapter fourteens that surely freshens your reading of either. And the meshing is worth continuing here.

Both chapters are concerned with the implementation of a quite new conception of metaphysics, a conception that has been the topic of these *Cantowers* from the beginning. Indeed, you might well consider that the *Cantowers* parallel the previous chapters of *Insight*. So, for instance, *Cantower XII*, on Spacetime, can be uncomfortably associated with the discussion of your notion of being as it is fostered by chapter 12 of *Insight*. The discomfort is that in reading the *Cantower* you may have had the honest discovery that you missed this bridge in the book *Insight*. The discomfort is part of the invitation of the conclusion of the section on "Absolute Objectivity" in chapter thirteen of *Insight*, but you may not have felt it on a first reading or even on a twenty first reading. If you grimly and honestly come to grips with your notion, your horizon, of being, you may find that, yes, you are really stuck with some view of us *being* in space and time, with lurking problems of edges and ends. *Cantower XII* brings you back to that "bridge too far"[65] for your previous efforts at reading *Insight*, of reading in particular the first sentence of the final paragraph of section 13.2, "Interpretations of being or of absolute objectivity in terms of space and time are merely intrusions of the

---

[63] *Insight*, 399[425].

[64] *Method in Theology*, 364.

[65] "The Bridge of Size" is one of the bridges considered as possibly too far for contemporary Lonerganism in the article, "Features of Generalized Empirical Method and the Actual Context of Economics," *Creativity and Method*, edited by M. Lamb, Marquette University Press, Milwaukee, 1983.

imagination."[66] What of chapter 11 of *Insight* in its relation to *Cantower XI*? If you move to a comparison you will find that there is a much more discomforting challenge of self-affirmation, a heavier "scientific moment," involved in the *Cantower*.

You might think here in terms of Joyce's *Ulysses*, how he managed to echo the sequence of the work of Homer. And so you will find it profitable, as you work through this present year's *Cantowers*, to stay alert to the parallel. The paralleling, indeed, becomes increasingly explicit, with the final 21st *Cantower* being paralleled by the Epilogue of *Insight*.[67]

But let me return to the present effort, which involves a triple relating. My hope is that the section to follow will help you to read chapter 14 of both *Insight* and *Method* with fresh wonder, freshening ayes. You will see the frightening improbability of the emergence of such a metaphysics as *Insight* describes, and appreciate the modest shift in probabilities that the revised metaphysics of *Method in Theology* promises. You will glimpse enlightening parallels between Plato's various efforts and hopes regarding Athens[68] and my hopes regarding New York or Dublin[69], or your hopes for your home town. You will sense a need for a massive shift of metaphysics towards realistic fantasy, and of the canons of inquiry of *Insight* chapters 3 and 17 to inquiries into the future. You will feel, and perhaps

---

[66] *Insight*, 379[404]. The intrusion referred to is a key reason for the canon of complete explanation in chapter 3 of *Insight*. *Cantower III* offers another entry into the problem of that intrusion by raising such questions as, What do you mean by *phantasm*?

[67] *Cantower XV* is to be taken in tandem with chapter 15 of *Insight*. It deals with the massive 1400-page final effort of Stephen Gould, *The Structure of Evolutionary Theory*, Harvard University Press, 2002. *Cantower XVI* will place the work and tradition of Kuhn in the context of the 16th chapter; *Cantower XVII* will focus on active interpretation, especially that which is associated with popularization. The title of *Cantower XVIII*, "The Possibility of Cultural Ethics," makes evident the parallel. The proposed titles of *Cantowers XIX* and *XX* are, perhaps, sufficient clues to their parallels, "Ultimates," and "Intimates." *Cantower XXI*, as promised in a previous *Cantower*, will be on the topic of contemplation, but it will also be sublational of the drive of the Epilogue of *Insight*. It will end the year 2003 and open up to the new *Cantower* rhythm of 2004, one which will pay a considerable amount of attention to the New Yorker, Richard Feynman.

[68] A context here is the third volume of Eric Voegelin, *Order and History*, Louisiana State University Press, 1957, where he deals with Plato's reflections on the structure of governance.

[69] In the conclusion of chapter four of *Lack in the Beingstalk* I note the achievement of Joyce in making present the 'usual' of 20th century Dublin: the forward-heuristic task is to ground a third *Ulysses* that pivots on epiphanies and aspirations.

be burdened with, the huge role and task of "The Shaking of the Foundations"[70] where the foundations in question are the professors of philosophy and theology comfortable in recurrence-schemes of tiresome and second-rate re-shuffling of past philosophic perspectives, recurrence-schemes that do not mesh with the ongoing recurrence-schemes of boroughs and wards and blocks that "make life unlivable."[71] You may even begin to glimpse your own small contribution to the rise of fresh Founders, ever ready to offset the Tammany Halls that foster the fester of politics, economics, health, protection, joy, education, that warps the reach of our globe.

So, returning to the beginning of the previous paragraph, the first stage of our effort is to freshen your interest-reading of the two chapters 14 so that you can envisage a pragmatic-reading that would ground personal efficiency and metaphysical beauty. The pragmatic-reading should move you back, or forward, into the context of your own problem of implementation that was a key conference topic both in 2002 and in 2003.

There is the suffering beauty and efficiency of withdrawal that pivots on a deep faith in the patience of God and a luminous long-term commitment "to implement in all things the intelligibility of universal order that is God's concept and choice."[72] That living is a living within a hidden effort to conceive ever more adequately the "three stages"[73] of metaphysics and the "three stages of meaning"[74] and to express the concrete possibility in effective fantasy. But there is, too, the beauty of proximate effectiveness, but even that commitment needs its patience: effects will rarely be immediate. "Practical people are guided by common sense. They are immersed in the particular and concrete. They have little grasp of larger movements and of long-term trends. They are anything but ready to sacrifice immediate advantage for the enormously greater good of society in two or three decades."[75] But metaphysics in both cases is to be "factual"[76] and a leavening of "the material that it generates, transforms, and unifies."[77]

The **material** that I have focused on mainly in these *Cantowers* has been the material of culture to be leavened in its needs, "a profound exigence in the

---

[70] The title of Tillich's book that lurks behind my title, *The Shaping of the Foundations*.
[71] *Topics in Education*, 232.
[72] *Insight*, 726[748].
[73] *Insight*, 391[416].
[74] *Method in Theology*, 85.
[75] *Method in Theology*, 360–1.
[76] *Insight*, 393[418].
[77] *Insight*, 393[418].

contemporary situation,"[78] by hodic method. But that material is within the material of local cultures, and proximate operations must be tuned to these cultures. Both long-term and short-term founders must "enlarge their horizons to include an accurate and intimate understanding of the culture and language of the people they address [and care for]. They must grasp the virtual resources of that culture and that language, and they must use those virtual resources creatively.... in a line of development within the culture."[79]

I am thinking here, and I would wish you so to think founder-fashion, whether long-term or short term, of an illuminating day spent wandering the area of Coney Island (in south Brooklyn), absorbing the sad needs of that recreational beach with its shabby subway-stop and battered play-zones where poorer people can still smile and share moments of light and flight. To move to such thinking you may avail of the multitude of books on cities and urbanization, Jane Jacobs or Lewis Mumford or Tom Wolfe. But you must reach out in your contextualized[80] sensability to local streets and struts and stutterings, to the universe in the here and now of its groaning finality. So you come to re-read the word *situations* as Lonergan uses it in that fourteenth chapter of *Method*. Whether in Brooklyn or Bombay or Beijing, "situations are the cumulative products of previous actions and, when previous actions have been guided by the light and darkness of dialectic, the resulting situation is not some intelligible whole but rather a set of misshapen, poorly proportioned, and incoherent fragments."[81] The following section is my small effort to tune you to this way of metaphysical and hodic thinking.

14.3 Founders of New York

I have been in and out of Manhattan, and indeed the other four boroughs of New York City, since my journey to the Florida Lonergan conference of Easter 1971. Only recently, however, did I luminously approach the city with my present perspective for ten days of "field work," where *field* has the strange meaning given it by Lonergan in his lectures on existentialism. "The field is *the* universe, but my horizon defines *my* universe. Both are relevant to metaphysics, for metaphysics

---

[78] *Method in Theology*, 367.
[79] *Method in Theology*, 362.
[80] The contextualization is briefly presented symbolically and diagrammatically in the fourth chapter of *A Brief History of Tongue*.
[81] *Method in Theology*, 358.

deals with *ens*, with *omnia*, with the universe. The field regards metaphysics as such, but the horizon regards metaphysics as possible-to-me, relevant-to-me."[82]

My present perspective is not *yours*, and if you have managed to open yourself to the notion of adult growth and you are under my age of seventy, you expect an existential gap. The gap is not closed by summary but by life luminously lived against all the odds. I have written previously—for example, in the final Bacchus pages of *Lack in the Beingstalk*—about incommunicability with the self of last week if one is living thus. My present inclusion of New York within metaphysics startles me, and could not be communicated easily to me of last month. Yet it is all there, "so obviously" in the claim of *Insight* that metaphysics is integral, concrete. Perhaps my few pages and pointers might shorten the climb to the obvious for you?

Why New York? Because at least the borough of Manhattan is familiar to many readers and its mapping is relatively simple: Avenues from 1st to 12th across the map, streets running from 1st (starting north of Soho and Little Italy) to 220th way up at Inwood, where few visitors go.[83] New York City has been five boroughs since 1898, but perhaps you might focus just on Manhattan for the present ride.[84] Or indeed you might attend to your own native place or where you now reside and handle it with the same stretching focus. All I can do here is resonantly invite. Walk with Jane Jacobs and James Joyce. Pause with Ignatius of Loyola's "Contemplation for Obtaining Love" haunting your sensabililty. Taste with Proust. But you are stretching for a self-luminousness that was beyond these four. And you must banish, to the best of your ability and time, amnesia: something of Toynbee's *Mankind and Mother Earth* in your bones. Probably you know of Peter Minuit paying the Indians sixty guilders (about $25) in 1626 for the Dutch

---

[82] *Phenomenology and Logic*, 199. It is worthwhile to check the index and the pointing at the end of the introduction to that index, 382.

[83] Below First Street is the sort of mess of streets that one associates with the core of older cities like Dublin or Jerusalem. Then there is Broadway, rambling up from Battery Park at the south end and cutting across from 4th Avenue at 8th street through the Theater district to beyond 10th Avenue on the Upper West Side.

[84] Here there is the obvious need of a diagram, which in this case is a map or a series of maps: streets, subways, wards, economic, racial, histomaps, population, etc etc. You may remember the boroughs: The Bronx (recalling a land grant in 1640 to Jonas Bronck, a Danish Lutheran farmer), stretching up to the northeast. Across the East River, on Long Island, there are Brooklyn and Queens (with its two airports, La Guardia to the north, JFK to the south). The less-populous Staten Island is to the south, accessible by the famous ferry (with its view of the Statue of Liberty) and by the Verrazano Bridge.

possession of the 25 square miles, but you might also walk the Bowery in the memory of the Dutch farms, Boweries, of that century. By 1776 the town stretched a mile up; by 1810 it was two miles; by 1974 there was 34th street, and the famous 42nd street was there in the 1880s.[85] And in the two miles south of 1st street there is a mesh of memories in street names and structure, not only of New York but of the globe. Joe Di Maggio Highway is not far from the hole in the ground that was the Twin Towers and a little north from there a quarter acre was dedicated, while I was in Manhattan in July of 2002, to the memory of the Irish Hunger.[86] But your reading of faces and streets must be a battle against naivety. You are poised in the problem of the Poise and the Protopossession raised in *Cantower IX*: the real Manhattan is in an embrace of the universe that lifts you and the scene toweringly up from the scene.[87] And the embrace should, for instance, include economics: perhaps, for you at present, a discomforting pointing. I recall the last time that I lectured in Manhattan—it was at the Fordham Law School.[88] I had worked my way in ten hours to some intimation of the meaning of the 'square diagram' of economic flows that is probably familiar to you.[89] I concluded by stretching the square into a rectangle so that it could overlay Manhattan (on its side, indeed!). It is a massive task to read the history of money in Manhattan through that overlay.

---

[85] Some idea of the growing population of New York is clearly relevant. The population of Manhattan was about 5,000 in 1700; it rose to 11,000 by 1740 and to 22,000 by 1772. The revolution reduced it almost by half, but it surged again to 33,000 by 1790. It had risen to 96,000 by 1810. The famine brought the Irish: by 1860 there were 200,000 of them, about a quarter of the population. The census of 1870 put the number at 942,292. In 1910 Manhattan—now within Greater New York—had a population of 2.33 million. By 1928 Greater New York had a population of 7 million, and it has oscillated above that since. These numbers need the enrichment of details of race, profession, micro-colonies etc etc. As well as Little Italy there is now Little Odessa, and less than half of the total population is white.

[86] The quarter acre is symbolic: there was a British Law that limited poor relief to those who had less than a quarter of an acre of land.

[87] I am recalling here the drive of *Cantower III* towards understanding's centrality, towards the Dark Tower.

[88] Fordham University is in the Bronx, where the town of Fordham was founded in 1673. The University was originally St. John's College, founded by Bishop Hughes at Rose Hill in 1841.

[89] I am referring to the fundamental diagram of Lonergan, twisted through an angle of 45 degrees as in the presentations of *Economics for Everyone. Das Jus Kapital.*

What is it to read Manhattan? I am speaking now of the reading that is a piece of the operation of dialectic, the operation described on that page 250 of *Method in Theology* to which I constantly return. Then the reading is both factual and contrafactual, a felt presence of fact and fantasy, of agony and aspiration.[90] One seizes the hustle and bustle of past and present, but also one sights roads not taken and one cherishes strangely that past and present as "something better than was the reality"[91]: the emergence of overway and subway travel that places faces in rattling silence on the edge, perhaps, of their real journey of inner contemplation. So, one freshens O. Henry's remark, "New York will be a great place if they ever finish it" or the comment of Ed Koch, the 119th mayor, "New York is not a problem. New York is a stroke of genius. From its earliest days this city has been a life boat for the homeless, a leader for the hungry, a living library for the intellectually starved, a refuge not only for the oppressed but also for the creative."

But one does not lose sight of the invention in 1788 by William Noonan of the Society of St. Tammany and the twisting story of Tammany Hall all the way up to the 1950s. One has to hold to the possibility of satirizing power lust and avarice in the tradition of Zenger's *Weekly Journal* of the 1730s. One has to push New York towards a larger worldview as Karl Marx did there in the *Tribune* more than a century later. And Marx brings to mind both the piano that he wished his daughter to have and the pianos that emerged from Henry Steinway's factory after 1853. There we find the echo of the realities of loneliness and longing that reach out globally in Marx's Soho or in Manhattan's Soho. The *Stranger's Handbook of New York* of that year of 1853 lists 7 theaters, 25 Broadway hotels, and 272 churches in the city. And, as with the flow of money and Tammany, so the twisted flow of piety needs a massive attention to reveal roads not traveled, a dire absence of ongoing founders. What did these 274 churches represent, dictate, demand, direct? And to the emergence of churches and concert halls one may add the emergence of educational structures on all the levels in the five boroughs. The warps in the recurrence-schemes that crippled these emergences and their orientations go back to the beginning of the axial period. Plato's efforts at founding were already too little too late.

So I slide forward to the question of my title: what might be meant by "founders of New York"? First, I obviously mean ongoing founders, and this is illustrated by Plato. Athens was there: how should it be organized, ruled? Plato

---

[90] This type of dialectic reading, both precise and existential, is a difficult and slowly-developed habit: it twines fantasy with accurate interpretation, lifting the object line by line into a perspective that seeks to echo God's agony with evil.

[91] *Method in Theology*, 251.

had a shot at thinking that out, especially in *The Republic* and *The Laws*. But it is a geo-historical issue: there are Chinese, Indian, Egyptian, etc. versions of the effort, or lack of it, and the resulting *polis*.

Recall now the work of *Cantower VIII*, on "Slopes," on the manner in which the various zones of inquiry move up through research, interpretation, history, converging "at different angles" on the dialectic task. There I noted that later I would deal with the move forward to the eighth specialty of executive reflection, but made the point that it is not symmetrical to the angling up of the previous four. The contrast can, perhaps, best be conveyed by noting that in Research, etc. one is picking up on random "sports," successful practical thinkings related to urban dwelling in any zone. But the aim is to shift from the random sports to "democratic spreads." You need diagrams here: can you manage some? I once presented the process—in New York in fact—in terms of two cones the top one resting, "point to point" on the vertex of the other. There is the move up in the lower cone to dialectic which, you remember, generates not only positional discoveries but also a richer gathering of culturally viable types.[92] What is specified in foundations, the connected point, is a foundational pointing: in a terrible pun I talked about a "Coney Island" of founding mothers. The way forward, mediated by these founders, is complex in that the richer dialectic gathering is not lost but lifted forward through the last three specialties to mediate a fuller urban life globally.

Have you got the picture, roughly? I do not wish to enter here into the complexities of the lifting forward, stuff for later *Cantowers* and for future collaboration. My main hope here is that you enrich you image of the Tower-climb of *Cantowers III* and *VIII*. And this also helps you to add a discomforting touch of realism to the modest shift from Plato to Lonergan. Functional specialization is not magic: but it will change the statistics of mediated happiness; it is an improvement on Plato's solitary reach.

This can best be seen by returning to our concrete reflections on New York, its history, its present structure. And perhaps you might find it useful to think at first merely in terms of architecture. A style can emerge, for example, pre-1940 in Germany or post-1960 in Japan, and can be spread—regularly uncritically, accidently: think of the Bauhaus invasion of New York; read Tom Wolfe's witty book *From Bauhaus to Our House*. Such uncritical accidental spreading is to be

---

[92] See *Method in Theology* 250. The paragraph on *Classification* and *Selection* ends with the words "and dismisses other affinities and oppositions." The dismissal may be only foundational; the last three specialties will pick up on some 'dismissed' seeds of progress.

replaced—I write with distant normativity—by a hodic structuring of the mediation of local building. It would be good here to recall the comments on the present inadequacy of aesthetic criticism exemplified by the writings of Seamus Heaney.[93]

But again I do not wish to enter here into detail. Indeed, I wish you now to focus on the present state of philosophy—and theology—in New York. It is not a matter of me giving the location of New York Universities and the history and statistics of philosophical allegiances in different departments. It is a matter of you thinking concretely about some department that you are familiar with, and asking, What happened to the care of Athens shared by Plato and Academes? A member of a department of philosophy and theology can certainly care about their city: but I am talking here about integral care, the integral heuristiks that they are called to be. Perhaps you notice that, whatever their commitment to the affairs of state and street, their academic bent is largely academic, in a shocking reversal of Plato's meaning of academic bent. Obviously you will not find the hodic division of labour luminously operative: that is something of the next century. But think broadly of the forward specialties: are their shadows present in present departments? For instance, there is such a thing as Systematic Theology in many departments: does it even vaguely anticipate the massive generative genetic pragmatics[94] that would powerfully mediate the gentle transformation of the interlocking recurrence-schemes of present institutions, roles, tasks, of religious and socio-economic theory and practice? Or is it rather some type of puttering with past systems, usually of the static axiomatic type? Indeed, what is found generally in departments of philosophy and theology is an evident lack of any serious commitment to the forward mediations.

Perhaps you are beginning to sense better "The Need for the Division"[95] of labour within a functional unity and beauty of methodological influence? Generalized empirical method would extend that unity into all the veins and capillaries of culture to reach this village and that suburb, this farmland and that rice paddy. Founders are to be the leaven of the cultural lift within and without the hodic tower, initially only a mustard seed.[96] But only the detailed accounting

---

[93] See *Cantower VIII*.

[94] See *Cantower VII*.

[95] The title of section 4 of chapter 5 of *Method in Theology*.

[96] Recall and enlarge Lonergan's reflections on present leading by the nose. ."... it will give new hope and vigor to local life, and it will undermine the opportunity for peculation corrupting central governments and party politics, it will retire the brains

of the random effects of such seeding will be solidly persuasive in our mad, hurried, yet relatively mindless, modern world.

Think again, for instance, of New York money: the graft and payoffs of the nineteenth century, the federal and state bailouts of the twentieth century, the mythology of Wall Street. What is needed in New York is a massive shift of economic thinking, and it seems good to quote here from the conclusion of Lonergan's reflections of sixty years ago on the challenge. "Now to work out in detail the conditions under which this must be done, and to prescribe the rules that must be observed in doing it, is a vast task. It means thinking out afresh our ideas of markets, prices, international trade, investment, return on capital. Above all it means thinking out afresh our ideas on economic directives and controls. And if we are to do this, not on the facile model of the totalitarian or socialist regimes[97] which simply seek to abolish the problems and with them human liberty, then there will be a need not merely for sober and balanced speculation but also for all the concrete inventiveness, all the capacity for discovery and for adaptation, that we can command."[98]

Directives and controls, that is the issue: and perhaps it is better to think of directors and controllers, but now in the fantastically new sense associated with microautonomy[99] and mesoeconomics.[100] You need to stretch your imagination to envisage new patterns of conversation in wards and boroughs, in theaters and banks, in school boards and stock-markets. But above all, if you are thinking hopefully and efficiently of the future, then you must think "of persuading eminent and influential people to consider the advance thoroughly and fairly,"[101]

---

trust but it will make the practical economist as familiar a professional figure as the doctor, the lawyer, or the engineer." (*For a New Political Economy*, 37)

[97] In 1942 Lonergan had mainly in mind fascism and communism. But sick centralisms are the order of the present day.

[98] *For a New Political Economy*, 105–6. It is the conclusion of his 1942 typescript of that title.

[99] The notion of microautonomy was first presented in chapter 10 of *Wealth of Self and Wealth of Nations*. It will grow in significance as we move through *Cantowers XIX and XX* on "Ultimates" and "Intimates."

[100] The notion of mesoeconomics was emphasized in my *Pastkeynes Pastmodern Economics. A Fresh Pragmatism* (Axial Publishing, 2002). Eventually the present non-empirical tradition of "general textbooks" in economics (regarding their disorientations, see Anderson and McShane, *Beyond Establishment Economics. No Thank You Mankiw*), Axial Publishing, 2002) will be replaced by local analyses. School texts should show even more local interest.

[101] *Method in Theology*, 366.

and you must think and talk of that advance as an advance in education from kindergarten to college.[102] But I have written of this already: perhaps I need only remind you of the slogan that gives popularly the core of the advance: "when teaching children geometry, one is teaching children children."

And from this invitation to read each and every classroom normatively I return to the problem of section 14.2, the question of reading more adequately chapter 14 of both *Insight* and *Method in Theology*. Perhaps you already notice the freshening of meaning of the few quotations given in that section from these chapters? So, **situations as cumulative problems** may now take on the shapes and tonalities of Manhattan's Chinatown or Greenwich Village or your local equivalents. But were not such shapes and tonalities already there, steaming from the typewriter of the 65-year-old Lonergan?

We are, of course, back to the question of interpretation in both the active and the passive sense.[103] The 48-year-old writer of *Insight* had already walked with luminous attention the streets of such cities as Rome and London. He had no doubt but that metaphysics included those streets and so he—much later—resonated with Jane Jacob's descriptions of city life. Nor, even if his own expression was flawed, did he doubt but that "all we know is somehow with us."[104] So, while he wrote of the goal of reorienting common sense and science in terms of major and minor premises,[105] he knew where those premises were to be; he took his stand on the fact that "the goal of the method is the emergence of explicit metaphysics in the minds of particular men and women,"[106] and that this goal required that "theology unites itself with all other relevant branches of human studies."[107]

Reading New York, or wherever, into chapter 14 of either work is not, then, reading in, but reading with a full metaphysical reach for the field, the garden, the town. And what of my own effort in section 14.1? Does it not seem remote from

---

[102] Recall the beginning of the first chapter of *Lonergan's Challenge to the University and the Economy*. (Axial Publishing, 1979: a copy is now available online at: http://www.philipmcshane.org/published-books).

[103] I discussed this previously in the final section of chapter one of *Lack in the Beingstalk*.

[104] *Insight*, 278[303].

[105] *Insight*, 399–400[424–5].

[106] *Insight*, 401[426].

[107] *Method in Theology*, 364. You might find it interesting, or startling, to read now the next very dense page of *Method* and discover the subtle patterns of dialectic practice in integrated studies, patterns related in particular to the effort, in *Cantower VIII*, to describe collaborative disciplinary slopes.

the present topic, from departments of theology, academic campuses, block associations in cities? Yet I wrote the chapter in the wake of an effort to point towards the rich complexities of Communications as a functional specialty. In that previous writing I was thinking concretely but writing symbolically of sets of systems, S_{ij} , and the intermeshing of such systems with actual contexts through the operations of the eighth specialty.[108] Within a developed heuristic science, such symbolism is recognized as reaching to the concrete realities of the globe.

The problem, THEN, is one of unshared context, and that is the problem being faced in these *Cantowers* with their drive to a communal sharing of the first and second words of metaphysics and a diagram of global collaborative endeavor analogous to the periodic table that guides chemical and biochemical collaboration.[109] Perhaps you might return to that diagram now and look for New York there. For instance, the diagram envisages the sequential operations of aggregates of viewpoints on viewpoints: so it includes, certainly for me the writer, my dialectically-twisting viewpoint on the viewpoints of the 120 or so past mayors of New York. The Founder's task, in any specialty, is to make such an inclusion a vibrant operative reality so that, like a good New York school coach, she or he is ready, ever ready, to nudge the specialized or local human team gamely forward.

---

[108] "Systematic, Communications, Actual Contexts" was not published until 1987 in *Lonergan Workshop* (7) 1987, 143–174. There were occasional concrete illustrations in the article: "So, French agriculture-based theory-policy of an earlier century, transposed by general functional economic categories, might be found relevant to a culture-sensitive economic transformation of a twenty-first century Indian province" (151).

[109] The diagram, from page 124 of *A Brief History of Tongue*, has been presented regularly.

F ~ THE FULL PROBLEM OF DEVELOPMENT

Why 'Full' in the title in this early essay of my series? Well, F is for Full! But there is a sound reason for this fulsome early ramble. The previous essay gives you some impression of my struggle, over one month in 2003, with aspects of the canons of hermeneutics in Lonergan. The high point of these canons in *Insight*, in my view, is densely presented in the paragraph that turns, in *Insight*, 609 to 610, a paragraph I have designated for years as 60910, and will continue to do so here. The word *development* occurs twice there: on the last line of 609, and the fourth line of 610. How did you read it, how do you read it? Did you Jay-walk through the paragraph and the word, rather than J-wrap?[1]

My first skimpy puzzling about the canons of hermeneutics began in 1958, but puzzling about development had its serious existential beginnings in the winter of 1958–59.[2] It blossomed in my focus on the problem as it occurred and occurs in biology, especially botany, in 1962–63, and my poise on it in 1964 was a slimly enlightened version of that of the biologist Paul Weiss. It seems best to quote here a full paragraph that I wrote on the topic in the spring of that year.[3]

Presently, we will touch on more complex aspects of the interplay of classical and statistical inquiry. Before doing so, however, we must turn our attention to a rather obvious question concerning the plant: how does it grow? More properly, we are asking about the understanding of the development of the plant, and, in an essay such as this, one cannot but raise the fundamental question: What is development? As Paul Weiss remarks as the beginning of his book,[4] this question

---

[1] I decided to throw this pointer ahead of its treatment. You can of course go straight to where I treat it formally, in Essay J. At present consider the distinction as between unenlightened commonsense reading and heuristically poised reading. Note that *jaywalk* is not, at least in its history, a neutral word: it is a compound word derived from the word *jay*, an inexperienced person and a curse word that originated in the early 1900s, and *walk*. Jaywalking is the curse of present Lonergan studies.

[2] I described this at the beginning of chapter 2 of the 1989 book *Process. Introducing Themselves to Young (Christian) Minders* (http://www.philipmcshane.org/website-books). The focus was on what Aquinas could possibly mean by "growing."

[3] "Insight and the Strategy of Biology," *Spirit as Inquiry. Studies in Honor of Bernard Lonergan S.J.*, edited by Frederick Crowe, Herder and Herder, 1964, 74–88.

[4] *Principles of Development*, New York, 1939. I am quoting this from page 80 of the article referred to in the previous note.

seems trivial. 'Does not everybody have some notion of what development implies? Undoubtedly most of us have. But when it comes to formulating these notions they usually turn out to be very vague'. Weiss himself seeks to get beyond this vagueness, beyond, too, the type of explanation which 'cannot survive the first rigid test on a concrete phenomenon of development,'[5] by staying as close as possible in his considerations to specific phenomena. Thus, while he sees progressive differentiation as the keynote of development, detailed illustrated discussion of differentiation leaves no room for an accusation of a mere shift of obscurity. Again, the hierarchy of organizations of the organism has to be explained, first by decomposing the complex phenomenon into simple processes of biological order, then further by attempting 'to trace the roots of biological process into the known realms of physical and chemical phenomena,'[6] the ultimate aim being 'to describe and understand any state of the living system as conditioned by the immediately preceding states.'[7] "

It seems useful to interject here that, if you have little interest in botany, pause and re-read this paragraph thinking of the Christian church and an ultimate aim of understanding 'any state of the living system as conditioned by the immediately preceding states.'

My next push on the topic came in the autumn of 1965, when I contemplated the topic as suitable for a doctorate in Oxford. I mused over the work of J.H. Woodger.[8] That work, however, did not ground optimism regarding solving the

---

[5] *Ibid.*, 75.

[6] *Ibid.*, 108.

[7] *Ibid.*, 120.

[8] I went on to write a thesis on the more manageable topic, "The concrete logic of discovery of statistical science, with special reference to problems of evolution theory," a fuller version of which appeared later as *Randomness, Statistics and Emergence* (Gill, Macmillan, and Notre Dame, 1970). Of course I touched on both the work of Woodger and the topic of development, (see, on both, the index) but the central focus in the book was in fact the central focus of the essay, J, below. The high point of the thesis, however, was the push towards "some kind of Markov matrix as giving the required picture of history." (*Randomness, Statistics, and Emergence*, 237), something within my present more elaborate view. Is that recent view of mine adequate? It is no more adequate than Woodger's in the limited zone. It is to this limitation that this essay, F, points and the point is nicely made in a comment on Woodger's work, (see *The Axiomatic Method in Biology*, Cambridge, 1937) regarding the problem of finding heuristic symbols. "One would be at a loss to get the square root of MDCDXXXVI, and a basic flaw in Woodger's efforts to axiomatize biology lay in his failure to find an apt symbolism." *Randomness, Statistics and Emergence*, 89: see the footnote there.

problem. Indeed, the problem of solving the problem is our topic here: I see it now as a mightier problem, a problem for the positive Anthropocene.

A help here is to bring you back to my memories of the four years I spent in the world of mathematics, and to refer you to a book I came to use much later as a guide to, well, the meaning of it title: *The Development of Mathematics*.[9] Unlike Paul Weiss, the author was not into the meaning of development, nor is this strange. Another companion of my thinking through those years was the classic, *The Development of Logic* by Kneale and Kneale. Again, the development of logic was—a curious claim—not the topic of the book.

The point of this ramble of mine is to get you to pause over the cultural ethos that does not raise certain questions. Think of my years of mathematics 1952–56: I simply did not advert to the topic of development in mathematics, though the years were haunted by my existential problem of growth. My first serious venture came, as noted above, in 1958, nudged by Lonergan and Aquinas. What about it as a serious venture of present culture? I do not wish to enter into that topic here, but I would note that in areas like botany the interest expressed by Paul Weiss and others in the mid-twentieth century has been replaced by a daft reductionism that chatters away about genes and information theory. Lonergan writes in *Method in Theology* about—LOL—the real problem leading "into the impasse of scrutinizing the self-scrutinizing self."[10] And is this not a good place to halt this piece of our venture?: giving you a pause, "eyes off the page,"[11] to think of your problem of perhaps falling short of the subtle self-scrutiny that would reveal stages in the development in you of an understanding of development. Then peruse Lonergan's suggestion, quoted below, about the required self-scrutiny in the simplest of areas, mathematics. But, as I remarked about biology, weave you perusing round the topic both of your own development and of the development of culture.[12]

> The history of any particular discipline is in fact the history of its development. But this development, which would be a theme of the history, is not something simple and straightforward but something which occurs in a long series of various steps, errors, detours, and corrections.

---

[9] E.T. Bell, McGraw Hill, 1945.

[10] *Method in Theology*, 167[158].

[11] A phrase used by Gaston Bachelard regarding creative reading in *The Poetics of Space*, Beacon Press, Boston, 1970. For details of his view see note 29, p. 98, of my book (1975), *Wealth of Self and Wealth of Nations: Self-Axis of the Great Ascent*: http://www.philipmcshane.org/published-books.

[12] To the context of *Insight*, chapters 6, 7, and 15, add that of *Phenomenology and Logic*, the two final chapters that I refer to regularly.

Now as one studies this movement he learns about this developmental process and so now possesses within himself an instance of that development which took place perhaps over several centuries. This can happen only if the person understandings both his subject and the way he learned about it. Only then will he understand which elements in the historical developmental process had to be understood before the others, which one mad for progress in understanding and which held back, which elements really belonged to the particular science and which did not, and which elements contained errors. Only then will he be able to tell at what point in the history of his subject there emerged new visions of the whole and when the first true system occurred, and when the transition took place from an earlier to a later systematic ordering, which systematization was simply an expansion of the former and which was radically new; what progressive transformation the whole subject underwent; how everything that was explained by the old systematization is now explained by the new, along with many other things that the old one did not explain—the advances in physics, for example, by Einstein and Max Planck. Then and then alone will he be able to understanding to understand what factors favoured progress, what hindered it, and why, and so forth.

Clearly, therefore, the historian of any discipline has to have a thorough knowledge and understanding of whole subject. And it is not enough that he understand it in any way at all, but he must have a systematic understanding of it. For the precept, when applied to history, means that successive systems which have developed over a period of time have to be understood. The systematic understanding of a development ought to make use of an analogy with the development that takes place in the mind of the investigator who learns the subject, and this interior development within the mind of the investigator ought to parallel the historical process by which the science itself developed.[13]

I leave you with that musing of Lonergan from 1959. The next essay goes back to view his climb during 1949–53 towards the understanding of development. View? Musings? I nudge you to begin to glimpse that we are puttering along in a slimly known unknown, tuning our W-enzymes into "all that is lacking."[14]

---

[13] *CWL* 23, *Early Works on Theological Method 2*, "Understanding and Method," 175, 177.

[14] *Insight*, 559, line 24, read in the indigestible context of the previous 10 lines.

G ~ *Insight*'s Search for Genetic Control

So we move to a larger context of that paragraph 60910: the full suggested self-scrutiny of *Insight*. Our question is, What is development?, where the what-focus is on a symbolism of control, a genetic control. You might push that, in this fresh "scrutinizing the self-scrutinizing subject," by thinking of a genetics of genetic control. Can you get some distance in figuring the duplication? A help here is to return to the first section of chapter 8 of *Insight*, "The General Notion of the Thing."

Consider whither Lonergan is pushing you to a heuristics of thinking "thing" or a genetic control of such a heuristics. A further disturbing help is to consider the motto of the book, reproduced here in italics as it was in the original text. Note that the fourth last word in the text is *developments*, and recall the quotation with which we ended the previous essay. Pause over the question, Is the motto an adequate expression of the challenge of the book, or of the challenge of the two volumes of his proposed work?

> *Thoroughly understand what it is to understand, and not only will you understand the broad lines of all there is to be understood but you also will possess a fixed base, an invariant pattern, opening up upon all further developments of understanding.*

Does our puttering in Essay F not lift the problem, and express a problem about the motto? Add problems posed by the previous essays. Indeed add problems, eventually, of the full "A to Z" in viewing the slogan. The slogan "happily enough sums up the positive content of the book,"[1] but what meaning had Lonergan for *enough*?

So we can move, happily or unhappily, to ask about *Insight* and the topic of genetic control. I suggest the odd view that the intent in the book was to get the subject to self-scrutinize sufficiently to open the door to the problem of genetic control. On the road there is the central section of the book, packaged nicely in the seeding beginnings of an obscure new metaphysics, sections 7 of chapter 15. He is finally ready to nudge you into thinking out those beginnings with him. Do you find this a little shocking? "To reveal the heuristic significance of the notion of development, and to prepare our statement of the integral heuristic structure that we have named metaphysics, attention must now be directed to genetic

---

[1] *Insight*, 22.

method."[2] Indeed, attention must now be so directed, where *now* means our now, your now with me. Because: the directing of Lonergan in the fifties just did not work. I recall chatting with Fred Crowe about the directing: he admitted finding this stuff quite beyond him. It remains beyond me but I struggle on with a startled open mind. How about you?

It may help to startle you if I recall one of my own daft efforts to come to grips with, well, with the flower and its place in the flowering of finitude. That daft effort was in fact a fresh beginning of my *Cantower* series, which I halted following a suggestion of collaboration on the topic which now claims my full strategic attention: Lonergan's brilliant focusing on effective dialectic collaboration.[3] The fresh beginning was a prolonged ramble—forty one essays[4]—round the meaning of that single paragraph on page 489 which begins, "Study of an organism begins from ..."

The oddity of those essays is that they stayed within the nudgings of that paragraph with no attempt to push forward from that "begins," that beginning. Page 489 ends with a turn to that push, or might I say a genetic push towards that push, or might I say a genetic push towards a genetic push towards that push?[5] The beginning has been a suggestion of getting to grips with the flower as integrator: "However, the organism grows and develops."[6] That little sentence points nicely to a central crisis in this millennium's thinking.

Pick up on the madness of the next two pages, and chortle—"proofless, purposeless laughter can dissolve honored pretence"[7]—at the closing line: "The matter may be clarified by an illustration."[8] The high-flying of the first half of page 490 leads to the three questions that lead into the three paragraphs leading to the comic sentencing of humanity to **what** its way towards genetic control. "What is the operator?" "Still, what is the operator?" "How is the operator studied?"

Drop the question mark, and scrutinize the dropper. If you, the dropper, are a serious self-scrutinizing self then the scrutinizing will make slowly luminous "all

---

[2] *Ibid.*, 484.

[3] The topic of chapter three, "Self-Assembly," of my *The Future: Core Precepts of Supramolecular Method and Nanochemistry*.

[4] Titled *Field Nocturnes* : http://www.philipmcshane.org/field-nocturnes.

[5] Pause and brood over the sentence which concludes this section 7.2: "In this fashion one's understanding of the operator begins to be an instance of higher system on the move in the development of scientific knowledge of development." *Insight*, 492.

[6] *Insight*, 490, line 3.

[7] *Ibid.*, 649, line 9: the context is the place of humor and satire in human progress.

[8] End of *Insight* 491.

that is lacking" in the study of the operator. What is the operator. Still and stilly, what is to be the operator, shifting into the positive Anthropocene of a blossoming of scrutinizing the stumbling self-scrutiny—"the reader already possesses some familiarity"[9]—of the closing century, perhaps, of the negative Anthropocene.

> The emergence of humanity is the evolutionary achievement of sowing what among the cosmic molecules. The sown what infests the clustered molecular patterns behind and above your eyes, between your ears, lifting areas—named by humans like Brocca and Wernicke—towards patterned noise-making that in English is marked by "so what?"[10]

Have I changed, even a little, your poise in reading those two frightful pages 490–1 of *Insight*? Then float on, yes, float on and over, the gap[11], the lack,[12] lurking in the dozen pages that follow there on your hidden "*moi intime*,"[13] your axial "I"[14]: hopefully with "heightened tension."[15] "Riverrun past Eve and Adam"[16] and Jesus and Muhummad,[17] screaming for us to notice that we are the stalk of the story, a so-far "Hole Story," to recall James Joyce.[18] That we are the stalk of the story I wish to make the talk of the town. I would have us read the end of those dozen

---

[9] *Insight*, 493: beginning last paragraph.
[10] The beginning of chapter one, "Sow What," of my *The Allure of the Compelling Genius of History*, Axial Publishing, 2015.
[11] The existential gap is the topic of the final two chapters of *CWL* 18, *Phenomenology and Logic*. To these I refer to regularly, giving their challenge different contexts.
[12] The central topic of my *Lack in the Beingstalk*, Axial Publishing, 2006.
[13] *Insight*, 495, line 21.
[14] Ibid., 499, lines 15, 16, 27.
[15] Ibid., 499, line 5.
[16] The first words of James Joyce, *Finnegans Wake*.
[17] "It would be misleading to see a chronological limit to the Axial Age that excluded those two mighty epigone (i.e., Jesus and Muhummad) of Zarathustra and 'Deutero-Isaiah'. Thus the Axial Age expands from a period of about 120 years to one of about seventeen centuries running from c. 1060 B.C., down to A.D. 632, which is the date of the Prophet Muhammad's death." (Arnold Toynbee, *Mankind and Mother Earth*, Oxford University Press, 1976, 178.) My larger perspective begins to emerge in "Middle Kingdom: Middle Man. (T'ien-hsia—i jen)," *Searching For Cultural Foundations*, edited by Philip McShane, University Press of America, 1980, 9–11.
[18] The "Hole Story" is a poise that dominates in John Bishop, *Joyce's Book of the Dark: Finnegans Wake*, University of Wisconsin Press, 1986.

pages soberly, humbly, committed to a shift to effectiveness in cherishing the stalk, indeed in what I write of later as a cherished "Stalking Jesus."[19]

> It has been possible, I believe, to offer a single integrated view that finds its point of departure in classical method yet embraces biology, the psychology of behavior and depth psychology, existential reflection upon man, and fundamental elements in the theory of individual and social history, of morals and asceticism, of education and religion.[20]

Thus I come to an apparent defect in *Insight*'s integral but incomplete push.[21] "It may be asked in what department of theology the historical aspect of development might be treated, and I would suggest that it may possess peculiar relevance to a treatise on the mystical body of Christ."[22] It may, indeed, be so asked. But let us leave musing on that puzzle to the middle section of the following essay on "A Potential Totality."[23]

---

[19] See below, 167ff.

[20] *Insight*, 503–504.

[21] Completing the push was the task of my *The Road to Religious Reality*, Axial Publishing, 2012.

[22] *Insight*, 763, lines 29–31.

[23] **Here you have my second of eleven (pp. 8, 62, 70, 74, 87, 92, 118, 140, 141, 150, 169) boldfaced notes. The last words above are "Potential Totality." Might you think of physics' reach for a TOE, a "theory of everything," so recalling the first note of this series, note 30 on page 8? A TOE-grip of Lindsay and Margenau, a TOE grip on the Mystical Body? Most of my readers have no toe-grip on L and M: heavens, they have not got a toe-grip on the first year physics course to which my website essays 7 and 8 are preliminary notes. If you are one of them, pause over the challenge of lines 14–25 of *Insight* 559, and mesh that pause into Lonergan's discomforting comments on *haute vulgarization* of *CWL 6*, 121 and 155. I ask you now, immediately, discomfortingly, about your doctrine, your policy, of and in your own thinking and prayer. "Doctrines that are embarrassing shall not be mentioned in polite company" *(Method in Theology*, 299[279]). I am now way beyond politeness! "In the Greek patristic tradition *theoria* became the name of contemplative prayer." *CWL* 13, *A Third Collection*, "Mission and Spirit," section 4. I am raising the question of a post-axial version of this. Do you take your what-call to *theoria* seriously? Have you ever been "bitten by theory" (*CWL* 6, 155)? Bitten by the Theory that is the Word?**

H ~ A Potential Totality

As I was winding this book to its conclusion I came back, for a third effort, to the craziness of trying to compactly intimate the meshing of Lonergan's discussion of the genetics [1] of humanity's leadership's viewpoint with his discussion of the Triune Leadership.[2] The cut back still leaves me with a weaving in of the leadership of Mystery's obscurity, and it seemed to me as I revised this that obscurity here is a help: I am thinking as I type this of a remark of James Joyce at the end of an instructive letter. "If I can throw any further obscurity on the matter let me know." We desperately need luminous obscurity.[3] But now, on with my cut-back venture.

****

So I invite you to take[4] as our question and quest the concluding poise of the previous Essay G, the puzzle-poise of Lonergan: "It may be asked in what department of theology the historical aspect of development might be treated, and I would suggest that it may possess peculiar relevance to a treatise on the mystical body of Christ."[5] I place it in the context of the climb sketched by Lonergan in

---

[1] The discussion is in *Insight*'s chapter 17, section 3.2, "The Notion of a Universal Viewpoint," but perhaps you share my problem of the pedagogical difficulty of that phrase. So I talk here of genetics and of the genesis of genetic viewpoints.

[2] *CWL* 12, *The Triune God: Systematics*, Part Six.

[3] Might you read such desperation into your W-enzyme as you take up and in Lonergan's first section of *Insight* chapter 17? The desperation is lurking there, in your W-enzyme's vertical finality, a "dynamic joy and zeal." *Insight*, 722, last words.

Put these five words of mine, *we desperately need luminous obscurity*, into your reading of Lonergan's comment on Aristotle's ideal (quoted below, differently, in note 14). "It is not hard to discern in this passage an acknowledgement of vertical finality in its multivalence and in its obscurity. In its multivalence, for there is in man a finest; it surpasses all else in power and in value; it is to be let go al; the way. In its obscurity, for what is divine in man, and what would be going all the way?" Lonergan, "Mission and Spirit," *A Third Collection*, Paulist Press, 1985, 27.

[4] Oh la la: *take*? By accident *take* was the 11th and middle word of the previous note's first sentence. What did it mean to you? What is your take on *take*? Yes, your present **what** is your take on *take*. Should I **boldface** the word as we go along here, to remind you, to rewind you?

[5] *Insight*, 763, lines 29–31.

the final sixth section of *The Triune God: Systematics*.⁶ That sketch, for students, ends gloriously thus:

> For the glory of the Father is this, that just as he eternally speaks the Word in truth and through the Word breathes forth Love in holiness, so also in the fullness of time he sent his incarnate Son in truth so by believing the Word we might speak true words and understand, and through the Word He sent the Spirit of the Word in accord with holiness so that joined to the spirit in love and made living members of the body of Christ we might cry out, 'Abba, Father!'⁷

Pausing over this properly can help us towards musing on the challenge of a potential totality of effectively engineering the road to the terminal value of those missions, that "greatest of all works."⁸ But what is a proper poise? That, really, is the question that haunts this entire book, indeed, is to haunt always the entire enterprise of theology and prayer. We are talking about a high incomplete achievement of Lonergan, of the future, of an excellence of humanity that is to end in an eschatological radiance. The core of our problem is our limp **what**, embedded at present in its proximate home, our floundering W-enzyme.

How is the core of that embedded problem to begin to see and be seized by the fullest meaning of the word *achievement*, or of the title of this Essay, *potential totality*?⁹ That problem is very simply stated by pushing the usual meaning of the what-question to the fullness that lurks in the question: What might this be?¹⁰ It

---

⁶ The discussion dates back to the first edition *Divinarum Personarum Conceptio Analogica*, 1957: the edition I began with in the late 1950s. Lonergan sent me his 1964 edition when it was published: it is a wrecked bundle of pages now: my extension, in the last century, of the Book of Common Prayer that is to become, globally, *Insight*.

⁷ *CWL* 12, *The Triune God: Systematics*, 519, 521. The translation is mine, but I stay close to the faulty translation in the text, although other subtle shifts would be good.

⁸ *CWL* 12, 491.

⁹ I quote the first line of section 17.3.2 at the bottom of *Insight* 587. Perhaps by the end of even a first reading, a first take, of this essay you will find your self-thinking of yourself as what is meant by *a potential totality*?

¹⁰ I could ask you to venture into the meaning of *exigency* in *CWL* 19, *Early Latin Theology*, "The Supernatural Order" (see 149) or the meaning of *exigence* in *CWL* 18, *Phenomenology and Logic* (see the index under *Exigence*) or the related meaning of natural resultance in *CWL* 2, *Verbum: Word and Idea in Aquinas* (see 144–48), but here I ask you to venture into yourself, your core W-enzyme self. With Graceful luck, the venture can **take** you out of the tradition of self-dodging that I write of below in note 16, to **take** you in "to dismiss those that would have us resign ourselves to our mortal lot" (see note 14 below).

A Potential Totality

is imaged nicely by the eye-straining involved in seeing my usual tower image of collaboration as leaning, indeed leaning spookily.[11] I note that I have not changed that tower image since I first concocted it: I leave that to the next generations.[12] One leans the image thus, and thus in the molecules of the incarnate subjects you and me, in the fullness of praying "Abba, Father" or "Thy Kingdom Come."[13] Behold the Tower now, tilted psychically by you: overlay it with the leaning that is your infant Interior Lighthouse.

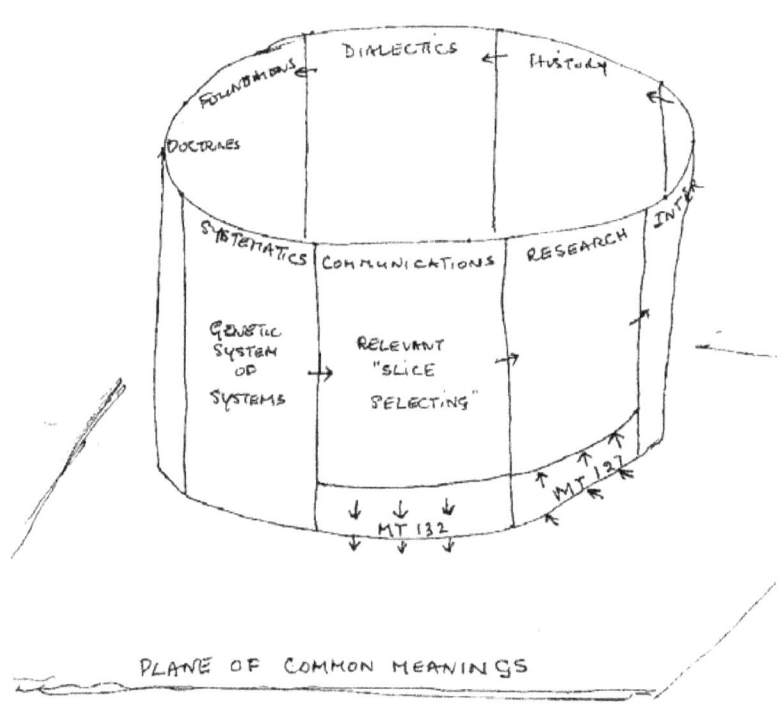

---

[11] I would ask you to lean with Lonergan's spooky writing to Fred Crowe of June 1954 as he leaned desperately after his first year of teaching in Rome. See my leaning to that leaning and its future in note 10, p. 95.

[12] I am obviously a long term optimist. The long term calls on you, cauls in you.

[13] The normative incarnate poise of this prayer is discussed in the final section of the fifth of my articles in *Divyadaan: Journal of Education and Philosophy*, vol. 30, no. 1 (2019).

But let us make a little start here by you **taking** seriously my suggestion of thinking of the little girl voice and lungs of Joan Sutherland or of Amy Winehouse, the little-boy fingers and spine of Glen Gould or of Art Tatum. Spread your fantasy to excellence in any zone of art, science, sport.[14] Thus tune into your own W-enzyme and find through the invitation of admiration some absence in you, some potentiality that is a genuine bent beyond in strange potential. Perhaps the relevant tuning is the twirling of personal darkness?

> This basic, indeterminately directed dynamism has its ground in potency; it Iis without the settled assurance and efficacy of form; it tends to be shouldered out of the busy day, to make its force felt in the tranquility of darkness, in the solitude of loneliness, in the shattering upheavals of personal or social disaster.[15]

We are now facing the reading of section 17.3.2 of *Insight* and without some such extravagant tuning it seems to me that the reading of section 17.3.2 of *Insight* will remain as it has been for sixty two years.[16] The first six words of its second sentence, "Our present concern will be to," sit there, looking you in the inner I... Please don't turn the page.

"Our present concern will be to." To what? Oh yes, to what. How far are you from one who is luminously "scrutinizing the self-scrutinizing self"?[17] Did

---

[14] I wish you to reach for analogies for "the theoretic life," the life, in my terms, of The Interior Lighthouse. The wish adds a nudge of repetition. "In a celebrated passage Aristotle granted that his ideal of the theoretic life was too high for man and that, if one lived it, one would do so not as a man but as having something divine present within one. Nonetheless he went on to urge us to dismiss those that would have us resign ourselves to our mortal lot. He pressed us to strive in the utmost to make ourselves immortal and to live out what was finest in us. For that finest, though slight in bulk, still surpasses by far all else in power and in value" (Lonergan, "Mission and the Spirit," *A Third Collection*, Paulist Press, 1985, 27). Think, now of the full potential of voice boxes and little fingers: what are those molecules reaching for? See further, note 16.

[15] *Insight*, 648.

[16] Recall my slogan of note 28, p. 8. I ask you to pause over one particular failure to scrutinize the self-scrutinizing self: that paragraph 60910. It is the central piece of Lonergan's reach for a science of interpretation. Are you one of the many who failed? It is pre-functional, so it need not be tied in with the general dodging of that challenge. Yet, week after week I see familiar names of Lonergan students in the flow of *academic.edu* "following the bent of their genius" (*Insight*, 602, line 5) not at all "bewildered and dismayed" (*ibid.*, line 4) at ignoring a central norm of Lonergan's pre-method metaphysics.

[17] My problem-slogan for this book! *Method in Theology*, 167[158].

you climb up through those six words in and to a hierarchy of turns?[18] How far are you from trying to get a grip on your kingdom, your queenly role?[19] But perhaps it is best for you to heart-hold that question of your inner I till I reach towards your Aye in the next essay and in the essay to follow, Essay J, where you find a shocking genetics of such reaching in, yes, in a semicolon. Meantime, we turn the page together to read those first three words of page 588, "clarify the notion," and perhaps now sense a little better what a misleading word *clarify* is.

Clarify is an unfortunate word, but Bernard is in a hurry that summer of 1953. He cannot pause to create a teaching, but rather writes, so to speak, from the top down. What am I to do? Go back to the top of page 586 and seize my problem here. What of my shooting for a simple interpretation? "The simple interpretation gives rise to further problems."[20] Think, humbly and sadly, of the habitual insights of Lonergan studies regarding Lonergan's viewpoint on viewpoints. Think, thus, of the quality of "deficiencies E and E'."[21]

Perhaps I should try a reflective interpretation, despite its "two obvious difficulties"?[22] "Reflective interpretation is a smart idea, a beautiful object of thought. But is it a practical possibility?"[23] Here I might have begun my wriggle with the complex dodges of a fuller interpretation by, oddly, homing in on the apparent deficiency, mentioned at the end of the previous essay, in Lonergan's achievement in *Insight*: should we call it E"?[24]

---

[18] *Method in Theology*, 167, top [158, top].

[19] I think of the science of humanity as engineering, and the queen as its effective heuristic W-enzyme presence. Lift, thus, this challenge of Lonergan: "If philosophy is to include a philosophy of science, if in some sense it is be a *regina scientiarum*, not merely a constitutional monarch—you do no wrong because you can do nothing at all—but an effective monarch that exerts a real influence within the fields of the sciences, then, as a philosophy it will have to be something fixed. But it cannot have the fixity of a monolith, one big stone, solid and homogeneous throughout. Its fixity has to be the fixity of form in which the sciences are included; but what are included are not fixed sciences but sciences free to develop," *CWL* 18, *Phenomenology and Logic*, 126. Relevant to this no-fixity and to the engineering poise is the solution to the problem of the chasm: see note 9 of p. 90.

[20] *Insight*, 586, line 7.

[21] *Ibid.*, line 6.

[22] *Ibid.*, line 26.

[23] *Ibid.*, 587, lines 3–5.

[24] See note 36 below, and think of the lift of the defect E" by the connection of **e** and **E** in our engineering sublation of that paragraph 60910.

The apparent deficiency is the problem left in the Epilogue of the book, left dangling at the end of the last Essay, G: the character and place of a treatment of the mystical body of Christ?[25] How would it fit in in a fulsome theology? The materials are there, but what of "its formal element"?[26] "I would be inclined to think that its formal element remains incomplete as long as it fails to draw on a theory of history."[27]

Here I flex my cut-back bent, cutting out outrageous reachings that we also float past in later alphabet essays. We are dealing with "the remote possibility of thought on the concrete universal,"[28] whose "proximate possibility resides in a theory of development"[29] that weaves natural and supernatural into a dynamics of humanity. There is work to be done here on the twists and turns of Lonergan's battered searchings throughout the next decade. It is simpler here to lift you forward through my own struggles with the topic that blossomed into a broad, if incomplete, treatment of the topic in my little book of 2012: *The Road to Religious Reality*.[30] The core of my struggle was with the meaning of *Comparison* in section 5 of *Method in Theology* chapter 10.[31] Here I nudge you to think in terms of the procedures either of modern physics or, more suggestively, in terms of medical searchings for adequate treatment of organic or even psychic disorientation.[32] In both there is the occurrence of **comparison** to what in physics is called *The Standard Model*. The struggle is to compare suggested 'pushing forward' in these or in any area of human engineering with the currently accepted best.

This is trickier than it seems, the seeming being connected with the word *currently*. But let us leave that issue vague till, in Essay O, we face the adventure of "Understanding the Object." What I wish now is for you to begin to resonate with the "shock value: the actual heuristic bringing together of the two topics, **Comparison** and **The Mystical Body**, was certainly a wild delightful shock for

---

[25] *Insight*, 763.
[26] *Ibid*., 764, line 3.
[27] *Ibid*., lines 2–4.
[28] *Ibid*., 764, line 27.
[29] *Ibid*., line 29.
[30] Axial Publishing. I would note that the full title has the odd pre-title, placed thus: *Method in Theology 101 AD 9011: The Road to Religious Reality*.
[31] On the context of this problem see Patrick Brown, "Functional Collaboration and the Development of *Method in Theology*, Page 250," *Himig Ugnayan. A Theological Journal of the Institute of Formation and Religious Studies*, (16) 2015–16, 171–200.
[32] I have regularly use pedagogically the TV program *House* as a way into the type of thinking that goes with the strategy named *Comparison* on *Method in Theology* 250[247].

me."³³ The effort of *Comparison* that is to control adequately theological progress is a *Comparison* of the *Assembled Completed* recent results with the front-edge of the sequence of geohistorical heuristic treatises on global progress. In theology that front-edge *Praxisweltanschauung* is to be the current treatise on the mystical body; in philosophy it is to be a limply adequate geogenetic heuristics of history.³⁴ This is a daftly compact statement of what is already quite compacted in *The Road to Religious Reality*. Perhaps a further heavy quotation from that little book could be a helpful nudge to your shock and searchings.

> What is to emerge is a Towering control of the spacetime of meaning in its full aggreformic dynamics. Fibre-bundle geometry will breed an image-adequate fulsome heuristic of the geohistorical complexity of local and personal viewpoints, so that we no longer speak vaguely of ongoing, overlapping, etc contexts, but gear up to the impossible dream of the second canon of hermeneutics. There is to be a new self-creating self-imaging in the Tower of Able. "It is, I fear, in Vico's phrase, a *scienza nuova*."³⁵

I find it breathtakingly encouraging even to re-type this piece of my writing of eight years ago. It weaves forward from the breathtaking encouragement of Lonergan's conclusion to his 1934 *Essay on Fundamental Sociology*. And as I view it now I am pushed to add two words to its middle sentence: "gear up to *and beyond* the impossible dream." The beyond is already there in the previous part of the sentence: did I not see that in my younger effort?

And do you sense the wildness of a beyond this section 17.3.2, that **takes** its new geohistorical flavor up into a controlling genetics of the genetics of efforts to reach geohistorical control of engineering the future?³⁶ Faced with that fantasy,

---

³³ *The Road to Religious Reality*, 13.

³⁴ For an earlier but relevant description of this geohistorical genetics see, in my series, *Questions and Answers* (http://www.philipmcshane.org/questions-and-answers), Question 36, "An Appeal to Fred Lawrence and Other Elders."

³⁵ I quote from pages 40–9 of *The Road to Religious Reality*. The concluding quotation is from Lonergan's review of books on Christian Philosophy by M. F. Sciacca and Maurice Nedoncelle: *CWL* 20, *Shorter Papers*, 223.

³⁶ Might you now reread this little essay, H, taking it into Lonergan's desperate discussion of general and special categories (*Method in Theology*, 285–91[267–73]) and find seeded in your take the Standard Model, a heuristic genetics of heuristic genetics of heuristics genetics, be that model the limp general categories or the glory of a full meaning of *Comparison*? And now have I not lifted your **take** on the words *Universal Viewpoint*, a problem-**take** of the first note in this Essay? And the end Word of *Insight*,

are we not breathless, not now with the poise of "breathless and late,"[37] but with the poise in existential hope, "an eternal fire of optimism and energy,"[38] that ends Lonergan's 1934 *Essay on Fundamental Sociology*.[39]

610, line 9 is a Viewpointing of the Universe, as you "fuse into a single explanation," Explanation. We are called to live in that explanation, Explanation.

[37] "a little breathless and a little late," *Insight*, 755.

[38] *Essay in Fundamental Sociology*, 43.

[39] Here you have my third boldfaced note of eleven such (pp. 8, 62, 70, 74, 87, 92, 118, 140, 141, 150, 169). Recall the first two notes of this boldfaced series of eleven notes. I am asking about the existential hope and energy of you as a minder of history. The brutal fact is that, without venturing into serious explanation in some years of your living, you are simply not in the ballpark of functional Tower work of redemptive engineering. *Serious explanation* are troublesome words: as minding goes up from the simplest of subjects, physics, to the difficult zones of psychology or sociology it tends to fade into meanings laced round non-scientific tinkerings, the disease of "academic disciplines. Clearly enough, these approaches to the problem of method do little to advance" (*Method in Theology*, 3–4[8]) serious thinking. And now I am mindful not only of those following such conventional pretense but also of those who already suspect this ineffective world of e.g. chit-chat about grace and art and conversion and culture, and who tend to take such challenges as mine seriously. Some of my friendly younger readers seem to roll through even such books as I produced in this last decade in a sadly non-growth fashion. Are they not thinking of growing up: and up and up and up, concavely? Their uncouth neurodynamics is against them, a neurodynamics that could carry Maslow's gloomy statistic through this millennium: "less than one per cent of adults grow." Such books as I have produced are deviously scientific, as are e.g. Lonergan's works. They are classy science but they are not classics in the simple sense of Friedrich Schlegel: "A classic is a writing that is never fully understood. But those who are educated and educate themselves must always want to learn more from it." I would have us weave round and away from such vagueness to lean into science that invites one, in precise if aesthetic terms, to genetic growth. Such invitations must, in the positive Anthropocene, carry with them techniques of exercising that discomfort conventions of learned discourse. *Insight* does not do that, except for oddities of stray suggestions: think of Archimedes at the beginning of chapter one. My own *A Brief History of Tongue* has only a single but biting instance: the Keller exercise of the first chapter. I was wiser with chapter three of *Wealth of Self* and the tail of chapter 2 of *Process: Introducing Themselves to Young Christian Minders*. Without exercises, introductions tend to be elaborate misdirecting *haute vulgarization*.

I ~ Self-Assembly: The I of the Storm

It's not, at present, a storm of course: it's a dreadful becalmed, be calm: one lacking any dread: at times a busy drifting.

Drifting is decently indexed in *CWL* 18, *Phenomenology and Logic*. I quote from the first of the references that I included. It hits the stale on the head. The quotation is from Lonergan's lecture notes.

> *Gerede, Bavardage quotidian,* Talk.
> Cuts articulation of *Verstehen* from real; means become an end; *Mitsein* becomes talking to one another, being preoccupied with the talking
> authoritative: things are so because said to be so
> all-embracing: only from and against talk can one reach genuine
> evident and certain: doubt excites indignation, resentment, because Talk hides inauthenticity
> curiosity: concerned with new because new; not wanting to understand anything but to be distracted, to escape
> ambiguous: talk about everything but really understand nothing; doing all sorts of things yet nothing that is *my* doing.[1]

There is then no "I cannot face Lonergan's demanding methodology of dialectic, the central acceleration point of his functional method." There is just business as usual.

I obviously do not want it to be business as usual as we turn now to the first three pages of chapter 7 of *Method in Theology*. "Our concern is with interpretation as a functional specialty," are the introductory nine words that follow that large print INTERPRETATION. Our concern, and Lonergan's, is dialectical, is it not? We are to reflect seriously on interpretation "as a functional specialty": which means, alas, that we are invited into a minding haunted by the first diagram that we "faced" in this book, the Preface's W_3. The end of the first paragraph gives us a merciless footnote asking us to "observe"[2]: what sort of observation can you

---

[1] *CWL* 18, *Phenomenology and Logic*, 190.
[2] *Method in Theology*, 153[145], note 1.

manage without W₃? And the "instance"³ of the final sentence in that note pitches us into its end word's referent, *dialectic*.

What is this "reflect seriously" that I have in mind, that Lonergan had in mind? He is quite clear and self-clear on it. "If more than general and vague, it is arduous and time-consuming; it leads to the impasse of scrutinizing the self-scrutinizing self."⁴

Scrutinizing the self-scrutinizing self is a phrase I repeat regularly in this work, a slogan, a name for a fundamental option.⁵ "What do I mean by interpretation?" is your suggested question in this section, in this book, in this exercise. Are you up to facing it arduously, scrutinizing the self-scrutinizing self?

And now here's the shift from becalmed to storm: it is a shift to my storming in on the settled present betrayal of Lonergan. For Lonergan suggests, brilliantly, that communal scrutinizing the self-scrutinizing subject is the key to a dialectic of progress. That communal self-scrutinizing is a "development and application of theological method"⁶ leading him or her to "the categories he is to employ, the language he is to speak."⁷

My thus storming in is the center—literally—of my recent book *The Future: Core Precepts of Supramolecular Method and Nanochemistry*. Lonergan's brilliant suggestion is isolated and identified in the third of five chapters.⁸

---

³ "For instance, what there is termed a universal viewpoint here is realized by advocating a distinct functional specialty named dialectic." *Method in Theology*, 153 [145], note 1, end.

⁴ *Ibid.*, 167[158]. That subtle scrutinizing is to lead us towards facing the problem of the chasm that Lonergan identifies in previous efforts. See note 9, p. 90. That problem weaves into the failure mentioned in note 15, p. 5. The massive challenge is lifting Lonergan's forward specialties into present and future effectiveness.

⁵ The option is for a genetic ontic and phyletic adherence to the fulsome expression of the top of page 141 of the first edition of *A Third Collection*: (yes, I repeat it, a fresh nudging!) "Generalized empirical method operates on a combination of both the data of sense and the data of consciousness: it does not treat of objects without taking into account the corresponding operations of the subject; it does not treat of the subject's operations without taking into account the corresponding objects."

⁶ *Method in Theology*, 155[147].

⁷ *Ibid.*, 155[148].

⁸ Details of my strategy are given as it develops through the book. The need was to relocate the sections of *Method in Theology*, Chapter 10, before and after section 5, thus giving that key section is proper place as THE identification of the strategy of functional dialectics. I suspect that the contextualization Lonergan gave it there was due both to tiredness and to the unsatisfactory struggle with the puzzles we shared in the summer of 1966.

Self-Assembly: The I of the Storm

The book bubbled forward in the summer of 2019 from my decades-long brooding over his distress in 1966 about going about writing *Method in Theology*. As I have noted repeatedly, I spent the summer of that year with him in the old Bayview Regis, grappling with his guidance of me into his view of functional collaboration, but also sharing jokes with him as he relaxed at the swimming pool, recovering for the surgery of 1965. Writing *Method* was a struggle with his limited energy and with the impossibility of presenting the stuff in decent genetic continuity with the climb of *Insight*.[9] His focus, as we chatted in his room, was the direction of chapter one and the problem of weaving *Insight* in.

My problem in *The Future* was rescuing his brilliant central advance that was embedded in other topics in the chapter on Dialectic.

Perhaps a touch of humor helps here, and a distracting of you into being your "little self" by recalling Lonergan cheerily claiming "I am to be my own little self"[10] as he ventured later in that essay to give the same key brilliant pointing of section 5, chapter 10, of *Method in Theology*. The little self is invited "to lay his cards on the table,"[11] indeed, "at pains not to conceal his tracks."[12] It is "a projective test in which interpreters reveal their own notions of authenticity and unauthenticity both to others and to themselves."[13]

Think of Kuhn's phyletic problem;[14] think of Max Plank's ontic problem.[15] Think of getting at a strategy that effectively grounded—in "a statistically effective form"[16]—scientific progress. Would that not be worth homing in on as the center-

---

[9] I have only skimmed past this topic here. It would be a quite large undertaking to envisage seriously a young man's venture into the "far larger" (*Insight*, 754) work that would "go on to a developed account" (*Method in Theology*, 287[269]) of the light treatment of *Method in Theology*'s topics that was produced at the end of the 1960s.

[10] "Philosophy and the Religious Phenomenon," *CWL* 17, *Philosophical and Theological Papers 1965–1980*, 392.

[11] *Method in Theology*, 193[180].

[12] Ibid.

[13] Bernard Lonergan, "Philosophy and the Religious Phenomenon," *CWL* 17, 403.

[14] "In brief, I am relying on the course that Thomas Kuhn has found to prevail in physics, namely, that mistaken ideas that once were dominant are not so much refuted but abandoned. They vanish when they prove incapable of gaining competent disciples." "Philosophy and the Religious Phenomenon," *CWL* 17, 403–404.

[15] "As Max Plank testified, a new scientific position gains general acceptance, not by making opponents change their minds, but by holding its own until old age has retired them from their professional chairs"(*Insight*, 549).

[16] I am recalling Lonergan at age 30 writing his *Essay in Fundamental Sociology*. He arrives brilliantly at an answer to his own question, "What is progress?" (20) in terms of

piece of a life of genius, a genius-move in any science: a genetic pain-whirl round and about concealment of incompetence?

I halt here abruptly and strategically. The present Lonergan leadership do not think the genetic pain-whirl relevant to their dialectic rambles. I wonder why?—well, really I don't. A younger generation is about to face the exercise of the three objectifications of the whirl.[17]

---

a cycle that is "statistically effective" (20) in seeding progress. The *per se* core of the seeding is the triple objectification suggested at the conclusion of section 5 of the tenth chapter of *Method in Theology*.

[17] In this 4th boldfaced note of my series (pp. 8, 62, 70, 74, 87, 92, 118, 140, 141, 150, 169) I ask you to carry the paragraph above leading into it, about leading and following, into the musings of the 5th note in the series, which is at the end of Essay K (p. 87). My immediate focus is on your growth-poise in relation to the Essay J that follows. It is a very existential question: are you willing to wrap yourself around the semi-colons whose meaning is poised between you and the animals and plants in the formula $f(p_i ; c_j ; b_k ; z_l ; u_m ; r_n)$? This is the bridge of asses in my tower geometry of your growth in relevance. Two million years ago there were migrations from Africa; you belong there. Do the real Tea-bags echoed in Essay L belong there with you? What is this belonging and longing? Yes, what is this belonging and longing. The what is W-enzymed in you in a genetic pain-whirl of present changes of climate and culture: are you bent towards being authentically in it? "The Lonergan leadership do not think the genetic pain-whirl relevant to their dialectic ramble" (I quote the last paragraph above) about, e.g., conversions. I add in here, quite disturbingly, note 100 (p. 203) of the Appendix of this book: "I am recalling Lonergan's appeal to a superior in 1935, when he wrote at the end of a ten-page letter, "what on earth is to be done?" I write here to theologians now e.g. who write abundantly on conversions. The writing requires deliberation; the conversions involve deliberation. Generalized empirical method "does not treat of objects without taking into account the corresponding operations of the subject; it does not treat of the subject's operations without taking into account the corresponding objects." (*A Third Collection* [1985], 141). Being scientific about deliberation is doubly dodged by those conversion-talkers."

J ~ INVENTING TECHNIQUES

"To this end there have to be invented appropriate symbolic images . . ."[1]

To what end?

To the terminal value?[2]

Well, yes: is that not obvious? No, obviously, it is not! Certainly not in an effective way. Might you, pretty please, join me in a key effectiveness? At least think about it. Or, more effectively, run this essay through the central brilliant technique of *Method in Theology*.[3]

On the effective road to the terminal value, the Field[4] of Dreams of "Developing Characters of Craving,"[5] there has to become operative and "statistically effective"[6] "at a rather critical moment in the historical process"[7] "a resolute and effective intervention in this historical process"[8] that I am asking you to pause over here. The pause is over the challenge to rise to engineering, in oneself and others, in this century—seeding and seething into the common sense

---

[1] *Insight*, 489.

[2] I am pointing you at the Spread of Words of *Method in Theology* 48[47], but pointing you urgently further at my musings about that display in *The Future. Core Precepts in Supramolecular Method and Nanochemistry* (Axial Publishing, 2019), 9–17. The Spread is reproduced there on page 16.

[3] I hardly need remind you? It is the concluding challenge of section 5, chapter 10, of *Method in Theology*: speaking yourself out in discomforting company.

[4] The speaking of the previous note aims at lifting the engineering of humanity closer to a fully effective science, dominated by a heuristic neuroecho of the field: "The field is *the* universe, but my horizon defines *my* universe" (*CWL* 18, *Phenomenology and Logic*, 199. The problem is escaping from "the blinkers of a personal or communal horizon. They have to be people in whom the horizon is coincident with the field. If they are not, then all they possibly can do is increase the confusion and accelerate the doom." (*Op. cit.*, 306). Add in the problem of the chasm: see pages 79–80 below.

[5] See pp. 121–25 of my "Finding an Effective Economist: A Central Theological Challenge," *Divyadaan: Journal of Philosophy and Education*, vol. 30, no. 1 (2019).

[6] I am recalling Lonergan's poise on the cycles of progress from his 1934 *Essay on Fundamental Sociology*, 20. See also *Insight*, 144, the top lines.

[7] *CWL* 18, *Phenomenology and Logic*, 300.

[8] *Ibid.*, 306.

of the entire future, including the *Eschaton*—what. Yes, what.[9] But what in particular? Surely I am thinking of the crisis of climate, fossil fuel etc? Well, no actually, though there is an abundance of inner and outer techniques to be invented to accelerate Gaia-care, with the inner pressing enzyme-wise on the outer. What I am thinking of is what's core companion, as it leans into the wild W-enzyme, presently boxed off by convention except in some artsy, neurotic, or archaic consciousnesses. I am thinking, with Poisson madness,[10] of its release, by some small percentage of you readers reading ";" seriously, as it occurs in my symbolic expression of you, Supermolecule. Here you have that expression: $f(p_i\,;\,c_j\,;\,b_k\,;\,z_l\,;\,u_m\,;\,r_n)$.

How seriously has it to be read?

****

I wrote that beginning at an early stage in my musings over this little book, but only faced the problem of serious reading when I was coming near the end, and in the intervening stages growing in my awareness that this essay was the crisis essay in the book, leading me to a distinction that might be effective in nudging those who follow Lonergan to shift to a serious explanatory honesty. The distinction is between what I came to call, in this winter struggle, J-wrapping one's reading of pieces of Lonergan and Jay-walking those words, sentences, paragraphs, chapters, books.[11]

I recall now my first effort at such J-wrapping, not then named thus by me, not then seen by me as massively revolutionary: J-wrapping Thomas' thinking about *vivens*. It was in the winter of 1963–64, battling my way to produce "*Insight* and the Strategy of Biology."[12] I focused on the one-cell animals. Were they not just highly and successfully organized chemicals? I still vividly recall marking my pages of scribbles alphabetically, and getting as far as page W, when yes, I had got the pointing. Then I dumped the pages and wrote a sentence in the article. What

---

[9] Perhaps a reading of the first paragraph of my *The Allure of the Compelling Genius of History* (Axial Publishing, 2015) would spread your attention? See page 61 at note 10.

[10] The Poisson statistical distribution is famous for its application to the problem of deaths by mule kicks in the Prussian army: a statistics of rare events. Of course, I hope for a long-term effect that will place the enterprise of this essay in a Normal Law curve.

[11] *Jaywalk* is a compound word derived from the word *jay*, an inexperienced person and also a curse word that originated in the early 1900s, and *walk*.

[12] Pages 74–88 of *Spirit as Inquiry. Studies in Honor of Bernard Lonergan S.J.*, edited by Frederick E. Crowe, S.J., Herder and Herder, New York, 1964.

sentence you might ask? But I point you now to the sentence in Lonergan that inspired my pause over *vivens*. I see it now as the crisis sentence of the book *Insight*. Best make it conveniently present to you here.

> To this end, there have to be invented appropriate symbolic images of the relevant chemical and physical processes; in these images there have to be grasped by insight the laws of the higher system that accounts for regularities beyond the range of physical and chemical explanation; from these laws there has to be constructed the flexible circles of schemes of recurrence in which the organism functions; finally this flexible circle of schemes must be coincident with the related set of capacities-for-performance that previously was grasped in sensibly presented organs.[13]

If you have read *Insight* you have certainly Jay-walked that sentence; with an equivalent certainty I would claim that you did not J-wrap it. So, your entire Lonergan chatting, I would claim, is a bluff, a biased commonsense bluff, made plausible, indeed inevitable, by the culture of our times. *Assemble* that, Ladies and Gentlemen![14]

My next effort in the area was to—LOL—communicate that key J-wrapping to my doctorate supervisor and the examiners in Oxford.[15] Sadly I would say that there is little evidence that I communicated the core-leap to them or to anyone, in the past fifty years, with that effort.

What effort, you say? Might you take it as a nice illustration of a faulty "reflective interpretation?"[16] More realistically, it was, then, a cunning reflective interpretation, fitting in with Lonergan's note to me in 1968 regarding my Oxford struggle, "Give the guy what he wants. It's only a union card."

Still, it was a decent shot at generating seriousness about the up-grading of Aristotle.[17] Check the index of *Randomness, Statistics and Emergence* under *aggregate*,

---

[13] *Insight*, 489, lines 22–30.

[14] I am recalling the Beckett quotation marked by Lonergan in my *Lonergan's Challenge to the University and the Economy*: see note 10, p. iii.

[15] The thesis title was *The concrete logic of discovery of Statistical Science, with special reference to problems of Evolution Theory*. To 'get through' I had to simplify parts, and omit chapter 8, "The Foundations of Statistics" of the subsequent book, *Randomness, Statistics and Emergence*. That chapter tackled a shift from the first to the second edition of *Insight* related to a convergence problem of statistics. The examiners considered it to be only mathematics.

[16] *Insight*, 586.

[17] We get to that shortly. See in particular note 22 below and its context. This flaw in Aristotle is merely his time in history: aggreformism was just not on with the science of the day. The larger up-grading of Aristotle involves upgrading his view of science, a

then take a run at the last reference there, "in biophysics and biochemistry, 180 ff." Ff.? Really ff. will get you to the end of the book, page 260: 80 pages of, yes, possible J-wrapping round evolutionary emergence and its statistics of recurrences, stabilizations, etc.

We are back, or forward, to that crazy first section before the **** , where I invited you to pause over the " ; " in the expression $f(p_i \,;\, c_j \,;\, b_k \,;\, z_l \,;\, u_m \,;\, r_n)$.

Here I am at a loss: is there any point in summarizing? The book *Randomness, Statistics and Emergence* is not easily found: perhaps I should jump to my next effort to communicate, one not handicapped by a thesis context. In my first paper for the Florida Conference of 1970, I had a shot at communicating the stuff to what I considered naively to be a group of enthusiastic revolutionaries.[18] Lonergan remarked to me at the time about the paper, "Well, it just opens up area after area!" Well, it didn't: I do not recall a single reference to it in the past fifty years.

It is curious that I have, in that last sentence, reached a decent high in the "offense" intended by my Frontispiece, though it took no great skill. But that high point is also a skillful strategic identification of the honest starting place of a genuine science of humanity.[19] It is, I might say, the bridge of asses,[20] and note that in that claim I am, apparently, deviating from a tradition that speaks and

---

point raised in the second paragraph of chapter one of *Method in Theology*. See the beginning of Essay B above. I would note that Lonergan's seminar of autumn 1959 hovered over this problem. Aquinas, too, juggled with it, as Lonergan indicates. The seminar weaved round the text "System and History" (*CWL* 23, *Early Works on Theological Method 2*, 231 ff.). Shaking off Aristotle in this is quite a task.

[18] There are some comments of the Florida Conference of 1970 about key issues taken with Lonergan in my *Lack in the Beingstalk* (Axial Publishing, 2006, 85), and the book indeed tackles these issues, among others. A mythic consciousness about initial meanings prevailed there.

[19] The Epilogue hovers over this question, indeed, expresses darkly a leap in the appreciation of our truncated axial struggle that goes beyond this book.

[20] *The Bridge of Asses* is a name given to Euclid's fifth proposition in the first book of his *Elements* (that the base angles in an isosceles triangle are equal). At times I have written about chapter 5 of *Insight* in parallel terms, "a natural bridge over which we may advance from our examination of science to an examination of common sense," *Insight*, 163, the beginning of that chapter. My examination of science leads me to see engineering progress as the central science of humanity. The point is made by Lonergan's inclusion of "implementation" in his definition of metaphysics, but he was not pushing the shift in *Insight*. The push is most explicit in the final chapters of *Phenomenology and Logic*. Might I suggest that detached science and art—'art for art's sake'—is somewhat asinine?

writes of the importance of conversions.[21] Anyway, take time out to ask yourself what sort of intellectual conversion it would be to claim to be in the position of critical realism regarding "is? is! is.", and slide over the effective meaning of discovering intelligence's human burden of the form-matter linkage? "Who am I as I 'What?'" is the key issue whether I am dealing with love or loneliness or climate crises. Moreover, the issue has to be faced in the contemporary reality of what I call *aggreformism*. Certainly Aristotle had a decent shot at facing it in his day and led Lonergan to claim that "strictly, then, it is not true that insight is a grasp of form; rather, insight is the grasp of the object in an inward aspect such that the mind, pivoting on the insight, is able to conceive, not without labor, the philosophical concepts of form and matter."[22] But I suspect that Lonergan was thus led in his very contemporary context. At any rate, read that claim now in secret honesty: might you suspect that the pivoting is not really in your ballpark?

Might you then be converted to the task proposed by that terrible pivotal paragraph of *Insight* page 489, beginning where it tells you, Organism, Supermolecule, to begin? "Study of an organism begins . . ."

My mind leaps now to a weaving of a Study by the Organism, the Supermolecule Lonergan at the age of 54,[23] into my own years focused, in my early seventies, on "study of the organism." I am not pushing you into a struggle with the entire work, "Understanding and Method," but only into a mood, a question,

---

[21] I am not taking a different tack from Lonergan's emphasis on conversions in section 5 of chapter 10. What I am doing is nudging us all towards a fuller heuristics of them. See, Question 36, "An Appeal to Fred Lawrence and Other Elders" (available at: http://www.philipmcshane.org/questions-and-answers). On the flaws in the discussions of conversions see note 100 on page 203 below.

[22] *CWL* 2, *Verbum: Word and Idea in Aquinas*, 38. As in note 4 above, I think now of the problem of the chasm, but in a precise and difficult way of scrutinizing self-scrutiny. Pause over my suggestion that a flawed 'spaced-out' reading of diagrams that deal with this, such as those of *CWL* 18, *Phenomenology and Logic*, 322–3, can build an internal neuro-block that can be thought of as an isomorphic chasm. Think, strangely, of correctly and psychically reducing the diagrammatic distance between "Q, ! and data." That pushes you to self-appreciate concept or system as a mediating layering of data, supporting the what-Q. It gets you towards an intussusception of the W-enzyme poise, towards a view of system as neuro-meshed. The topic is too large and novel to say more here: but it seems a road towards solving the chasm problem.

[23] *CWL* 23, *Early Works on Theological Method 2*, "Understanding and Method." It was the matter of a seminar in the spring of 1959.

a problem, that lurks there. It is a problem "of separation,"[24] of chasm[25], of "character,"[26] of spookiness[27] of spirituality.[28] It is a problem of present systematic theology: "there is nevertheless a difference between the systematic mode of understanding and the other mode which pertains rather to a mode that is intersubjective, symbolic, and characteristic of commonsense or everyday understanding."[29] The problem is "how those who are dedicated to theology might effect a synthesis between their thinking and their spiritual life."[30]

Attention to this mood that weaves existentially into that chasm—self-attention, "scrutinizing the self-scrutinizing self"[31]—lifts my own effort into a deeper existential context, indeed I might call it, with fresh meaning for me now typing, "The Character of a Field Nocturne." Perhaps I should lead into my point by putting in the description of the Field Nocturne project on the website:

> This series of forty-one essays was undertaken as the 300-page project of reading the single paragraph in *Insight* that begins "Study of the organism begins from the thing-for-us, from the organism as exhibited to our senses." *Insight, Collected Works of Bernard Lonergan*, vol. 3, 489. *Field* refers to Lonergan's use of the word in *Phenomenology and Logic* (*CWL* 18), while *Nocturnes*, a reference to both Chopin and John Field, points to a community of functional collaborators, each member of the community in his or her luminous darkness.[32]

The issue of the effort was indeed a self-searching leading to an invitation to members of the Lonergan community to find themselves, "each member of the community in his or her luminous darkness." Providentially, the central essay,

---

[24] *Ibid.*, 5: see the note there.

[25] See the index to *CWL* 23, *Early Works on Theological Method 2*, under *Chasm*.

[26] "Character" occurs significantly in Lonergan's treatment of the ontology of communication: *Method in Theology*, 356, line 12[328, line 17]. See also the beginning of the Aristotelian *Magna Moralia*.

[27] See note 9, p. 172 and the context there, which weaves forward our searchings in the present essay.

[28] I have written abundantly on the challenge of apokataphatic contemplation under the title *Interior Lighthouse*. We are dealing here proleptically with a refinement of that poise.

[29] "Understanding and Method," 177: see note 23 above.

[30] *Ibid.*, 47.

[31] My recurrent slogan, from *Method in Theology*, 167[158].

[32] Thanks to James Duffy for this description.

Field Nocturne 22, "Aggreformism" is on point here as well as being on the point of ";".

In that essay I moved, on the second page, to sadly point to

a massive missing of the data on being human in a sincere effort of a scholarly group. A similar context of motivation is one that preoccupies me at present: the sincere and prolonged efforts of Julia Kristeva's dedicated life to handle the split subject that is our reality in human life, a reality muddled immensely by the subtle distortions present in conceptualism and its apparent rejections. In a simple way one might settle with the question, Is there a way out of the either-or of reductionism and dualism? But the existential question is not so simple and that complexity is laid on us mercilessly by Kristeva as she invites us to envisage pragmatically some dark aesthetic, here-ethic, way towards a cloudy identity.[33]

I conclude here and now by returning to the fresh-pointing of my phrase, "The Character of a Field Nocturne." The issue is your character as a Field Nocturne,[34] as a Supermolecule whose W-enzyme[35] is ever-tuning to the Field in a resonance of genuineness, tensions, harmony.[36] It is an ontic and phyletic cycling[37] round the self-luminosity of " ; " that sees and seizes and sizes to it that "good will wills the order of the universe and so it wills with that order's dynamic

---

[33] A very shabby intimation of a massively complex thinking. I am indebted here to the doctorate thesis of Christine Jamieson, *The Significance of the Body in Ethical Discourse: Julia Kristeva's Contribution to Moral Theology* (1998: St. Paul's University, Ottawa). Again, we meet the problem of the chasm: see note 25 above.

[34] I am pushing forward here from the concluding pointers of the volume *Divyadaan: Journal of Philosophy and Education* vol. 30, no. 1 (2019), where I write of "Developing Characters of Craving," 121ff.

[35] I introduced the name and notion of *W-enzyme* on page 2 of *The Future: Core Precepts in Supramolecular Method and Nanochemistry*. It fits neatly into the present sense for integral meaning. Begin with the Greek: *en-*, in + *zyme,* leaven: a catalyst, initiating, boosting, or speeding reactions. W can obviously be taken to refer to What or to Wonder, but it covers all the Wantings of you, supermolecule, and nudges you to think integrally, as this essay climbs to suggest.

[36] The challenge now is to a fresh shocking intussusception of the concluding sections of *Insight*'s chapter 15.

[37] Here the issue is a sublation of the demanding meaning of the final two chapters of *CWL* 18, *Phenomenology and Logic*.

joy and zeal."[38] It is a *humus* self-luminosity that lives in the prayer, "Grace, Grace, Grace, Attune me to the Allure of the Scent of a Nomen."[39]

---

[38] *Insight*, 722, the end lines.
[39] *The Allure of the Compelling Genius of History*, 199–200; 223.

K ~ A Universal Language

> Such a study **will** not be possible without a prior development of sciences and the long clarification of more general issues of philosophical inquiries and debates. Nor **will** the scientific development themselves **be** possible without a prior evolution of language and literature and without the security and leisure generated by technological, economic, and political advance.[1]
>
> Still, there would be in principle no difficulty in reaching a universal language, for any term that was offensive to anyone could be replaced by some arbitrary name or symbol that was free from all associations of human imagination and feeling.[2]

This "reaching for a universal language" is not an enterprise for the fainthearted but for the frontliners, and therefore a central focus of the dialectic struggle that battles gallantly from *Assembly* to a third objectification that hands the baton for "providing a statistically effective form for the next cycle of human action"[3] at the geohistorical front by the better fantasizers among foundation folk.[4]

Now an honest scientific-minded reader—are you slowly tuning to its beginnings, its stretching of your fantasy?—will pause over that last paragraph and the two quotations from Lonergan, and will I hope do so positively. But please please just don't float on. Might I say that KLM is not just the flag-carrier airline of the Netherlands, but the flag-carrying core of **K**ultivating **L**eaps of **M**inding in Interpretation? But the goal of the Leaps has to become a global ethos in these

---

[1] *Insight*, 558–9. I have bold-faced three replacement words that pitch Lonergan's statements of 'would be possible' into a fantasy of a distant future.

[2] *Ibid.*, 591, lines 5–9.

[3] *Essay in Fundamental Sociology*, 20.

[4] More and more I see this as the challenge focused in in the third chapter, "Self-Assembly" of my book *The Future: Core Precepts in Supramolecular Method and Nanochemistry*. Essay I is the lead into the zone in this book. Think of it, of its core "three-objectification" strategy, as I do now: in terms of the final paragraph of section 3.3, "Levels and Sequences of Expression" of *Insight*'s 17th chapter, which I quote at the end of Essay Q here. I focus there on the challenge expressed here, on the challenge expressed in a dense symbolization at the end of the present Essay K.

next millennia, starting today with you, you finding new courage of symbolization.[5]

Only you, now, can check the honesty of your poise recalling your reading of the previous essay, J. In that essay I proposed a definite unit of a needed universal language, the unit symbol "; ". Its key occurrence is in the variable display that we paused over in that essay: "$f(p_i ; c_j ; b_k ; z_l ; u_m ; r_n)$." Its fullest relevant operable context is another piece of the future universal language of culture, and it seems good to face that piece again here now, putting you face to face with it that you might puzzle over it with me. The honesty is to be the pressured ethos of the third objectification of dialectic, but here I wish for a simple reaction. I think now of the simple reaction of Fred Crowe when he read an early effort of mine to find symbols that would carry philosophy and theology forward: "do we have to learn mathematics to do theology?" On the next page, at all events, is the key piece.

Look seriously at W_3's complexity, meant to suggest the control of meaning that is to slowly emerge.[6] A decent undergraduate degree round it would give you a beginner's control of it. A serious reading of *Insight* and *Method* and *The Triune God* volumes of Lonergan would give a better control. But where is such decency and seriousness to be found? It is, alas to be found in later generations. How late? That depends on you. Not that you have to reach mastery, but that you have to tune in imaginatively to all that is lacking. "Most of all, what is lacking is knowledge of all that is lacking, and only gradually is that knowledge acquired."[7] Presenting the diagram now is like presenting the periodic table of chemistry to the chemists of the late 17th century, when the *terra pinguis* of Johann Becher was been turned by Georg Stahl into a phlogiston view of combustion. Is this not a quite offensive view of, say, present Lonergan studies? On the contrary, Becher and Stahl were in an ethos of scientific seriousness not paralleled by late 20th century phlogiston Lonergan studies. "What is lacking is a cultural milieu habituated to the use of

---

[5] I refer you to the challenge expressed by Lonergan in the concluding page of the *Essay in Fundamental Sociology*. It points to the fulsome graceful commitment to The Kingdom: that gracefulness is to wrap round the "three-objectification" strategy" mentioned in the previous note. It is the form and the formatting of religious conversion for our present millennium.

[6] The emergence is compactly fantasized in the previous two notes. The actual emergence of the complex symbol W occurred in the writing of *The Future: Core Precepts in Supramolecular Method and Nanochemistry*. See there, page 2.

[7] *Insight*, 559.

abstract[8] concepts and trained in the techniques[9] that safeguard their employment."[10]

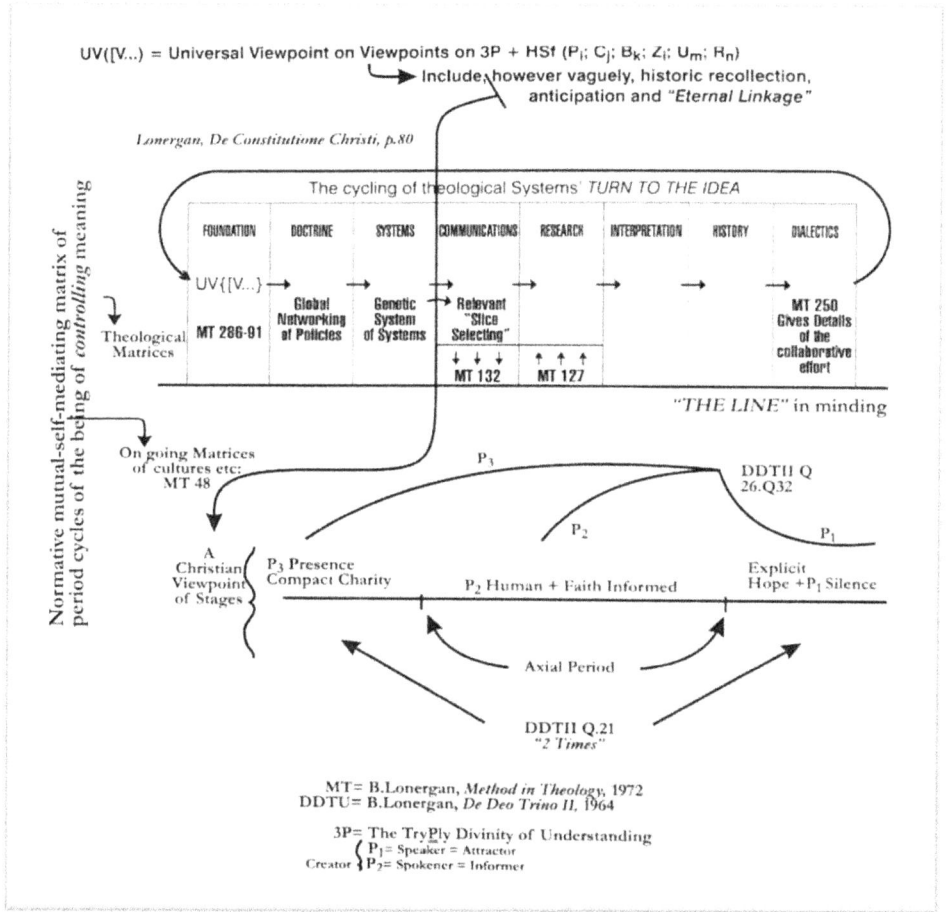

---

[8] Need I point to the challenge of the meaning of this word, the challenge expressed in *Insight* and *Verbum: Word and Idea in Aquinas* (*CWL* 2) as an *enrichment*? To abstract is to tiptoe towards the world of The Word of God. The point of this essay is that we need to mark our tiptoeing, not just in liturgy and daily rituals but in a radiant cloud of contemplative knowing and unknowing that is so-called *abstract symbolization*. Further on this: notes 14 and 15 of Essay Q (p. 122).

[9] Essay J focused on a single "simple" technique: the present essay points to a distant radiant cloud of such techniques. "Where God stood on a cloud and sang" (see 180).

[10] *Insight*, 559.

I have very deliberately pointed you toward a fresh read of the subsection on *The Genesis of Adequate Self-Knowledge* in *Insight*, a piece of the cutting-edge reflection on **Metaphysics, Mystery and Myth**.[11] Pre-phlogiston Lonergan studies has no grip on this cutting edge.

I recall now the shock of being at the Florida Conference in Easter 1970, getting my first suspicion of this. Two particular zones of Lonergan's work came under attack. There was a spectrum of problems about the 'proof' of God's existence in chapter nineteen of *Insight*. There were objections to Lonergan's cutting-edge view of myth. The origins of both counterpositions was a mythic consciousness that still dominates Lonergan studies.[12]

But why go on here? The opposition to my view and Lonergan's is the solid wall of "the arrogance of omnicompetent common sense."[13] Let's hear, please, commonsense talk its way out of the following requirement of Lonergan for the control of serious comprehension.

> The comprehension of everything in a unified whole can be either formal or virtual. It is virtual when one is habitually able to answer readily and without difficulty, or at least 'without tears', a whole series of questions right up to the last why? Formal comprehension, however, cannot take place without a construct of some sort. In this life we are able to understand something only by turning to phantasm; but in larger and more complex questions it is impossible to have suitable phantasm unless the imagination is aided by some sort of diagram. Thus, if we want to have a comprehensive grasp of everything in a unified whole, we shall have to construct a diagram in which are symbolically represented all the various elements of the question along with the connections between them.[14]

I move to conclude now by noting the ridiculous compacting here of that brilliant and neglected first section of *Insight* chapter 17. It raises the question of a new positive Anthropocene culture in which "the earth and every common sight take on the glory and the freshness of a dream."[15] To ground that move there

---

[11] I used boldface here. Might someone recognize it as the name of a very big book to be written about the profound message in the first section of *Insight* chapter 17, weaved round the problem of the chasm (see pp. 79–80 and note 9, p. 90) and the problem of living in the "absolutely supernatural" (*Insight*, 747)?

[12] See note 16, p. 66.

[13] *CWL* 17, *Philosophical and Theological Papers, 1965–1980*, "Questionnaire on Philosophy: Response, 370.

[14] *CWL* 7, *The Ontological and Psychological Constitution of Christ*, 151.

[15] *Insight*, 556.

must emerge a theology dominated by symbolisms of the "'known unknown'"[16] that support rituals and artistries of human loneliness.[17] In Christian thinking we have to leave the commonsense God of Abraham and of the philosophers behind in favor of the Christoffer[18] obscurity, G^i_{jk}.[19]

I pause now, wishing you to pause with me, hovering over that symbol, G^i_{jk}. Would you like me to go on? Would I like me to go on? Compacting the fantasy of a millennium-long beginning is pretty silly. "We are not there yet,"[20] even in sniffing the need for the fantasy. Try a little of it before meeting me in my silliness at the end of Essay Q.[21]

---

[16] *Ibid.*, 557.

[17] A context for musing here is *Insight* 498.

[18] The word twists us creatively towards the later explanatory theology of Jesus's offer by echoing the simpler meaning of space-time associated with the Christoffel tensor (See Lindsay and Margenau, *Foundations of Physics*, Dover pb, 362.)

[19] G^i_{jk} carries the associations mentioned in the previous note, and could have a larger weave up through the more complex sciences, till it glories explanatorily in an appreciation of peculiarity of a Trinitarian God having an incarnation, "i" that grounds a strange weave of humanity's subjectivity with the Divine Subjectivity. See further, note 20, p. 124.

[20] *CWL* 21, *For a New Political Economy*, 20.

[21] **My 5th boldfaced note of eleven (pp. 8, 62, 70, 74, 87, 92, 118, 140, 141, 150, 169)** is in the context of the discomforting paragraph that ended Essay I, on leaders and followers in what may be called "the Lonergan movement." I wish to turn that so-called movement—for going round in ever decreasing circles is an odd movement—back to the beginning, the beginning that is the 1st boldfaced note at the end of B, the beginning that is our beginning, John's Gospel's beginning, the Christoffer, the offer of G^i_{jk}. Who are G^i_{jk}? And now, yes, the beginning in Lonergan, to which you are asked to climb in 19 chapters of *Insight*, thus to rise to a "twenty-sixth place, God is personal" (*Insight*, 691) in a climb that tunes you to the 27th question of Thomas that invites a further climb, but in a vastly new context that leaves the God of Abraham and the God of the philosophers behind. Please pause now freshly over that paragraph of Essay K that edges you into the diagram W_3 on page 85. "Double You Three"? What can that possibly mean if you have not been invited to climb by a competent leadership? You must make a fresh beginning, at best not alone. Groups are to emerge that cherish W-enzyme's caul.

L ~ BRIDGES

> Tea-Bag finished talking and sat down. The blank page of paper she was holding she now folded and laid it in front of her on the table. Everyone in the room was silent and still. Humlin wondered what they all felt, if they had been through something earth-shattering, as if Tea-Bag's narrative had painted the room in new colours. It's deeper than that, he thought, but it goes so deep I can't express it.[1]

Tea-Bag is a central character of the Henning Mankell novel *Tea-Bag*, a refugee African woman surviving street-wise in Sweden. Humlin is an odd poet finding reluctantly the voices of such young women and eventually coming towards "dreaming about that cool, clear river with its source far away in Tea-Bag's mountain."[2] These Shadow Girls are incarnations of strange lonely elements of meaning. "If people were shown how to find in their own experience elements of meaning" that echoed that shadow loneliness, and my shadow loneliness in the Sweat Den of Lonergan studies. If, If, If! If "assembled."[3] Yes, "they would find themselves in possession of a very precise tool, they would know it in all its presuppositions and implications, they could form for themselves an exact notion,"[4] but only if the self-assembly were luminous and patient and foreign to present lands and glands. Tea-Bag and I and Hermine and Harry Haller speak[5] **into** those lands and glands but the **into**'s entry normally shrinks the words into sound bites. Are the words thus shrinking in you or do you sniff effectively[6] a

---

[1] Henning Mankel, *The Shadow Girls*, 243.

[2] The final words of the novel. The original novel was first published with the title *Tea-Bag* by Leopold Forlag, Stockholm, 2001. I am quoting the English translation by Ebba Segerberg, published in Britain by Harvel Secker, 2012 with title *The Shadow Girls*. I am quoting from the New Press, New York, version, and refer to the book throughout as *The Shadow Girls*.

[3] *Method in Theology*, 172[163]: linking this with "assembled" of *Method in Theology* 250, line 30[235, line 25] would be quite an enlightening enterprise.

[4] *Ibid.*

[5] Hermine: "Ah, Harry, we have to stumble through so much dirt and humbug before we reach home. And we have no one to guide us. Our only guide is our homesickness." Herman Hesse, *Steppenwolf*, Penguin, 179.

[6] I surely need not repeat Lonergan's challenge to become effective (*CWL* 18, *Phenomenology and Logic*, 306).

strange interpretation of *"The Genesis of Adequate Self-Knowledge"*[7] an interpretation that is, in present times, a rare and lonely journey, a possession, a being possessed, "only at the summit of a long ascent,"[8] only in the Shadows?

My trembling reach, in this little ell and Big L of my bridge-building fantasy, is **into**[9] your molecular yearnings. Would it not be wonderful to say, past 'tense', together, like Tea-Bag—who speaks always in italics, *"the bridge lay before us and the very last part of our trip was a single jump into a weightless vacuum"*?[10] Would it not be wonderful if you jumped away, here hear now, from the sick shrunken babbling of present Lonergan studies to face the apprenticeship needed "to speak effectively to undifferentiated consciousness."[11]

> Such speech, however, is found clear and accurate and explanatory only by those that have done their apprenticeship. It is not enough to have acquired common sense and to speak ordinary language. One has also to be familiar with theory and with technical language. One has to examine mathematics, and discover what is happening when one is learning it and, again, what is happening as it was being developed. From reflecting on mathematics one has to go on to reflecting on natural science, discern its procedures, the relations between successive steps, the diversity and

---

[7] *Insight*, 558, where Lonergan, like Tea-Bag, speaks in italics. Think of him adding these words to the text by hand, as he did.

[8] *Ibid*.

[9] The *into* involves facing the challenge, Supermolecule, of evolving integrally your W-enzyme, "the elimination of the chasm or gap between the intellect and senses. This means [to abandon the false notion that] the intellect has to do solely with universals and necessaries, utterly ignoring the fact that understanding is had in sensible data, as well as the fact of the manifold mutual influence by which the intellect and the senses spontaneously and naturally work together to form a single human consciousness that is both sentient and intellectual. There must be developed, therefore, a psychology of the 'incarnate spirit'; a theory of the pictorial and plastic arts, of music and literature; a theory of the primitive, the mythic, the popular, and the semi-educated mentality. {Lonergan inserts here on the margin by hand 'Marcel, Merleau-Ponty, De Waelhens'} All of these must be integrated with theology, with Christology, grace, ascetical and mystical theology, ecclesiology. All this together would contribute greatly to solving the problem of history." (*CWL* 23, *Early Works on Theological Method*, page 635, a piece on the 'problem of the chasm' connected with the 1959 Spring seminar on "Understanding and Method" in the same volume).

[10] *The Shadow Girls*, 328.

[11] The concluding words of *Method in Theology*, chapter 3, on "Meaning." The task of note 9 above, a task talk in "Nanochemistry" (The final chapter of *The Future. Core Precepts of Supramolecular Chemistry and Nanochemistry*.

relatedness of classical and statistical methods, the sort of world such methods would reveal—all the while attending, as well as one can, to the conscious operations by which one intends the objects. From the precision of mathematical understanding and thought and from the ongoing, cumulative advance of natural science one has to turn to the procedures of common sense, grasp how it differs from mathematics and natural science, discern its proper procedures, the range of its relevance, the permanent risk it runs of merging with common nonsense. To say it all with the greatest brevity: one has not only to read *Insight* but also to discover oneself in oneself.[12]

I have written before about bridges,[13] bridges too far for our sick humanity to sense or seek, for we are busy on The Bridge, a sloping rotten bridge that has rattled us down the mountain for millennia into a vomit swamp of academic disciplines and arsehole dodges of directing us and Gaia further down.

Might I be a Tea-Bag for you in a Proustian cup[14] of "sensing and tasting internal things,"[15] wings in your W-Enzyme?[16]

So I wind my plea round to echo Tea-Bag, speaking in italics from a blank page, "*from which an invisible bridge led to paradise,*"[17] weaving its apokataphatic[18] way towards draining the vomit swamp, towards cusping the sloping rotten bridge effectively into a thin-aired humus in which then "*every grain of sand was a watchful soldier,*"[19] but not yet, not yet, not yet. "We are not there yet."[20] It is the thin air of a later millennium, cleansed slowly slowly slowly by some few "*people now

---

[12] *Method in Theology*, 260[244].

[13] "Features of Generalized Empirical Method and the Actual Context of Economics," *Creativity and Method*, edited by Matthew Lamb, Marquette University Press, 1980, 543–71.

[14] Proust (*The Remembrance of Times Past*) contributes, on the level of literature, the potential of a sublation towards redeeming linguistic time and thyme and enzyme.

[15] Recall St. Ignatius's "*sentire et gustare res internas,*" but assuming the present context's pressure for a massive sublation, the fresh "scrutinizing the self-scrutinizing self" (*Method in Theology* 167[158]) pointed to especially in note 9 above.

[16] The mention of wings reminds you of the butterfly (see the beginning, 175, and the conclusion of the Epilogue, 183) bent on ranging, with Grace, into spooky living.

[17] *The Shadow Girls*, 327.

[18] Apokataphatic sublates the two ways, apophatic and kataphatic into the concrete rhythms of subjectivity. The sublation, a task of the slow climb into the Interior Lighthouse, pertains to the solution of the problem posed in note 11 above.

[19] *The Shadow Girls*, 327–8

[20] *CWL* 21, *For a New Political Economy*, 20. The beginning of a page-long paragraph that I refer to regularly: the present flow of text and notes gives it fresh meaning.

humming melodies under their breath and moving in slow measured victory dances," dancing on the ceiling in the strange displaced fullness of their W-enzymes' orders and order, finality's Dionysian steps, "with that order's dynamic joy and zeal."[21]

> *I survived. I was not consumed by the sea and by the betrayal, cowardice and greed. I met a man who held a palm frond in his hand and said there were people in this land who wanted to hear my story and who would let me stay. But I never met these people. I have given my smile but what do I get in return?*[22]

---

[21] *Insight*, 722, the final words.

[22] *The Shadow Girls*, 328. **And here I add my 6th boldfaced note of eleven (pp. 8, 62, 70, 74, 87, 92, 118, 140, 141, 150, 169). In the 5th boldfaced note I weaved you and me into the migrants of Africa of today and of 2 million years ago. Tea-bag is a fictional migrant, "not consumed .... by cowardice and greed." But now I think of real migrants into the world of explanation that are lonely whats by-passed by those global pseudo-thinkers who "do not think the genetic pain-whirl relevant to their dialectic rambles" (Quoting again the final paragraph of page 74). Some of those migrants care about the redemption of history, and are appalled by the pretense of those pretenders of global care. I am appalled. Are the Who of G^i_{jk} appalled? Is the "i" of G^i_{jk} appalled? Is Lonergan appalled with those travelling "breathlessly and a little late," (*Insight*, 755), with those who dodge "their apprenticeship" (*Method in Theology*, 260[244]), and have no serious intention of being "bitten by theory" (*CWL 6*, 155)? The fresh start faces the present generation of beginners, or perhaps, sadly, a later generation of another millennium, masked against the foul heirs of sick cultures. That delay depends on you taking a bite.**

M ~ 60910

> I thought I saw the fallen flower
> Returning to its branch
> Only to find it was a butterfly.[1]

I hardly need to identify the reference of the title to that turn-of-the-page paragraph in *Insight*.[2] With that paragraph I regularly associate Lonergan's "sheer mystery" comment at the top of page 604 about the dynamics of its actuation: he parallels that actuation with the struggle with tensors and eigenfunctions in the early decades of the 20th century. That parallel might well be developed as a way of indicating the struggle we face in, so to speak, getting the show on the road, but the indicating would not be of much value to those not some way in tune with physics. So here I invite you to move in another direction, a direction that you may find useful in talking to others, in persuading others that this venture has its encouraging parallels.

I invite you to return to that page 604; note with a grin that Lonergan thinks is "sheer mystery;"[3] and that his pointing just a pointing to minor difficulties. Wander down the page about the major difficulty and settle with me in a dodging round that difficulty that may be realistic in attempting to get the hunt for "genetically and dialectically related determinations"[4] into the interest zone of Lonergan studies, into the seeding zone of the positive Anthropocene.

Pause then with me at the end of page 604.

> The artist and the teacher, no doubt, will endeavor to reconstitute the sights and the sounds, the feelings and the sentiments, that help us recapture the past; but such recapture is educative; it makes ascent to the universal viewpoint possible; it prepares us for an understanding, an

---

[1] "*Rakka eda ni / Kaeru to mireba / kocho Kana.*" The haiku is quoted from L. van der Post, *A Portrait of Japan*, (photographs by Bert Glinn), William Morrow, New York, 1968, 107. My objective here is to nudge you to rise to a fantasy of another Portrait of Japan.

[2] *Insight* 609–610.

[3] *Ibid.*, 604, line 2.

[4] *Ibid.*, lines 16–17.

appreciation, an execution, of scientific interpretation; but in itself it is not science.⁵

My focus in this essay is on a recapture that is educative, a recapture of the sights and sounds and sentiments of a sequence of particular hospital situations presented with some artistry on television. The presentations are those of the series titled *House*, perhaps familiar to you. My focus here seems quite deviant: we have been flying high in strange ways in this sequence of essays, and shall continue to do so, even in this deviance.

Humorously—I hope for both of us—I think of Namaan the leper travelling far for a cure, and getting the seeming low-grade advice of taking a dip in the Jordan.⁶

My recommended dipping in the Jordan is here your dip into one or many of the series of 177 episodes that ran initially from November 2004 to May 2012, and are still available.⁷ But my recommendation is to try for a peculiar dipping that lifts you some way—might it rise to all the way in this millennium?—to a benefitting from "scrutinizing the self-scrutinizing self."⁸ Of course, self-scrutinizing, you surely would claim now, is not at all the name of the game when watching television. But, might I respond, you are talking in the now of the negative Anthropocene age, and indeed that stage of it that covers the psychic skin of the self-neglected with a further skin of truncation.⁹

---

⁵ *Ibid.*, 604, lines 34–39.

⁶ I refer to the story in *2 Kings* Chapter 5, about Naaman the army commander who travelled in regal style to Israel and "was indignant" (v.11) when Elisha suggested he bathe seven times in the Jordan. Naaman talked of the great rivers of Damascus, suitable for a stately healing. LOL: how do you feel about 7 dips in a TV show?

⁷ They can be tracked on various sites and also purchased on Amazon.

⁸ *Method in Theology*, 167[158]. Take note here of my trickery. The self-scrutinizing self on my mind is the self that has taken up the *House* series because of one of my earlier hintings. Then one's self-scrutiny tries to intussuscept the patterns of behavior in any episode of the series as a nudge towards thinking out how an international group collaborates, in view of a standard model, an SM,—the best available end-product of the geohistorical effort of the medical community's long story of searching ways of engineering healing. 60910 then is viewed as the common possession of the 'House team' in the struggle of any episode. Is the answer to healing in that SM or does the team push forward? But now I am asking for a new level, scrutinizing the scrutinizing.

⁹ "The neglected subject does not know himself. The truncated subject not only does not know himself but also is unaware of his ignorance and so, in one way or another, concludes that what he does not know does not exist." Bernard Lonergan, *A Second Collection*, 73. It is quite a geohistorical task to delineate the manner in which the

Perhaps I might, with effective statistical success, put the problem of adequate poise this way. As you watch Hugh Laurie portraying Gregory House, are you meeting either of them? The question puts us in the realms of what I call *spooky intersubjectivity*.[10] But we need to climb to that, the long ontic and phyletic story of humanity. We have before us competence in action: a competence—genetic if battered—refining itself in the geohistorical genetics of healing the battered genetics of individuals.

Refining itself? Let us move towards detail to find a massive plurality of selves, within which the series isolates small international groups of selves: all competent, and increasingly so in a quite deliberately operational way. But be realistic. Is it Hugh Laurie or Gregory House who is thus growing; Omar Epps or

---

negative Anthropocene moved from neglect to truncation in these last millennia, a truncation that spread, particularly in the last millennium, from high civilizations to native peoples. Students of Lonergan should beware of assuming that truncation is not lurking in their reading of Lonergan. Indeed, were it not, this little book would not be "a resolute and effective {I hope!} intervention." (*CWL* 18, *Phenomenology and Logic*, 308). The problem is our existential poise regarding the field as basic horizon. (See, *ibid.*, the index under *Field*). The leprosy is a cultural reality, boosted by general bias (*Insight*, chapter 7). "The real issue" of the dipping "has to do with how you pick out the right horizon" (*ibid.*, 311), how you are effectively poised regarding 60910's engineering role in your life and in history.

[10] The spooky intersubjectivity is associated with Lonergan's leap of 1954, expressed in a letter to Fred Crowe. It seems good to inflict on you, in this context (see note 24 below) the fullest hint about the topic that I gave in the second last footnote of *The Future* (p. 111). "My stare at you is incomplete, and the final note will put that incompleteness in context. But here I think of the short-term context, the context of my brief introduction (above, p. 28) of Aristotle and Drucker as pointing to the stairs inadequately, (R, I, H and D_{oc} S C) and my pointing inadequately there to the bridge between them (D_i, H): a context for the *Duffy Exercise* that is to dance round the third chapter of this book. The short-term fuller context to my "Openers of the positive Anthropocene" in the book is your picking up on my nudgings given in the repeated mention of problems associated with the words *intersubjectivity* (xiv, xvi, 8, 9, 34–5, 40, 54–5, 80, 92, 96, 103) and *spooky* (3, 8, 13, 17, 66, 116) and the 6 repetitions (xiv, 8, 34, 54, 80, 103) of Lonergan's 1954 challenge regarding the future of theology. You find now, perhaps, that you did not climb in each occurrence to a fresh meaning of the word or the challenge? Such a climbing in reading belongs to the positive Anthropocene. But we need to climb towards that climbing: try climbing over the stile named by my repetitions, my petitions, Lonergan's petition. I return to your aid in "On the Stile of a Crucial Experiment," *Divyadaan: Journal of Philosophy and Education*, vol. 31 (2020). That is to be followed by the aide-mémoire, *The Future as Life Stile: From Mild Mess to Wild Bliss*."

Dr. Eric Foreman, Charlyne Li or Dr. Li Park; etc.?[11] Whatever. What is obvious is that the growing is invisible, a within of portrayer or character, but with lagging expression, be that expression a shift of verbalization or of operational complexity.

The issue is, how obvious is it to you? Are you at least somewhat "bewildered and dismayed" at the human talents that generate the operational complexity? So that that bewilderment invites you to adjust your notions to "being there"?[12] It is an adjustment seeded by your W-enzyme, the psychic spread of what Lonergan names *the protean notion of being* when he writes "that interpretation aims at differentiating the protean notion of being by a set of genetically and dialectically related determinations."[13]

Think of the protean notion of being an exceptional doctor that seems to haunt the show *House*. Does that protean notion of being haunt you in some way, pose an ideal, that "the ideal of the cinema and sound track is the ideal not of historical science but of historical fiction"?[14] Yet is not *House* cinema and sound track? And, indeed, is the haunting not just a seeming, an artistry locked in the psyche of the negative Anthropocene? The protean notion needs fresh doctoring, right across the worlds of art, science, technology. Peter Robinson's hero, Alan Banks, may well claim that "he felt a new hunger to understand, from a different perspective, the world in which he had grown up,"[15] but the hunger has no serious genetic dimension. Might one claim that neither Robinson nor his hero, neither Hugh Laurie nor his portrayed Gregory House, are in the ballpark of a luminous acceptance of the ideal of growth?

Follow the characters: House through a series that runs through 117 episodes, Banks that runs through a plethora of novels. Follow the character that watches those episodes, that reads those novels: you, in some parallel hobby or enthusiasm. Move that character study back from the fictioning to those addressed by the fiction. Move those character together to conversations at dinners or in coffee shops.

What do you find by the fresh self-scrutiny? Capitalize *house*, as I do now, in the comment of Gaston Bachelard when he writes of the protean challenge: "Late in life, with indomitable courage, we continue to say that we are going to do what

---

[11] One can Google the entire range of characters over the years.
[12] I think both of Heidegger and of Peter Sellars.
[13] *Insight*, 604, lines 15–17.
[14] *Ibid.*, lines 27–8.
[15] Peter Robinson, *Friend of the Devil*, Hodder pb, 2011, 2.

we have not yet done: we are going to build a House."[16] Think Proust, as he seeks "to recapture the past."[17] "Employ the utmost freedom of imagination"[18] to weave Proust and Bachelard and Maslow, and others into your seeded suspicions about some strange not-yet humanity, into 60910, to get some sense of the future glory of history. It is a struggle to come to effectively "distinguishing the successive stages of this, the greatest of all works."[19] That heuristics, to be effective, reaches, J-wrapping, "Stalking Jesus,"[20] for all situations and all persons, none of them "an animal in a habitat."[21]

I am suggesting densely here sublation of Lonergan's compact pointing to art's function.[22] I am pointing to *Pericles* as the rule not the exception.[23] I am pointing, yes, to a chasm-cancelling normativity of adult growth in the positive Anthropocene Age.[24]

And I am pointing to a massive effective sublation of my Preface of forty years ago to *Searching for Cultural Foundations*: the title of it is "Distant Probabilities of Persons Presently Going Home Together in Transcendental Process."[25]

---

[16] *The Poetics of Space*, Beacon Press, Boston, 1969, 61.

[17] *Insight*, 604.

[18] *CWL* 12, *The Triune God: Systematics*, 503.

[19] *Ibid.*, 491.

[20] The title of Essay Y here. Add some heavy musing on the notion of rescuing the stalk of the flower of history, battered by the negative Anthropocene: one seeks to stabilize the stalk of the Sonflower. The seeking is to carry the forward-looking specialist sub-communities into the huge creative effort associated with note 15 of Essay A, p. 5, and of the Epilogue's notes 7(p.177) and 18(p.181).

[21] *Insight*, 498, line 11. Weave in lines 15 and 22 to your puzzling, then add the fuller context of notes 10 and 24.

[22] *CWL* 10, *Topics in Education*, the ninth chapter.

[23] I refer to Shakespeare's *Pericles*, especially as interpreted by Patrick Kavanagh. His comments on the play and the character are reproduced from a radio talk on pages 56–65 of my *Lack in the Beingstalk. A Giants Causeway*, Axial Publishing, 2006. Pericles rises finally to tune into "the music of the spheres!" (*Pericles* V. i. 228).

[24] Adult growth has been a puzzle to me since the late 1950s (See the beginning of chapter two of my book, *Process. Introducing Themselves to Young (Christian) Minders* (1989.) There are relevant comments on the problem in the final pages of *Lack in the Beingstalk*. The puzzle fits, in a simple way, into the problem of spooky intersubjectivity (see note 10 above). If adult growth is an accelerating process, what are the normative neurochemical resonances in our exchange here?

[25] *Searching for Cultural Foundations*, edited by Philip McShane, University Press of America, 1980, page i.

Interpretation from A to Z

And it seems to me now that, in this little trickle of essays, it's best to cut short my musings on future adulthood by simply recalling that Preface's conclusion.

> Part of the glory of history is man's envisagement of its schedules of probabilities and possibilities. If the sapling of history is cut down from within, still it can have, within, a vision of the temporal nöosphere that, paradoxically, redeems God The envisagement is the core of future academic growth: its opposite is an elderhood that is the fraud of being in reality "not old folk but young people of eighteen, very much faded."[26] Our molecules, "our arms and legs filled with sleeping memories,[27] passionately demand that we fly after the butterfly.

> There the butterfly flew away
> over the bright water,
> and the boy flew after it,
> hovering brightly and easily,
> flew happily through the blue
> space. The sun shone on his wings.
> He flew after the yellow and flew
> over the lake and over
> the high mountain,
> where God stood
> on a cloud
> and sang.[28]

---

[26] Marcel Proust, *Remembrance of Times Past*, Random House, New York, Volume 2, 1042.

[27] [This long note is from the original Preface.] *Ibid.*, Volume 2, 874. I would enlarge the meaning of *memory* here beyond Proust. Enlist St. Thomas' meaning of *memoria* (see *CWL* 2, *Verbum: Word and Idea in Aquinas*, 93–94). The incarnate subject can move to remember, re-member, the *intentio entis et valoris* that subjects are and might be, can remember differentiatedly the eightfold spiral of *anamnesis* and *prolepsis*. At this stage, perhaps, the compendious meaning of the title word "Presently" has been noticed. A psychological presence in history is envisaged that presents, aims, with a transposed differentiated *prudentia,* towards the movement of history in its revelation of presences and presents (see *Method in Theology*, 1972, the index under *gift*).

[28] Herman Hesse, *Wandering*, translated by James Wright, Farrar, Straus and Giroux, New York, 1972, 89.

N ~ Abstruse Principals

My title comes, with a twist—*Principals* is not a typo!—from the disturbing remarks of Lonergan on the top of page 604 of *Insight*:

> One may expect the diligent authors of highly specialized monographs to be somewhat dismayed when they find that instead of singly following the bent of their genius, their aptitudes, and their acquired skills, they are to collaborate in the light of common but abstruse principles and to have their individual results checked by general requirements that envisage the totality of results.

Hidden here is the pushy optimism of Lonergan at 49, typing his way to the end of the astonishing solitary climb of *Insight*. What abstruse principles had he in mind? It is no stretch to say that a central place in his thinking was in *The Sketch* of the previous section, spelled out later in the canons of hermeneutics. What I consider the centerpiece of those canons was the topic of the previous piece here, M. But I consider too, and I wish you here to consider, that Lonergan knew his climb was incomplete, though I do not wish to attempt a spelling out, a "hypothetical expression,"[1] of that knowledge.[2]

My difficulty now is communicating the character of the incompleteness that I suspect lurked in this project of chapter seventeen of *Insight*. The difficulty is that analogies from sciences are the way towards that communication, and most of my readers are alas not in that ball park at the beginning of the 21st century. Might I talk of music, of early plain chant compared to Handel's *Messiah*? Then you get a very odd nudge here to think of, for example, the topic of section M in terms of plain chant with its broad rules. A scientific nudge that might not be totally lost is the thinking of Faraday as he weaved forward his broad notion of field, but not at all poised to speak out and about the field operators that Maxwell provided.

I doubt if these pointers are helpful, so I twist into another pointing, a pointing that is not caught in the same incompleteness but in what seems quite a

---

[1] *Insight*, 602, "Fourthly."

[2] Ponder over the meaning of the final sentence of "Thirdly" on that same page 602. Think both of the later discovery of the splits in a functional audience and of Lonergan interpreting Jesus to his audience in his Gregorian University courses. See note 28 of Essay Q, 125. Think, now, of the geohistorical stretching that might bring forth a hypothetical expression.

different incompleteness.³ The twist is in the shift from "abstruse principles" to the title.

"Abstruse Principals." Pause now, surely startled, to think of your interpretative effort as "to collaborate in the Light of Common but Abstruse Principals" where the capital letters and the twist of "principals" are faintly recognized as the blossoming, in the positive Anthropocene, of our self-luminosity regarding and guarding John's Jesus's claim. "When the Advocate comes, whom I send to you from the Father, the Spirit of truth who comes from the Father, he will be my witness."⁴ This lifts stunningly "The Sense of the Unknown" haunting *Insight* chapter 17 into a glorious intersubjective darkness and light that, I would surmise, was on Lonergan's mind when he wrote to Fred Crowe in June 1954 that "the Method of Theology is coming into perspective."⁵

What further can I write here that would be helpful towards entering this shocking spooky collaborative Intimacy? I finally decided that I had best just add a context from elsewhere, the context of the two final essays of my series "LO and Behold": two essays that are on the edge of my present reaching. The first of these is here below. The second forms part of the Essay V.⁶

Before facing that adventure it would be well to muse over my vague remark above about "darkness and light," about the Abstruse Principals as Friends. The topic is that of the fifth thesis of *CWL* 11, *The Triune God: Doctrines*. But let me simply nudge towards the task of slowly, mindfully, reaching and character-incarnating self-luminosity in the ontic and phyletic radiances of the positive Anthropocene's culture, the triplicity of analogy. One then seeks to rise to a mutual affirmation of clear friendship with the Abstruse Principals, sinks that friendship incarnately into glorious darkness, that glory being the weave in of the

---

³ An obvious component is the claim of the note on *Insight* 754 (see also the "b" comment on page 806) that the meaning of personal relations is in the ballpark of the supernatural. Does this not give a quite clear Dionysian boost to the third line of the word-spread on *Method in Theology* 48[47]?

⁴ John 15: 26. The fuller Spirit-identification is in chapter 16. And then there is the challenge expressed in this little book in sections C, H, V.

⁵ The passage is quoted shortly in *Lo and Behold 10*.

⁶ Obviously, the essays in the series leading up to those final essays are relevant. Indeed, my message to the reader is that some equivalent expression of climbing is needed in the task—my slogan again, of Essay A, note 28, p. 8,—of scrutinizing the self-scrutinizing subject that is committed to growing as an adult engineer in effectively "distinguishing the successive stages of this, the greatest of all works" (*CWL* 12, *The Triune God: Systematics*, 491). You need to speak to yourself in your own *Cantos* or *Cantowers*. If others, of our axial stage, listen: well and good.

third of the three meshed poises, eminence-bent. The seeking is apokataphatic, generating a core culture of the Interior Lighthouse, lifting into the absolutely supernatural "every common sight"[7] into "the glory and the freshness of a dream,"[8] not only a dream but a fact of personal molecularity.[9]

LO and Behold 10

Assembling $[1 + 1/n]^{nx}$

The original context of what we are assembling is a piece of a letter written by Lonergan to Frederick Crowe in June 1954. Crowe and I began our long sharing of the struggle to understand Lonergan in the early 1960s, and sometime later he shared the letter with me, focusing on the passage that made little sense to him. Over the years I have struggled with its meaning and shared the struggle with others.[10] My climb led me eventually to the essay in the *Journal of Macrodynamic Analysis*, volume 10 (2018), 105–35, titled "Method in Theology: From $[1 + 1/n]^{nx}$ to $\{M\ (W3)^{\theta\Phi T}\}^4$." Since then there has been the struggle expressed in *Divyadaan: Journal of Philosophy & Education* vol. 30, no. 1 (2019), and the book of the summer of that year, *The Future: Core Precepts in Supramolecular Method and Nanochemistry*, both of which efforts subtly pushed me towards the present problem of *Assembly* and my reach for an answer that could constitute my first and second objectifications of the *Lonergan's 1833 Overture*.

Best add here and now the relevant piece of the letter, where I bold face the two bits of present interest:

> The Method of Theology is coming into perspective. For the Trinity: Imago Dei in homine and proceed to the limit as in evaluating **$[1 + 1/n]^{nx}$** as $\underline{n}$ approaches infinity. For the rest: ordo universi. From the viewpoint of theology, it is a manifold of unities developing in relation to one another and in relation to God, i.e., metaphysics as I conceive it but plus transcendent knowledge. From the viewpoint of religious experience, it is the same relations as lived in a development from elementary intersubjectivity (cf. Sullivan's basic concept of interpersonal relations) to

---

[7] *Insight*, 556.

[8] *Ibid.*

[9] This weaves into the problem that Lonergan writes of as the problem of the chasm. See note 9 of Essay L, p. 90.

[10] On this see Patrick Brown, "Interpreting Lonergan's View of Method in May 1954," *Seeding Global Collaboration*, edited by Patrick Brown and James Duffy, Axial Publishing, 2016, 45–80.

intersubjectivity in Christ (**cf. the endless Pauline [suv- or] sun-compounds**) on the sensitive (external Church, sacraments, sacrifice, liturgy) and intellectual levels (faith, hope, charity). Religious experience: Theology:Dogma :: Potency : Form : Act.

My struggle with Crowe's struggle led me to work on the meaning of **[1 + 1/n]^{nx}**. What was Lonergan thinking of when writing "n" or "x"? I won't go there now, since it leads into, e.g., a musing over the oddity of e^x that is expressed in the equation $d/dx\ (e^x) = e^x$.[11] Indeed, my present poise exposes the focus on that first bold-faced piece as an unfortunate distraction. Lonergan, it seems to me now, was typing hurriedly in the mood of a thrilling grip on a possible genetics of expansion, an exponential bubbling, to which he was led by circling round—his early reading of Sullivan is in there—"the endless sun- compounds of Paul." And, you may ask—that is the task of a first and second objectification in Lonergan's Overture—what else is in there, for him then, for him eleven years later, for you now, for the millennial future of theology?

But first, a little help on the road: a pause over *The Letter of Paul to the Colossians*, verse 14 of chapter three. "Above all, clothe yourselves in love, which binds everything together in perfect harmony." If you have the Greek to hand, well and good, but no panic. The third last word in the Greek of the verse is "*sundesmos.*" There you have the sort of compound to which Lonergan was drawing attention. *Sundesmos*, as a noun, is a compound word comprised of *sun*, meaning "with" and *desmos*, meaning "a band, fetter, anything for tying"[12] So: you have a, well, a Super-tying. How Super? Who Super?

?"anything for tying"? What flows through your W-enzyme here, what flights of fancy? What-flights of fantasy?[13]

How can I help forward my short appeal for an *Assembly* on [1 + 1/n]^{nx}, an Assembly on Lonergan's excited passage, journey, of that piece of a 1954 letter?

I think, now, of two potential tyings-together, from previous efforts of mine, spanning fifty years. [A] There is the tying together of subjects in simple

---

[11] Pages 116–18 of the article mentioned in the first paragraph give pointers on this.

[12] I am relying on dictionaries here, as in my background puttering, but in that puttering I benefited from sun-conversations with scholarly folk, in particular with Conn O'Donovan, who did oceans of Pauline research in our climbing.

[13] The effort here is best made integrally, compactly. A W-enzyme poise (see pp. 2–3 in *The Future: Core Precepts of Supramolecular Method and Nanochemistry* on the dense meaning of *W*) that anticipates the harmonies and genuinenesses mentioned in *Insight* 498–504.

conversations talked of in my *Music That is Soundless*;[14] [B] there is the potential tying together [yes, long run e^x!] of the conversing community that was Lonergan's Dream of 1965.[15]

> [A] The basic question to raise is, *when did I last*[16] *have a real conversation?* That question must be asked in an authentic personal memory search, and its answer is aided by its threefold specification: *when was I last understanding, understood? When did I last speak? When did I last listen?* The process is an effort to locate personal data—and one may honestly find that one has little or no data. Some people pay their psychiatrist $100 an hour to attempt conversation—no one should assume that they achieve it every day. Contemporarily, for instance, real conversation rarely occurs in an institutional context: if this seems an exaggeration it is no worse than the psychologist Maslow's contention that less than one per cent of adults grow. In so far as one has had some experience of real conversation—indeed even if the question raised produces only a glimpse of its

---

[14] The extract [A] is on p. 7–8 of the third edition, *Music That is Soundless: A Fine Tuning for the Lonely Bud A* (Axial Publishing, 2005). The book originated in 1968.

[15] I have regularly symbolized Lonergan's dream as a tower:

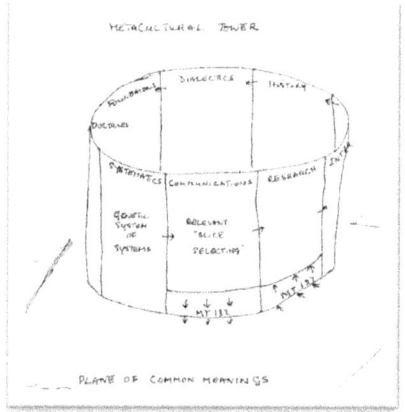

[16] [Notes 16 and 17 here are in the original text]. The word *last* here might seem superfluous. Its use relates both to the strategy of attention to a concrete particular (*Insight*, 274) and to the rhythm of the question. "This rhythm of language is a mysterious trait that probably bespeaks biological unities of thought and feeling which are entirely unexplored as yet." (Susanne Langer, *Feeling and Form*, Scribners, New York, 1953).

absence[17]—one has data for the understanding of conversation. But only data, only a beginning, as the Epilogue reiterates.

[B] Below is the matrix of Communications presented in chapter 16, "Communications and Metaphysics as Science," *The Allure of the Compelling Genius of History*.[18]

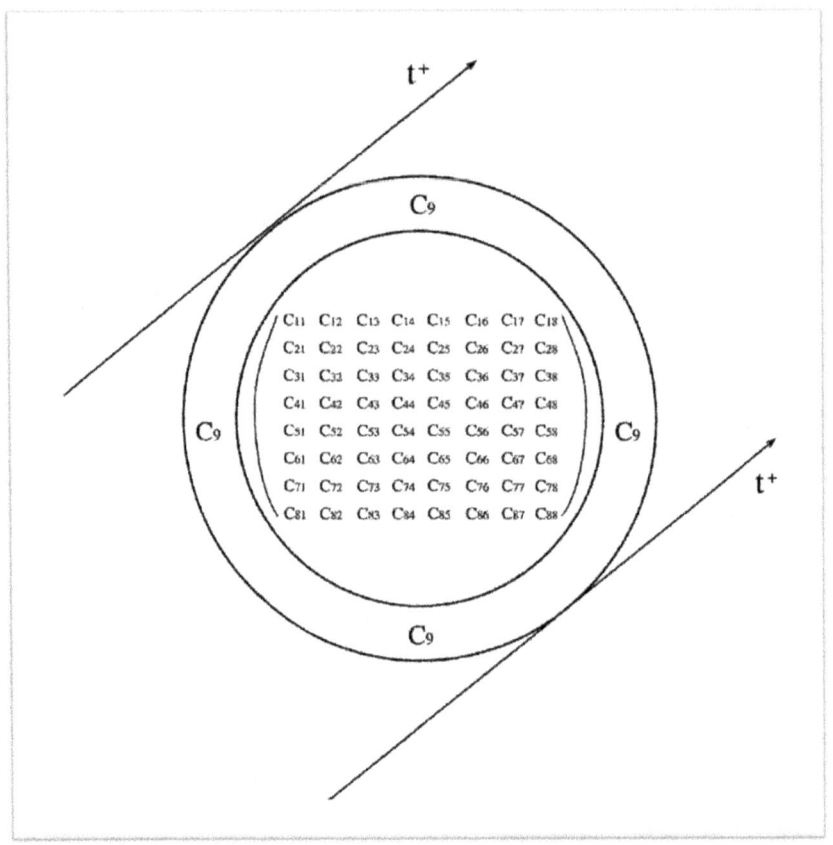

---

[17] This parallels Lonergan's point in "Christ as Subject," *Collection, CWL* 4, 174. "If anyone cares for clarity on this issue, he can begin from the statement, '*non si riesce a comprendre*' (one fails to understand). He can contrast that experience of not understanding with other experiences in which he felt he understood. Then he can turn his efforts to understanding and not understanding."

[18] It occurs on page 188, in chapter 16, "Communications and Metaphysics as Science." Note the meshing of chapters of *Insight* and *Method in Theology*, a strategy of illumination. The eight specialties are paralleled to *Insight* eight chapters, 9–16.

Now pause over another of *Colossian*'s verses: 1:17. "He himself is before all things and in him all things hold together." The verse in Greek ends with the word "*sunesteken.*" A *sun*-hold. Does the Son hold and host and hoist the molecules of our conversations in a symphony of words in which "God is not an object"?[19]

In both [A] and [B] you are invited to sun-hold together the spooky sun-hold together of networked and networking conversations. And have I not intimated that this is the invitation of finitude, a holding-together mediation of the holding together that is the oneness of minding, the minding of oneness?[20] Can you hear here hear the finger-springing Interior Lighthouse[21] of Lonergan's end-typing of *Method in Theology* in the early 1970s? It points to "the fruit of Christ's prayer: '. . . may they all be one . . .' John 17:21).[22]

Networking conversations: about pushing the "all be one" of all of the mediating situation rooms of all the homesteads and hovels and hotels of humanity's trek towards the home-stretch of the Eschaton.

These few pages, of course, are an invitation to group's Assembling $[1 + 1/n]^{nx}$ so that the invitation of Lonergan's Overture to converse freshly with oneself in the first two of three objectifications would bring your living as a theologian "from being a sort of vegetative living to being a conscious living."[23] There is the seed of carrying theology, *From Mild Mess to Wild Bliss*. Here hear here: if only some significant few would leap out of the messy vegetable garden into guarding the *sun-* garden of Paul and Jesus.[24] More about that guarding in the next

---

[19] *Method in Theology*, 342, line 2 [316, line 15].

[20] Pause now over the word "with" in the end line of *Insight* 722: "Good will wills the order of the universe, and so it wills with that that order's dynamics joy and zeal." A fresh reading for you? Recall our focus on that page and its difficulty in *LO and Behold 9*, "Assembling *Insight.*"

[21] I have elaborated abundantly on The Interior Lighthouse, a tradition of Kataphatic Prayer. For beginning reflections see *Disputing Quests* 14 and 16 (available at: http://www.philipmcshane.org/disputing-quests). The challenge was expressed earlier in the five (4–8) *Prehumous* essays on "Foundational Prayer" (available at: http://www.philipmcshane.org/prehumous).

[22] *Method in Theology*, 367[338].

[23] *Philosophical and Theological Papers 1958–1964*, "The Mediation of Christ in Prayer," *CWL* 6, 179, lines 9–10.

[24] This is a massive challenge. It obviously relates to facing the challenge of the second canon of hermeneutics and that turn of a page and a culture of *Insight* 609–10. Helpful leads are *Disputing Quests* 10, "Paul's Epistles and Functional Systematics," and the three *Disputing Quests* essays titled 4, 5, and 8 "Turn Wright."

essay. Meantime, I leave you dangling in the second last footnote of *The Future: Core Precepts in Supramolecular Method and Nanochemistry*.[25]

> My stare at you is incomplete, and the final note will put that incompleteness in context. But here I think of the short-term context, the context of my brief introduction (above, p. 28) of Aristotle and Drucker as pointing to the stairs inadequately, (R, I, H and D_{oc} S C) and my pointing inadequately there to the bridge between them (D_i, H): a context for the *Duffy Exercise* that is to dance round the third chapter of this book. The short-term fuller context to my "Openers of the positive Anthropocene" in the book is your picking up on my nudgings given in the repeated mention of problems associated with the words *intersubjectivity* (xiv, xvi, 8, 9, 34–5, 40, 54–5, 80, 92, 96, 103) and *spooky* (3, 8, 13, 17, 66, 116) and the 6 repetitions (xiv, 8, 34, 54, 80, 103) of Lonergan's 1954 challenge regarding the future of theology. You find now, perhaps, that you did not climb in each occurrence to a fresh meaning of the word or the challenge? Such a climbing in reading belongs to the positive Anthropocene. But we need to climb towards that climbing: try climbing over the stile named by my repetitions, my petitions, Lonergan's petition. I return to your aid in "On the Stile of a Crucial Experiment," *Divyadaan: Journal of Philosophy and Education*, vol. 31 (2020). That is to be followed by the aide-mémoire, *The Future as Life Stile: From Mild Mess to Wild Bliss*.

---

[25] Note 50, page 111.

O ~ Understanding the Object

I wish us here to approach our problem—not specified till the second part here—by first doing what I call a simple first reading, then I change gear into a second musing over the text in as large a context as we can muster, climbing especially from the two essays G and H.

But the first simple reading requires a sense of humor, a twist of the title: Oh! Understanding the Object?!!" Was there a twinkle in Lonergan's eyes as he typed that title? I suspect he was into a pedagogical minimalism, but not unaware of doing that. He does not use the word *theory* lightly,[1] and it occurs three times in the conclusion of the second paragraph. "Our present concern is with theory, and indeed, not the general learning theory that regards students but the special learning theory that regards exegesis."[2] What is special there is indicated by him in the final long sentence of the first paragraph: already knowing all about the object leaves the task of finding out what this person means in the text. But here you are allowed —is Lonergan not encouraging it?—to take "know all about"[3] in a low-level sense. "Such knowledge, of course, is general and potential. Reading the text, when its meaning is obvious, makes the general knowledge more particular and the potential knowledge actual."[4] Muse over "low-level sense" towards glimpsing that it ranges—in, say, reading Paul's New Testament writings—from what we may call lay-competence to the powerful low-level sense that N.T. Wright brings to that reading.[5]

Did the end of that paragraph catch your attention? There seems nothing low-level about Tom Wright's grip on Paul. Pause, then, over the end of that third

---

[1] A nice exercise is to check occurrence of *theory* in *Method in Theology*.

[2] *Method in Theology*, 156[148].

[3] *Ibid*. In the third paragraph "knows all about."

[4] *Ibid.*, 156[148–9].

[5] Consider his *The Day the Revolution Began. Reconsidering the Meaning of Jesus's Crucifixion*, Harper Collins, 2016. "Theology, after all, was made for the sake of the church, not the church for theology. I hope the present book will help ordinary Christians grasp, and be grasped by, the multifaceted glory of Jesus's cross, rather than getting bogged down in complex and apparently irrelevant problems." (*op. cit.* 22). In the previous paragraph is the remark, "doctrinal definitions can only go so far. Shorthand slogans and technical language are helpful when making sure that we are not losing something vital, but they must not be mistaken for the real thing."

paragraph: "the greater the exegete's resources, the greater the likelihood that he will be able to enumerate all possible interpretations and assign to each its proper measure of probability."[6] What greatness has Lonergan in mind here? A page later he remarks, "the wider the interpreter's experience, the deeper and fuller the development of his understanding, the better balanced his judgment, the greater the likelihood that he will discover what the author meant."[7] Suppose, then, that the exegete had the resource that is *The Sketch* on page 602 of *Insight*, had the deeper and fuller development of his understanding that "Thirdly"[8] points to: would he or she do a better job in helping forward the functional cycling to pulpit talk and street smarts? In that functional cycling there is to be a collaboration pivoting on "pure formulations."[9] "They are pure formulations if they proceed from an interpreter that grasps the universal viewpoint and if they are addressed to an audience that similarly grasps the universal viewpoint."[10]

Does such a norm of a "better job" not lurk behind the kindly ramble of this section 2 of *Method in Theology*, chapter 7?

I cannot help here sharing the distraction of an old musing of mine on that quotation from "Thirdly," and the pointing to "an audience that similarly grasps." Lonergan, I surmise, had little or no anticipatory grasp, as he typed in 1953, of the vision of the "split audience"[11] that would leap up in his molecules in February of 1965. The problem of his typing this section in the late 1960s was that he could not fly forward in his writing on exegesis in this chapter. His pacing and puzzling with me in the summer of 1966 comes to mind and are relevant to your reading of, and musing over, this short section. How much of *Insight* could he roll into this short introductory book?[12]

---

[6] *Ibid.*, 156[149].

[7] *Ibid.*, end of both 157 and [149].

[8] *Insight*, 602, line 26.

[9] *Ibid.*, line 26.

[10] *Ibid.*, lines 30–33.

[11] It is interesting to pause over this business of "similarly grasps" in the light of his later splitting of the group of interpreters. The split leaves a "similarly grasps" : a common vision of the cycle of collaboration that *per se* grows through the procedures of Section 5, chapter 10, of *Method in Theology*. The **similarly grasps** is to be the current Standard Model.

[12] That he did cunningly roll *Insight* into the book is the thesis of website article 10: "A Paradigmatic Panel for (Advanced) Student (of Religion)," available at: http://www.philipmcshane.org/website-articles.

So on we go to "listen with sincere respect to the Stoic description of the Wise Man, and then requests and introduction."[13] Back we go, indeed, to smile again at his title: "Oh! Understanding the Object??!" We are picking up particularly on the pointers to be found in essays G and H, connecting the effort there with "the deeper and fuller development,"[14] "the greater the habitual knowledge one possesses,"[15] that ends the short section "Understanding the Object." What might be this "richest possible development of his individuality" that ends the quotation from Bultmann in the note that concludes that section?

I am pointing you towards the genetic drive of *Insight* for a "potential totality"[16] up to and beyond "the level of one's times."[17] Let's enjoy straining towards the fantasy of an effective science of the future. Even in the case of a lily or a mustard tree this is a fantasy.

But now I wish you to face a fantasy which might not have been a fantasy-strain had we not been led astray by "bolder spirits"[18] like Aristotle. "I advanced that Aristotle was a bourgeois, that he introduced the distinction between the speculative and practical to put the 'good' as Socrates and Plato conceived it out of court."[19] I have kept this 'good' news relatively quiet till now in these essays so that you might be shocked at its absence and its obviousness. You are in 'good' company in that the 'good' Fred Crowe missed the point in his first index of *Insight*: the point that implementation is essential to the poise of whatting, of understanding.[20] This is true whether you are dealing with an orchid or an oak or an okie or an oral tradition. How does that resonate with your reading of the title

---

[13] *Insight*, 649.

[14] *Method in Theology*, 157[149].

[15] *Ibid.*, 158[149]

[16] *Insight*, 587: the beginning of the section on the Universal Viewpoint,

[17] *Method in Theology*, 350[323]. The rest of that section weaves round the topic.

[18] *Ibid.*, the beginning of the second paragraph of chapter one, a key pointer to the over-reach and the *scotosis* of Aristotle.

[19] I am quoting a 1935 letter of Lonergan to a Jesuit superior. The ten-page letter is fully reproduced on pages 144–54 of Pierrot Lambert and Philip McShane, *Bernard Lonergan. His Life and Leading Ideas*, Axial Publishing, 2010. The quotation is on page 152.

[20] The poise, in its fullness, is to be an effective emergence of characters who personally have solved the problem of the chasm. See note 9 of Essay L, p. 90. This raises again the problem mentioned in note 15 of Essay A, p. 5, and note 16 of Essay C, p. 18, and the beginning of Essay D, p. 19ff. Solving globally the problem of the chasm requires a quite new poise of Doctrines, Systematics, and Communications, one that is to lead to an effective structuring of what I would call *situation analysis*. See Essay P, note 12, p. 115.

"Understanding the Object," or indeed with your reading of the slogan of *Insight*: "*Thoroughly understand what it is to understand, and not only will you understand the broad lines of all there is to be understood but also you will possess a fixed base, an invariant pattern, opening upon all further developments of understanding.*"[21]

We shall return regularly to the key word in that statement, "possess,"[22] but first, alas, we must do some elementary puttering, or at least I must point to the need to perhaps go against the grain and do such puttering. Perhaps I could annoy you forward into that puttering by placing you in front of the fridge with the problem of cooking dinner. You open it, scan its contents and ask "what might that be?"

What is going on here? If you are the achievement of a basically adequate self-scrutinizing self, then you are at home in those "sixty three articles in a row"[23] of Thomas, but now your deliberation is twirled and screwed freshly into creativity.[24] Getting to grips with the question, 'What is going on?' "if more than general and vague, is arduous and time-consuming; it leads to the impasse of scrutinizing the self-scrutinizing subject."[25]

Does it take much self-scrutiny to become a little luminous about you and the universe going on? Might we say, brightly, that "what is going on in the universe," where there is no question mark? Might we part with Aristotle and take a stand on fulsome science as: engineering that is going on? So we find ourselves

---

[21] *Insight*, 22: the italics are in the text.

[22] The lead-into reflection on the word for me was through my musing, in the context of my five articles in *Divyadaan: Journal of Philosophy and Education*, vol. 30, no. 1 (2019), on *Whitson's Coming Convergence of World Religions*. I returned to the discussion that begins at line 29 of *Insight* 766: "theology possesses." Our problem is that it does not, in any religion, possess an effective relevance. How then is one to conceive of moving towards such a possession? What is needed is a massive climb to an effective heuristics countervailing contemporary warps in all the heuristics of sciences and in their referents. Such a climb involves the genesis of a full global topology of situation analysis. For more on that see the final chapter, "Nanochemistry" of *The Future: Core Precepts in Supramolecular Method and Nanochemistry*.

[23] *CWL* 1, *Grace and Freedom: Operative Grace in the Thought of St. Thomas Aquinas*, 94: the articles are *Summa theologiae*, 1-2, qq. 6–17.

[24] I would draw attention to the inadequacy of the entire philosophic tradition in its consideration of deliberation: think of the full challenge engineering the future and the massive heuristics of deliberation it is to involve. See the final chapter, "Nanochemistry," of my *The Future: Core Precepts in Supramolecular Method and Nanochemistry*. And of course there is my Appendix here.

[25] *Method in Theology*, 167[157–58].

Understanding the Object

in a sort of Leonardo da Vinci poise, say, with regard to wood and air, and envisage taking flight. And does not that poise weave nicely into the present crisis of the negative Anthropocene? "Understanding the Object" as a norm leans us forward to save us and Gaia. So, we are into a "deeper and fuller" reading of "the deeper and fuller development of his understanding"[26] and hers. Indeed, I would have you think quite oddly and newly about the end of the second paragraph of this section of chapter 7, on "understanding the object," an oddity that changes leapingly the reading of the paragraph to follow.

"Our present concern is theory and, indeed, not the general learning theory that regards students but the special learning theory that regards exegesis,"[27] and that concern and special bent leads you and me to think freshly, with positive Anthropocene hope, about the beginning of the next paragraph and the key advance towards that positive Anthropocene: Lonergan and you and I shift to claim effectively that "I have said that the whole exegetical task remains to be performed."[28]

You are poised here, in the interpretation of "the actual task of interpretation,"[29] over the seed of a quite new meaning of the word *envisage* in "First, then, envisage the materials. They consist of the totality of documents and monuments."[30] The **envisage** leans forward, the second of nine cycle-weaved meanings of *interpretation* that sublates that *Sketch* of *Insight*, that "First, Secondly, Thirdly, Fourthly, Fifthly" of the paragraphs there. But the poise of *Insight*'s *Sketch* remains, a poise of genetic sequencing.[31] That poise is to become the *nomos* of the ninefold enterprise, a rolling stone that aims to gather no moss or *mos* of negativity, but the *nomos* of engineering the future.

---

[26] *Method in Theology*, 157[149].

[27] Ibid., 156[148].

[28] Ibid.

[29] *Insight*, 602.

[30] Ibid.

[31] This little book is drawing attention to the massive sublation of the Sketch by the full Standard Model envisaging of the genetics of layers of genetic and geohistorical controls of layers of genetic realities. The drawing attention is a drawing of you, by the entire book, to the details of the climb of self-scrutiny that calls to you in the sacrament of the present moment, of the present millennium. Perhaps note 2 of Essay N, p. 99, encourages.

P ~ Understanding the Words

> The essential observance is to note one's every failure to understand clearly and exactly and to sustain one's reading and rereading until one's inventiveness or good luck have eliminated one's failure in comprehension.[1]

I begin this section—should I call it Please Please?—by asking for your Patience in the Potential discovery of a massive "existential gap."[2] I begin it with the concluding words of the section in chapter 7 of *Method in Theology* that is my present concern, which I wish you to share at least faintly but, yes, effectively.[3] I begin by asking you to pause regarding that concern, reading that sentence about "essential observance" with the seeds of a new seriousness that, yes, can boggle one's minding in a self-recognition about this section as it "leads to the impasse of scrutinizing the self-scrutinizing subject."[4] My Webster dictionary gives as a meaning of impasse "a situation offering no escape," but I am pointing here vigorously—and section Q adds to the distress—that the community following Lonergan has, not escaped, but simply carried on in reading and thinking patterns of old stale conventions of theology and philosophy.

Read again, Please, from the beginning, starting with the title's *P*. Does that quoted end-sentence boggle the mind not a little? It demands a terrible Dionysian

---

[1] *Method in Theology*, 159-60[151].

[2] The reference is to *CWL* 18, *Phenomenology and Logic*, chapter 13, section 2, the first of two final chapters on this topic.

[3] I keep repeating the key text on this: *CWL* 18, *Phenomenology and Logic*, 306: "a resolute and effective intervention in this historical process." It is to be the ethos of functional collaboration in the positive Anthropocene. Note its anticipation in Lonergan's 1934 *Essay in Fundamental Sociology*, "providing a statistically effective form" (20).

[4] *Method in Theology*, 167[158].

madness of creativity[5] in this "rather critical moment in the historical process."[6] It demands a pause over your possible *drifting* meshed publically—there is a comfortable "autonomy of the splinters"[7]—only slightly tinged with a neuro-hidden *dread*.[8]

I am poised here in the mood—Please Please Poise with me—of that brilliant section 1.4, "Resolute and Effective Intervention in the Dialectic," of the last chapter of *CWL* 18, *Phenomenology and Logic*.[9] I am poised to take Lonergan's advice of the end of that section 1.4, savoring also the advice of Fred Crowe in 1964 about what we must do. We **must**? How might that ***must*** be effective? Might you crazily step out of the NO-drift and become one of the ***they*** who effectively agree. "I think **they** will agree also that unless his readers are ready to undertake a parallel labor (not necessarily so prolonged inasmuch as they may be less tardy of intelligence) they have little chance of understanding what Lonergan is doing and talking about. This is rather bluntly said, I am afraid, but is there not room for a measure of bluntness at this stage?"[10] The stage is still the same: we are in the

---

[5] See my *The Future: Core Precepts in Supramolecular Method and Nanochemistry*, 15–16, and its comments on the third line of the *Method in Theology* 48[47] spread of words. The key nudge from Lonergan is "Man as insisting on the good of order is Apollonian; but as ready to tear it down is Dionysian."(*CWL* 10, *Topics in Education*, 40, line 1). I seek to tear down creatively and effectively the settled conventions of Jay-walking of Lonergan studies. Your help would be welcome. The book, *The Future*, is referred to below as simply *The Future*.

[6] *CWL* 18, *Phenomenology and Logic*, 300.

[7] *Ibid.*, 252. There are various splinter-folks and splinter groups within Lonergan studies, but all working within "a background of merely traditional norms that are not questioned."(*Ibid.*, 252–3).

[8] The pause is made existentially obviously by tracking the meanings of *drifting* and *dread* through the indexed references in *CWL* 18, *Phenomenology and Logic*, page 390.

[9] *Ibid.*, 305–308.

[10] F. Crowe, "The Exigent Mind," *Spirit as Inquiry: Studies in Honor of Bernard Lonergan S.J.*, 27.

same "slum"[11] **situation**[12] as we were in 1964. But now might you and I take Lonergan's advice at the conclusion of this section 1.4, advice and section ramped up into "a statistically effective form"[13] by his brilliant move towards a novel and effective dialectic?[14] Let us read that conclusion slowly now, trying a little or a Dionysian lot to enter the lunacy of "scrutinizing the self-scrutinizing self."[15]

> You can utilize the **situation** produced by the current mentality to manifest the defects in current mentality. Insofar as you are doing that, you are heightening the action of the dialectic that produces unsatisfactory **situations** as manifestations of unsatisfactory minds It produces these manifestations so that we may react to them and correct them. Again, intervention not only clarifies the **situation** but also drives home the point. You can show the evils of the **situation** are due to these errors, and that the evils of another **situation** are due to the same errors again and that to retain these errors is to perpetuate the evil. The argument will be entirely in the concrete. You will be making manifest to people what everyone knows is bad, what they do not want, and you will be showing the connection between what is bad in the **situation** and its ground in the limitations of their thinking.[16]

You and I have a **situation** here and now. Might you intervene? Yoohoo! You? Who? I nudge you back, or forward, to the simple technique of J-wrapping

---

[11] "The slum is not properly simply a poorer quarter, but a place where there congregates the failures of our industrial society, the people who have no hope and no ambition" (*CWL* 10, *Topics in Education*, 253). Think of the industrious society either of Lonergan studies or of the academy generally. I recall Voegelin remarking about the academy being a brothel of opinion. The hopes and ambitions of such people are not in the Field. The challenge of J-wrapping is to meet the demand that "they have to be people in whom the horizon is coincident with the field. If they are not, then all they possibly can do is increase the confusion and accelerate the doom." *CWL* 18, *Phenomenology and Logic*, 306.

[12] I boldface the word **situation** above, and 7 more times in the text that follows. The 8 occurrences echo the 8 occurrences in the last paragraph of section 2, "Common Meaning and Ontology," of the final chapter of *Method in Theology*. The final chapter, "Nanochemistry" of *The Future* sublates this into a statistically effective heuristics of the engineering of progress. NANO in the context means Not Alone Not Opaque. See Essay O, note 22, p. 110.

[13] *Method in Theology*, 167[158].

[14] The effective form, almost hidden in *Method in Theology*'s chapter 10, is the topic of the central chapter, chapter 3, of *The Future*.

[15] *Method in Theology*, 167[158].

[16] *CWL* 18, *Phenomenology and Logic*, 307–308.

as opposed to the convention of Jay-walking.[17] Might you here and now, or firmly later this year, pause to disconcertingly J-wrap a little your reading of "scrutinizing the self-scrutinizing subject"? Yoohoo, Supermolecule, $f(p_i\,;\,c_j\,;\,b_k\,;\,z_l\,;\,u_m\,;\,r_n\,)$.

What do I need from you, what do you need from yourself?

I am distracted here by—and indeed paused to listen and to watch—Billy Joel singing in 1978 about honesty,[18] with its repeated lines adding vibes to that word as I would wish to vibe altogether up up up your vibes of the word *word*.[19]

> Honesty is such a lonely word
> Everyone is so untrue
> Honesty is hardly ever heard
> And mostly what I need from you

So might we, starting with you, startlingly begin again at P, a Plea, "it is not only to read *Insight* but also to discover oneself in oneself."[20]

I think now too of website lectures of presently senior Lonergan colleagues on the book and the topics of *Insight*, disgustingly Jay-walking, and guiding the next generations towards Jay-walking. "Honesty is hardly ever heard, And mostly what I need from you" is to halt the "merely drift, choose to be like everybody else"[21] poise of present Lonergan studies. Might you begin by sniffing what it is to reach towards "understanding the words"?

---

[17] This is the central topic of Essay J above. J-Wrapping lifts reading to an incarnate luminosity regarding and guarding the " ; " of W_3. Jay-walking is the subtle disguising of common sense—especially by proper-name referencing—strolling around texts of Lonergan.

[18] I add this odd note that, while I point here to a male singer, integral honesty seems to flow better from the female voice. Again, I go onto mention the Bee Gees, but think of the lift given to their song "Immortality" by the presence of Celine Dion. Think of Pavarotti learning to breathe from Joan Sutherland while touring Australia in 1965. Is there not some deep truth in Molly Bloom's plea in her famous soliloquy: "I don't care what anybody says itd be much better for the world to be governed by the women in it" (James Joyce, *Ulysses*, 1961, 778). We are into tricky evolutionary problems here. Might not integral J-Wrapping women of the positive Anthropocene lead in humanity's learning to breathe and read?

[19] Lonergan, in writing on linguistic meaning in section 5 of chapter 3 of *Method in Theology* give a one-sentence pointer to Helen Keller's leap in word-use. But what about the leap into that leap by the self-scrutinizing subject, answering luminously the question: What is a word? On that leap beyond Helen Keller see my *A Brief History of Tongue. From Big Bang to Coloured Wholes*, 31–37.

[20] *Method in Theology* 260[244].

[21] *CWL* 18, *Phenomenology and Logic*, 306, top.

Understanding the Words

So, we begin a third time. Has this not something to do with the third objectification of Lonergan's strategy of dialectic? But your *Assembly* of "Understanding the Words" is, here and now, a possibility of a lone ranging round your understanding of *understanding*, your understanding of *the*, your understanding of *words*.

Understanding? Think now of my vibing with Robin Gibb as he sings "I started a Joke."[22] Imagine Lonergan, recalling, in the summer of 1966, his climb through *Insight* and his lonely longing to invite a massive cultural twist in that climb. The joke started in *Insight*, was carried feebly on in *Method in Theology*. Here, hear, the start of the joke: "*Thoroughly understand what it is to understand …*"[23] LOL.

The? A cousin of *this*, and "a theorist would explain 'this' as the return from the field of conception to the empirical residue in the field of presentations."[24] Are you that theorist, capable of explaining your return in *this* and *that* and *the*? "Being a circle is the same as the circle . . . when we come to the concrete thing, e.g. *this* circle, i.e. one of the individual circles . . . we must meet the inquiry by saying that the question cannot be answered simply."[25] This word *the* in the middle: might it push your neuromolecules to ting-a-ling with 'The Man in the Middle,"[26] Maurice Gibb, bringing you so so slowly "Closer than Close"[27] to your "ostensive gestures"?[28]

Words? And we pause with the third brother, Barry Gibb, and perhaps his familiar, "It's only words, and words are all I have …"[29] But what is a word, a *word*, and have we noticed "that the question cannot be answered simply," that there is a quite new level beyond the five week struggle of Helen Keller that is to make us humans self-luminous in an effective way in the positive Anthropocene age, to which you can say "hello"[30] this year if you would move cunningly away from the NO-drift?

---

[22] See *Æcornomics 6*: "I Started a Joke," http://www.philipmcshane.org/ecornomics.

[23] *Insight*, 22.

[24] *Ibid.*, 369.

[25] Aristotle, *Metaphysics*, VII, 1036ᵃ.

[26] "Man in the Middle" is a Bee Gee song associated with Maurice Gibb.

[27] "Closer than Close": again, associated with Maurice Gibb. See also note 3, page i, of *The Future*.

[28] *Method in Theology*, 77[74].

[29] The song referred to was a big hit, always sung by Barry Gibb. Regarding the group, note the point made above in note 18.

[30] I am recalling a conversation with Lonergan about Dante, and about the greeting of Beatrice, when Lonergan waved his hand in the air and remarked, "that's what life's

INTERPRETATION FROM A TO Z

Would it not be cunning to plan a venture of reading this little section 1.4 later in this day or in this year, to reach for a distant 2020 vision of you in your layers of ";"? There is the dreadful fact of unfolding self-scrutiny—not, sadly, dreaded by common sense—that "the meaning of a text is an intentional entity. It is a unity that is unfolded through parts, sections, chapters, paragraphs, sentences, words."[31]

---

about: saying 'hello'." Do I succeed in this little essay in saying an effective 'hello' to you, Supermolecule?

[31] *Method in Theology*, 159[151]. **And on we go, with our 7th boldfaced note of eleven (pp. 8, 62, 70, 74, 87, 92, 118, 140, 141, 150, 169).**

There is, then, the topic of the next Essay Q, the intentional entity that wrote *Insight*, unfolding his missionary self in "chapters, paragraphs, sentences, words" with a following who do not wish to say "hello." I heard a so-called Lonergan expert lecturing publically about how he "read *Insight* in three weeks and it changed me profoundly." What can I say about such a trivial and trivializing greeting? But alas, it is the ethos of the self-disregarding experts, even if they have spent years—apparently self regarding and guarding—skipping along the paragraphs of the Opera's melodies after dodging the "natural bridge" (*Insight*, 163) of chapter five of the book. The dodging leaves them scurrying past page 537 in *Insight*, and so missing the friendly intimate cauling that is the fourteenth place of *Insight* page 683, a ReG$^i_{jk}$arding of them as Ours. G$^i_{jk}$ would have their W-enzyme's weave aesthetic explanatory lives round Their Presence, lightsome in the fact that "God is not an object," (*Method in Theology*, 341, 342 [316]) but a deliberative Threesome of their slightest deliberations. Both our and their slightest deliberations push us forward to the "large global problem that awaits global self-attention" (Essay T's note 25, page 140), a problem that leads into our 8th boldfaced note, note 26 on that page). "What effective situational aggregate of deliberations must we possess," (*ibid.*) possess as engineers of history?

And now try to take note of the horror of our times and of our Lonergan peddling. The absence of luminous deliberation clouds all the other transcendentals in deceptive *haute vulgarization*, leaving us in a world of nominalist pretense. What, now, of the title and content of this present Essay P?

Q ~ Understanding the Author

I referred forward, in **A**, to this section of my musings and the three paragraphs of section 4 of *Method in Theology*, encouraging a relating of it to the work of N.T. Wright. Earlier there I posed the questions, "What on earth are Wright and Lonergan really doing? Are they not trying to engineer the Kingdom?" Here I give the section a twist by turning to "what on earth is Lonergan really doing?" and nudge you to share my musings about the first sentence of that section 4. The author is Lonergan; the words are those of *Insight* 17.3 and *Method* 7: so "then with the author by his words we understand the object."[1] But now I wish you to pause over the beginning of that sentence: "the meaning of a text is plain." Pick some text of Lonergan and muse over its plainness for you. Perhaps, at this stage in your reading of my alphabetic ramble, you share my view that the meaning of any of his texts is not at all plain. Yet it can be deceptively plain. This morning I push again through the mid-paragraph of page 601 of *Insight*. I read it first sixty years ago, and of course have been reading it since. I paused over the pointing of lines 19–20: "Unless they can envisage the range of possible meanings . . . .." What a daft condition! The plain paragraph's meaning is altogether remote, with the remoteness of, yes, the object talked of in this chapter, this book, the *Opera Omnia*.

Follow along with me here in my ongoing messy struggle with Lonergan's meaning. Be amused in the section Q, assuming now that Q is Lonergan in the following quotation, and P is, of course, Phil at trying to figure out, in his 89th year, what he is at in *The Sketch*.[2] Here we are, then, poised over a brilliant paragraph.

> Fourthly, there are hypothetical expressions. Suppose P to be interpreting Q. From his immanent sources of meaning P will work out a hypothetical pure formulation of Q's context and of the content of Q's message. But the pure formulation of the content of Q's message proceeds from a universal viewpoint. It has to be transposed into an equivalent content that would proceed from Q's particular viewpoint. That particular viewpoint is assigned in the pure formulation of Q's context. Finally, in as much as this transposition is effected under the limitations of the resources of language

---

[1] *Method in Theology*, 160[151].
[2] *Insight*, 602–603

and of the channels of communication available to Q, there results the hypothetical expression.³

Surely you admit that this is pretty crazy stuff, as indeed, hilariously, his titling of the section *The Sketch*. But then the entire book is the first of two volumes planned to be a sketch of the future of methodological thinking. Here he is writing in haste probably in early summer of 1953. Go back two pages to his "recalling the structure of classical empirical method."⁴ He hurries past "its upper blade consists in a heuristic structure."⁵ He could have enlarged on this, say, from Lindsay and Margenau, to get the reader to effectively notice that the upper blade, at any period in the history, requires a Standard Model with an "extraordinary array of techniques."⁶ Did you, my good reader, miss the point in that slim paragraph? So that when you arrived at "there has not been available an appropriate upper blade" you were not pushed to muse over the problem of a developed overview, a standard model, one globally accepted in a complex pure formulation? I think now of the push in physics expressed in *Gauging What's Real. The Conceptual Foundations of Contemporary Physics.*⁷ It is not, then, a matter of a vague heuristics of four imperatives, "Be attentive, Be intelligent, Be reasonable, Be

---

³ *Ibid.*
⁴ *Ibid.*, 600, line 6.
⁵ *Ibid.*, lines 7–8.
⁶ *Ibid.*, lines 24–25. Note that I have jumped you into the next paragraph in the page, into his musings on the potential science of interpretation. I recall now how, more than 20 years later in a Boston Workshop question session he was asked "how much physics should a theologian knows?" His reply, "well, he should be able to read Lindsay and Margenau!" Their book *Foundations of Physics* was his standard reference in *Insight*. On models and techniques see Essays H and J above.
⁷ Richard Healey, Oxford University Press, 2007, pp. 297.

responsible."[8] It is the shocking matter of sensing "all that is lacking"[9] and humbly seeking to seed the shift from present "*voraussetzungslos*"[10] to a massively detailed genetics of a situation[11] ethics of the future. Might you imagine a thousand page book on Method of late in the next century, dancing round the gauge title of Essay B above, "{Assembling (Interpretations)³}⁴"? Can you push your imagination, in a lower level of stress, to see Lonergan's efforts of *Insight* and *Method in Theology* "pushed to a far further development"[12] that "satisfy a genetic and dialectic unfolding of human intelligence"?[13] And weaved into that explanatory unfolding are to be the religious writings of all nations, the efforts of N. T. Wright, the efforts of us all to gesture out our native graceful exigence for characterhood. I am reminded now of how I began *The Allure of the Compelling Genius of History*.

> The emergence of humanity is the evolutionary achievement of sowing what among the cosmic molecules. The sown what infests the clustered molecular patterns behind and above your eyes, between your ears, lifting areas—named by humans like Brocca and Wernicke—towards patterned noise-making that in English is marked by "so what?"

Does this big bang nudge not put into a fresh context Lonergan's sentence, "the one point that we wish to make is that specialized modes of expression have to be evolved"? The sown seeds of the what that is humanity were cast, in the negative Anthropocene, on the naturally stony ground of potency, but in the recent millennia of that negativity the ground has been layered with a plastic

---

[8] *Method in Theology*, 53[52]. There is a deep and simple issue about these transcendentals that needs to be faced. It is neatly brought out by Lonergan a line later: "Being intelligent includes a grasp of hitherto unnoticed or unrealized possibilities." See now my Appendix A, "Two Diagrams," in *CWL* 18, *Phenomenology and Logic*, 319–24. The second diagram, as I note in the text (end of 319) is "pedagogically important." It lead me to include a transcendental "Be Adventurous," so that the list becomes "Be attentive, Be intelligent, Be reasonable, Be adventurous, Be responsible." This inclusion helps to clear up much messy writing in Lonergan studies, about being reasonable: even sometimes giving the impression that having a plan is not relevant to reasonableness. Furthermore, the pedagogy points students to the prime present need of engineering the future, of an increase in the sub-community focused on the forward specialties and their push forward in C_9. The issue, then, is adventuresomeness, indeed, with a pressure of Dionysian fantasy.

[9] *Insight*, 559.

[10] *Ibid.*, 600, line 28.

[11] See Essay P, note 12, p. 115.

[12] *Method in Theology*, 160[152].

[13] The final words of *The Sketch* (*Insight*, 603).

truncation. Our native graceful exigence for characterhood has been neurodynamically blocked, so that the need for specialized modes of expression is not recognized in the push for explanation in human studies. That need, in theology, is symbolized by symbols like ";" and W_3 and G^i_{jk}.

Thus I have brought us back to where I left off at the end of Essay K. And we are brought back to the strange solitary typing of *Insight*, on an old-style typewriter, in the years up to the summer of 1953. He was typing in and to a culture that I wrote of compactly in that Essay K, knowing the need for symbolization,[14] knowing the tune played by Lindsay and Margenau,[15] knowing the needs for a symbolic control of meaning in explanatory Christology.[16]

The problem we now face—one sadly presently dodged in studying Lonergan—is the problem of "determining the operators" when the heuristics of operators is not recognized as a serious challenge beyond their feeble beginnings in the simple science of physics. What to add here in silly compactness?

I talked of this silly compactness at the end of Essay K and then promised it here. It fits nicely into the challenge of "understanding the author." So, why not take a discomforting illustration that links various difficulties together: the challenge to understand oneself and the challenge of reaching an effective genetic perspective on finitude's blossoming. Understanding the author Lonergan

---

[14] Recall note 8 of Essay K, p. 86. I point now to that neglected little essay, "A Note on Geometric Possibility" in *CWL* 13: *A Second Collection*.

[15] See Section 2, "Lindsay and Margenau," of chapter ten of Pierrot Lambert and Philip McShane, *Bernard Lonergan. His Life and Leading Ideas*, Axial Publishing, 2010. The chapter is titled "The Dominant Context of Lonergan's Life," a context quite remote from that of his followers. See section 4 there, "Lonergan's Reach for the Character of Energy" (178–88).

[16] Useful to pause now freshly over Lonergan's pointer towards a geometry of incarnation: "The comprehension of everything in a unified whole can be either formal or virtual. It is virtual when one is habitually able to answer readily and without difficulty, or at least 'without tears', a whole series of questions right up to the last why? Formal comprehension, however, cannot take place without a construct of some sort. In this life we are able to understand something only by turning to phantasm; but in larger and more complex questions it is impossible to have suitable phantasm unless the imagination is aided by some sort of diagram. Thus, if we want to have a comprehensive grasp of everything in a unified whole, we shall have to construct a diagram in which are symbolically represented all the various elements of the question along with the connections between them." *CWL* 7, *The Ontological and Psychological Constitution of Christ*, 151.

genetically fits nicely in between those challenges and seeks to surround them in this present silly culture.[17]

But simply think now of a silly reading of three pages of *Insight*: pages 281, 463–64. Might it have been your silly reading in your first encounter with *Insight*? You encounter Lonergan managing, with his old-style typewriter, a little technical symbolizing. Take first the paragraph beginning on page 281, line 15, with the word *Consider*. LOL: we could pause over the reading of that word, musing about Jay-walking it! But on we go to T_i, C_i, S_i.: not too frightful, those single subscripts. But now we move, with Lonergan beginning the next sentence, "Suppose": might this have been, be now indeed, another Jay-walk? He pitches "E_{ij}" at you. What did you, do you, make of that? Think $f(p_i ; c_j)$: something you surely did not think of in a first reading? What images support your thinking, ??: the thinking of the bundles of sequences of physics' secondary determinations of relations of that level of realities that begin to look like water. Shift your thinking up a level, perhaps to a more apparent comfort, and think of and about $f(p_i ; c_j ; b_k)$. Simplify, if you like, to suit the E_{ij}, thus $f(c_i ; b_j)$. Now you are thinking about the chemistry of a plant, but—since there are really no unicellular plants, you might find it easier to cheat a little and think of the amoeba, a cheery little monocellular thingy that, when it's lonely, splits into two cheery little things.[18] So, we are thinking now—a handy piece of cheating—of $f(c_i ; z_j)$. And thus you have a neat further cheating-image of a little chemical blob rambling round, sticking out pseudo-feet to eat. How much chemistry have you in the image? Perhaps not much, but you see my point and my pointing? I am pointing way beyond that page of chapter 8—in which Lonergan is neatly cheating. I have you now in the ballpark of "to this end, there have to be invented appropriate symbolic images of the relevant chemical and physical process." But that end is being talked of, at this stage in the book, under the control of a metaphysics of meaning. The talk has changed in meaning, Even T_i , C_i , S_i , now seem simpler in presentation—no troublesome E_{ij}—yet with a suggested hierarchy, $X_i X_j X_k$ …

---

[17] "Surround" is a tricky word that really points to a confinement in openness. Think of the word "confinement" as it is occurs in *Insight* (509, line 4; 545, line 20; 593, 2nd line from end) and boosts its meaning by a fullness of meaning given by "engineering the future" to the word *implementation* in the definition of metaphysics (end of *Insight*, 416). We are in the stalk of a week-old sunflower **confined** to becoming a brown and yellow smile.

[18] I am recalling a song of *The Incredible String Band*.

The "measure of bluntness" here, a *nomos* of this "resolute and effective intervention in this historical process"[19] of your reading and rereading, is my question, "Did you notice the difference of the print-in-your-face of T_i, C_i, S_i from its facing you in 281 and facing you in 463?" "One has not only to read *Insight* but discover oneself in oneself." It reminds me of my two weeks in Dublin, 1971, of nightly conversations with Lonergan. We were hovering one night around "is? is! is." and I asked him when he sorted out **is**. His reply: "When I got that far in *Insight*!" Few have got that far in reading *Insight* even for years: a shared intellectual conversion is a silly myth of the Lonergan community. And what of the intellectual conversion to luminous reading in the J-wrap mode? And what of J-wrapping Jesus?

So, we arrive back at the puzzle of G^i_{jk} raised in Essay K, in particular at the meaning of "i." We are "on to" the challenge of note 16 above. For the Christian theologian the symbol G^i_{jk} is to haunt[20] the climb of *Insight* and to radiantly rise, indeed literally,[21] in the final place of the chapter's 'hypothesis' climb. "In the twenty-sixth place, God is personal."[22] It is an evident step to a twenty-seventh place, a 27th question of Thomas' *Summa Theologica*, "The hypothesis of intelligible emanations in God."[23]

For me, the symbol G^i_{jk} (G^i_{jk}), or indeed, $\{G^i_{jk} (G^i_{jk})\}^3$, symbolizes the challenge honest Christian "gown" readers are to face if Lonergan's inarticulate

---

[19] *CWL* 18, *Phenomenology and Logic*, 306.

[20] I am thinking of the range of old senses of *haunt*, such as are associated with the word *haim*: it is to be a Graceful home-bent. But I would ask you to simply think of the Christian, you and Lonergan, as climbing slowly over the years—I think of this as rising in the Interior Lighthouse—then the climb is four-fold interpersonal all the way. You are "The Well of Loneliness" (the title of chapter 19 of *The Allure of the Compelling Genius of History*) in both senses of well. You are present to the print as the present section. The present section occurs eleven times in *Insight* (see note 14, page 239, ibid,). Might you read it thus? Then in the 14th place (*Insight*, 683) the secondary intelligible that you radiantly are, in God as real, not spaced out elsewhere (see *Insight*, 537). There is the dark illumination of the fact that "God is not an object" (*Method in Theology*, 342[316]) and an anticipation of eschatological subjectivity—the goal haunting Lonergan's spooky identification, in 1954, of theology's growth (see note 10 of Essay M, p. 95, note 22 of Essay S, p. 134, and note 9 of Essay Z, p. 172).

[21] Add to the pointings of the previous note the context of note 10 of Essay T, p. 138.

[22] *Insight*, 691. We are in the world of serious religions, but at an explanatory level not yet shared by world religiosity.

[23] The title of my article in *Theological Studies* (23)1962, 545–68; available as *Published Article* no. 1: http://www.philipmcshane.org/ published-articles.

efforts are to lead the effective redemption of the message of Jesus to the town in this millennium. It points neatly to the simplest of the sciences, pushing on discontinuously in its invention of symbols.[24] Its operators stumble around in need of a better weird logic of genetic operators of meaning and expression. As one moves up into the visibilities of the higher sciences the stumbling worsens and is disguised by various reductionisms.[25] We need an infant heuristics of "determining the operators that relate the classifications relevant to one level of development to the classifications relevant to the next."[26] I am tempted to rewrite that sentence replacing 'level' by 'hovel' for the level of our times in the humanities. That hovel held Lonergan down, "was an impediment which the writer's thought could not shake off."[27] Might we take his talking and stalking of Jesus[28] into the engineering effectiveness of remote symbolizations?

---

[24] This is a huge future task of a surround of affect-laden imaging, radiant with explanatory understanding, that bridge what Lonergan calls *the chasm*. See the index to *CWL* 23, *Early Works on Theological Method 2*, under *Chasm*. Pause especially over the conclusion of no. 5 on page 635.

[25] Comically symbolized by Serge Haroche's title, "Breeding Schrödinger cats: a thought-experiment to explore the quantum-classical boundary," 280–305 of *Science and Ultimate Reality. Quantum Theory, Cosmology and Complexity*, edited by John Barrow, Paul Davies and Charles Harper Jr., Cambridge University Press, 2004. The volume contains a tragi-comic 6th part on "Emergence, Life and Other Topics."

[26] *Insight*, 595: I quote the final paragraph of the section on "Levels and Sequences of Expression."

[27] *Ibid*. His brilliant strategy of shake-off is the strategy of the three objectifications that concludes *Method in Theology*, chapter ten, section 5. Might you run this Essay through the Assembly Exercise of Duffy?

[28] I use the word *stalking* in a mesh of peculiar senses. But focus here on the problem of cherishing the stalk of a plant, such as the one-week-old sunflower; the cherishing is directed to its eventual full blossoming. It is worth considering my peculiar language, like *stalking* and, say, *W-enzyme*, *Sonflower*, in terms of the demands of Lonergan's *The Sketch* (*Insight*, 602). Recall note 2 of Essay N, p. 98. Let me quote the sentence referred to there, the end of "Thirdly" on page *Insight*, 602. "They are pure formulations if they proceed from an interpreter that grasps the universal viewpoint and if they are addressed to an audience that similarly grasps the universal viewpoint." I pick a pure formulation, with Lonergan's comment, out of "Preliminary note 5: The Manner of Union," pp. 231–41, of *CWL* 8, *The Incarnate Word*. "In God hypostasis and nature are distinguished only notionally, while in creatures they are really distinct, by a real minor, inadequate distinction. But these are later discoveries" (235). My language points genetically towards later discoveries of the standard model. That standard model, however, is to include the chasm-breaking (see note 24 above) which loosens the shackles of "explanation does not give man a home." *Insight*, 570, line 19.

R ~ Understanding Oneself

We find ourselves here half way between N and V.[1]

What a wonderful start—at least I think so!—to interpreting this page and a half of *Method in Theology* that points to "a revolution"[2] in outlook.

We have, in this now half-weigh or one-tenth-weigh reading of yourself, your invitation to "making history,"[3] effective only if you pause sometime in 2020, to existentially refuse to "fit into the assumptions and convictions of those that have dodged the issue of radical conversion."[4] What is that radical conversion? It is the conversion to roll with, crave in, "with joy and zeal,"[5] the wit and With of finitude. "What on earth is to be done?"[6] about your slim reading of that last sentence? **Wit** and **With** point to the two books that Lonergan faced into in the late 1940s,[7] but

---

[1] N contains the previous essay, *LO and Behold 10*; V contains the essay *LO and Behold 11*. I would suggest that—a later venture—you think of the sequence of essays O, P, Q, R, S, T, U, as being between those two final essays of the *LO and Behold* series.

[2] *Method in Theology*, 161[153].

[3] *Ibid.*, 162[154].

[4] *Ibid.*, 162[153].

[5] *Insight*, 722: the concluding words. Notice how the reading of those words are lifted by the astonishing meaning of "with": indeed the reading of the entire book. But we are here on the edge of the problem of the cunning poise of the author: see *Insight*, 754.

[6] From the conclusion of a ten-page letter written by Lonergan to his Jesuit Superior in January 1935. The full text is available in Pierrot Lambert and Philip McShane, *Bernard Lonergan: His Life and Leading Ideas*, 144–54. The letter was not well-received. Think of the problem we are dealing with here. It is the problem of a deeply faulty "*Vorverständnis*" (*Method in Theology* 162[153]. Shift Lonergan's comment on the effect of the classics to the effect of twentieth-century theological and philosophical education on the reading of Lonergan's *Opera*. I return to this topic in the final essay here, Z.

[7] Lonergan wrote as follows to his friend Eric O'Connor in 1952, brooding over the cut-off of his climb by being shifted to Rome in 1953. "I must finish and try to arrange for the publication of the first part of my work before my departure. It would be entitled Insight, and the remainder could be named Faith, or Insight and Faith." Rome cut back his climb. The letter is reproduced in the biography named in the previous note: page 156. Titles are not italicized in it.

only in 1954 did he sniff the core of **With**.[8] Only in 1965 did he sniff the effective cycling of that core that he so neatly anticipated in 1934.[9]

"A classic is a writing that is never fully understood."[10] Is *Insight* a classic? Please, skip **with** me the question: forget now about classics. Think—slimly, yes, but think, tinker—science. Not just a shift of science such as Maxwell's or Mendeleev's but the invention of integral genetically self-luminous human science, luminous in and articulate about its absolutely supernatural context of friendships.[11] "Did not our hearts burn within us, when he spoke on the way and opened to us the scriptures?"[12] I write reverently and spookily[13] about Lonergan with Jesus,[14] **in** the Spirit, writing *Insight*, turning Wright.[15]

Are you now rolling a little better with that strange and strangely-printed sentence?

---

[8] On the core of **With** see note 21 of Essay Q, p. 124.

[9] I refer regularly to the text, *Essay in Fundamental Sociology*, and the particular starling anticipation. Why not peruse it again in this context? To his own question 'What is progress?' Lonergan replies: "It is a matter of intellect. Intellect is understanding of sensible data. It is the guiding form, statistically effective, of human action transforming the sensible data of life. Finally, it is the fresh intellectual synthesis understanding the new situation created by the old intellectual form and providing a statistically effective form in the next cycle of human action that will bring forth in reality the incompleteness of the later act of intellect by setting new problems" (*Lonergan's Early Economic Research*, 20.)

[10] *Method in Theology*, 161[153].

[11] Recall Essay C, "Interpreting *CWL* 12, *The Triune God: Systematics*, section 6."

[12] *Ibid.*, 162[153].

[13] Lonergan, *A Third Collection*, begins his reflection in the third section on "The Supernatural" by talking of the word "spooky." In this little essay I am pointing both to it's fuller minding in a later theology and to its broader incarnation in "the flow of psychic events" (*Insight*, 556, line 2) of the global culture of the positive Anthropocene.

[14] In his *Christ and History* (Novalis, 2005) Fred Crowe raises the issue of the causality of Christ (157, 151–2). I give pointers to facing that issue in various parts of *The Allure of the Compelling Genius of History* —see, e.g. 170, note 56; 244, note 36; 248, note 44. An integral account requires meshing the pointers regarding primary and secondary relations of *Insight*'s sixteenth chapter with the full sweep of a decent explanatory account of the Divine Missions. We are back with **With**, and InWithTo, the problem of Essay C. Add the context of Essay Q, note 20, p. 124.

[15] Recall note 24 (p. 105) of Essay N, and the reference there to the three *Disputing Quests* essays titled 4, 5, and 8 "Turn Wright."

Is there stirring in your W-enzyme some creepy, spooky, sense of what it might be **to roll with, crave in, "with joy and zeal,"**[16] **the wit and With of finitude?** So that *W* of your W-enzyme has a shocking and Intimate Intersubjective new meaning weaved into its molecular loneliness?

> Vertical finality is obscure. When it is realized in full, it can be known. When it is in process, what has been attained can be known, but what has not, remains obscure. When the process has not begun, obscurity prevails and questions abound. Is it somehow intimated? Is the intimation fleeting? Does it touch our deepest aspirations? Might it awaken such striving and groaning as would announce a new and higher birth?[17]

Lonergan, I and Jesus, **Graciously**, are staring you, Supermolecule, **in** the race. I stared you, on a lower level, in the race and face in *The Future. Core Precepts in Supermolecular Method and Nanochemistry*, but wrote of the incompleteness in the second last note, note 50 on page 111. Should I not end here, abruptly, with that stare, that stair? Indeed, it is a stair, a stare, which I intend to repeat.

> My stare at you is incomplete, and the final note will put that incompleteness in context. But here I think of the short-term context, the context of my brief introduction (above, p. 28) of Aristotle and Drucker as pointing to the stairs inadequately, (R, I, H and D_{oc} S C) and my pointing inadequately there to the bridge between them (D_i, H): a context for the *Duffy Exercise* that is to dance round the third chapter of this book. The short-term fuller context to my "Openers of the positive Anthropocene" in the book is your picking up on my nudgings given in the repeated mention of problems associated with the words *intersubjectivity* (xiv, xvi, 8, 9, 34–5, 40, 54–5, 80, 92, 96, 103) and *spooky* (3, 8, 13, 17, 66, 116) and the 6 repetitions (xiv, 8, 34, 54, 80, 103) of Lonergan's 1954 challenge regarding the future of theology. You find now, perhaps, that you did not climb in each occurrence to a fresh meaning of the word or the challenge? Such a climbing in reading belongs to the positive Anthropocene. But we need to climb towards that climbing: try climbing over the stile named by my repetitions, my petitions, Lonergan's petition. I return to your aid in "On the Stile of a Crucial Experiment," *Divyadaan: Journal of Philosophy and*

---

[16] *Insight*, 722: the concluding words. Notice how the reading of those words is lifted by the astonishing meaning of "with," indeed the reading of the entire book. But we are here on the edge of the problem of the cunning poise of the author: see *Insight*, 754.

[17] Lonergan, *A Third Collection*, the third last paragraph of section 3, "The Supernatural."

Education, vol. 31 (2020). That is to be followed by the aide-mémoire, *The Future as Life Stile: From Mild Mess to Wild Bliss.*

S ~ Correct Enclosing

Might we here verge on "the aide-mémoire, *The Future as Life Stile: From Mild Mess to Wild Bliss*"?[1] For me it is the radiant memory of starting out on Easter Monday, April 1st {!}, of 2002, with *Cantower 1*. The venture had been inspired by Ezra Pound, to climb to Lonergan's meaning through a monthly effort for 117 months, the number of Cantos Pound wrote. Might I inspire you to such a correct enclosing? I quote now the beginning of the Fifth *Cantower*, titled "Metaphysics THEN."[2] I started it by quoting one of two final poems of Samuel Beckett:

> go where never before
> no sooner there than there always
> no matter where never before
> no sooner there than there always[3]

I had more written here for this essay but cut it off now to make a fresh beginning for both of us, but different beginnings, different freshenings. The cause of the cut-off and the freshening of my challenge to you is the leap that I describe in the Epilogue to the luminous discovery of "all that is lacking."[4] That leap of my epilogue-writing remains vibrantly open and searching, but naming it

---

[1] The conclusion to the previous essay.

[2] *Cantower 5* was added to the series in August 2002.

[3] It is useful to add in here the original *Cantower 5* footnote: "These four lines and the five lines that end this note are previously unknown lines from Samuel Beckett, recently printed in *The Irish Times*. My source for them is Dr. Conn O'Donovan. Both short pieces were sent a few months before Beckett's death in 1989, the first two to his biographer, James Nelson, the second to his publisher, John Calder. How does one contextualize the concrete quest for luminously dark luminosity that is Metaphysics Then? Obviously, *Lack in the Beingstalk* is an immediate context that I would wish you to share: but that is asking too much. At least take the Endtakes of Shakespeare (end, chapter 2) and Joyce (end chapter 3) and Donne (the Epilogue) into your Thentake. Obviously, the problem of the nature and future of metaphysics cannot be solved in a single Cantower. Further clues emerge in *Cantower VII*, section 3, and in *Cantower IX*, section 6. The problem of hermeneutics as metaphysics will haunt the 84 *Cantowers* XXII–CV. And indeed might one not read that same problem haunting the last lines of Beckett: "go end there / where never till then / till as much as to say / no matter where / no matter when"

[4] *Insight*, 559.

for you is only just that. Unless? Unless my nudgings have worked you into and beyond J-wrapping my text, firmly leaving Jay-walking behind,[5] except for playing the necessary games to "get the union card"[6] of degrees and even tenure in some department that is lost in present conventions. If you are studying Lonergan in a place like Marquette or Boston College or Regis in Toronto, it might not be good to express enthusiasm for my goings-on, or even to let this little book be seen in your hand. In most Lonergan groups "what is lacking is the cultural milieu habituated to the use of abstract concepts and trained in the techniques that safeguard their employment."[7]

I am now bringing you into the ballpark of interpreting this little book, but I am, not at a loss, but poised in puzzling over what I might add. My puzzling about what to write included a contextualized pause over Lonergan's three-page essay, "Openness and Religious Experience."[8] It is a powerful and dense communication, beginning with the quiet comment, "I can do no more than set down certain headings which, perhaps, will be found suggestive." He might well have written the same at the beginning of the two-and-a-half pages of this section 6 of *Method in Theology*, chapter 7, "Judging the Correctness of One's Interpretation," that we pause over here. My pause is, as I say, contextualized, and indeed now shockingly contextualized, by overarching insights that "hit the bull's eye."[9] McShane hits that bull's eye so that he can "say just what was going forward"[10] in these two millennia of Christian theology in a manner that weaves into a fresh reading of the final section of Lonergan's little essay, where Lonergan weaves

---

[5] I repeat note 11 of Essay J: *Jaywalk* is a compound word derived from the word *jay*, an inexperienced person, and also curse word that originated in the early 1900s, and *walk*.

[6] I am recalling Lonergan's letter to me in 1968 regarding my Oxford work.

[7] *Insight*, 559, lines 18–20.

[8] *CWL* 4, *Collection*, 185–87.

[9] *Method in Theology*, 162[154].

[10] Ibid., 164[155]. I would note, helpfully I hope, that the leap to envisage a structured effective future to theology lifts the entire book, *The Allure of the Compelling Genius of History* to a new level of meaning. Might you sense that lift in you possible lifting of the meaning of the closing words of its Epilogue, titled "The Birth of Christianity," recalling a work of Dominic Crosson. "Alas, many, in town and gown, are caught in twirling endlessly and ineffectively around initial meanings of the mysteries named *life* and *resurrection*. The slim salvific answer to the question of adequate meaning demands that we go beyond such twirlings to the structured vortex of Cosmopolis and its Tower surrealism. We are thus, in a fulsome subtle sense, at the birth of Christianity."

three aspects of openness together into a fundamental pointing regarding "man's making of man."[11]

There is the fundamental inner self, the W-enzyme, "the self as ground of all higher aspirations."[12] There is the highest openness, the gift of personally relating, perhaps seeding Lonergan's 1954 view of lifting theology up up up.[13] Then there is that middle ground and grinding of reaching to hit the bull's eye. Might you read the second paragraph of section 6 freshly now, regarding McShane's venture, in order to sense what it takes "to reconstruct the context of his thought"[14] of the beginning of theology as an engineering science that is radiantly intimate? We are into the challenge of a heuristic precision in "Gauging What's Real,"[15] and I recall that work to have you pause effectively over the concluding words—but now replace in it *science* by *physics*—of Lonergan's fifteenth chapter of *Insight*. "Modern science has made it possible to distinguish very sharply between preliminary description and scientific explanation."[16]

I have arrived at a fertile startling view of the sharp "enclosure" involved, leads to which enclosure certainly haunt all my alphabet soup, but particularly the essay O, titled "Understanding the Object." "It is the emergence of that enclosure that enables one to recognize the task as completed and to pronounce one's interpretation as probable, highly probable, in some respects, perhaps, certain."[17] Might you be enabled, by my rambles, to recognize effectively that exclusive enclosure "at a rather critical moment in the historical process,"[18] air-pressured and heir-pressured by the wake-up call of Gaia? Might my broodings of 18 years ago in *Cantower 5*, "Metaphysics, THEN," help?

---

[11] "Openness and Religious Experience," 187.

[12] *Ibid*.

[13] Should I not write rather "in in in"? The problem is the genesis of characters that are integral incarnate solutions to the problem of the chasm. See note 9 of Essay L, p. 90.

[14] *Method in Theology*, 163[154].

[15] The title of a recent book on fundamental physics: Richard Healey, *Gauging What's Real: The Conceptual Foundations of Contemporary Gauge Theories*, Oxford University Press, 207.

[16] *Insight*, 511. The changing of the word *science* to *physics* is not a correction to Lonergan's conclusion. He had no doubts about the leading role of this most elementary science, nor about the shambles that passes for the more complex higher zones of "The Field" (*CWL* 18, *Phenomenology and Logic*, 199, 306).

[17] *Method in Theology*, 165[156].

[18] *CWL* 18, *Phenomenology and Logic*, 300, line 11.

Interpretation from A to Z

I am back at the challenge of intimating the leap mentioned at note 4. But I resist any inclination towards summary. My broodings of *Cantower 5*, at the age of 70, obviously do not help, or do they? They are the searching of a younger minder. The first section is bold-face titled, "**I will build my Love a Bower**" but the *Cantower* is moving to turn the B into a T. The next essay here, Essay T, is titled "A Clarification": think then—LOL—of the title of Essay B: "{Assembling (Interpretations)³}⁴" as somehow made to suit you to a .... to a T. LOL again, and consider the meaning of *made*: the making is in your pause, your patience, your normative adult growth. Yes, over generations the content of that growth improves: Newton would make little sense of Feynman. But climbing remains a norm for the authentic human, especially for the human inclined towards the building of the Bower, the Tower. It is the task of all religions that I sketched out in my five articles of *Divyadaan* 2019.

After the title "**I will build my Love a Bower**" in my *Cantower* 5 comes a quotation from an early Canto of Ezra Pound:

> upon the gilded tower in Ecbatan
> Lay the God's bride for ever, waiting the golden rain.[19]

"The place of gathering"[20] of the Tower that I have in minding is the community of "Arriving in Cosmopolis"[21] of the 10th millennium, waiting, in the enclosure of a shared open vision, for the golden rain of the *Eschaton*: in wild bliss, yes, in the creative recollection of the mild mess of the millennia that were the first stumbling, and sometimes shockingly poor, reach for the historical meaning of God, G^i_{jk}.[22] The waiting then is to be a creative waiting of The Interior Lighthouse. But the waiting now can also be in that integral aspiring interiority of the W-enzyme. Such a waiting in you could bring the "Arriving in Cosmopolis" a millennium or eight closer. See, then, seize now, at best in Dionysian madness,[23] the image of the enclosing, spiraling, Tower.

---

[19] Ezra Pound, *The Cantos of Ezra Pound*, New Directions, N.Y., 1970, 16.

[20] Ecbatana was an ancient city of western Iran. The name means, literally, "the place of gathering."

[21] The keynote Address at the First Latin American Lonergan Workshop, Puebla, Mexico, June, 2011, available in both English and Spanish at: http://www.philipmcshane.org/website-articles.

[22] See Essay K, note 19, p. 87, and Essay Q, note 20, p. 124.

[23] Recall note 3 of the Preface, p. i. The problem of this book is that it is an invitation to read the first two lines of the spread of words on *Method in Theology* 48[47] from a Dionysian poise, a poise reaching for a solution to the problem of the chasm that Lonergan raised in the late 1950s (See note 9 of Essay L, p. 90). Recall that the spread of

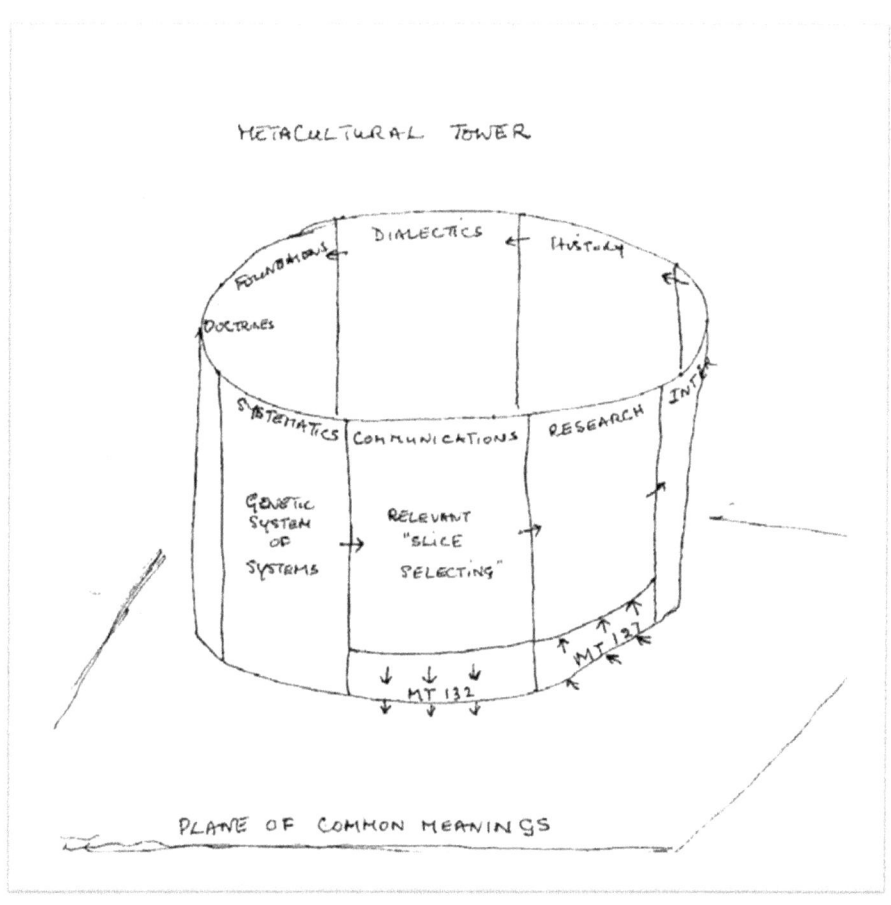

words in *Method in Theology* has a source in the lectures on education. Think of the good of order as Apollonian, something we cling to in our Axial weakness. Then pause again over Lonergan's remark, repeated here once more. "Man as insisting on the good of order is Apollonian; but as ready to tear it all down he is Dionysian" (*CWL* 10, *Topics in Education*, 40). Our problem is to tear our way forward creatively.

T ~ A Clarification

What a marvelous title to this seventh section of Lonergan's chapter on "Interpretation." Lonergan goes old-style here,[1] pulling on Collingwood, Schleiermacher, Aquinas, in the hope that he "may add clarity to what I have been saying."[2] But he is only pulling along the reader through what I might disrespectfully call *the tinkerings* of those three, to the real problem, which he comes at another and sounder way in *Insight*, with his tinkering around varieties of expression. The real problem bubbles out at the end of the first paragraph, the problem of a grip on "a single development." All three of the hot shots—and also you now—are conscious[3] of the broad reach into and of history and even to varying degrees articulate about them. Still

> **the process from consciousness to knowledge, if more than general and vague, is arduous and time-consuming; it leads to the impasse of scrutinizing the self-scrutinizing self and into the oddity of the author who writes about himself writing; such authors are exceptional.**[4]

I have spread out and bold-faced these words of Lonergan because their clarification is the core of this entire project from A to Z. We need to pause over them in our weaving round Lonergan's little clarification and my larger one. The millennium's challenge is the passage from exceptional to normal.

Scrutinizing the self-scrutinizing self? I am thinking now, I am inviting now, a scrutinizing of the awareness of the self-scrutinizing self. The issue of awareness is a fundamental topic regarding and guarding finitude. It is the issue of the presence in finitude that is in us, seed, stalk or flower. The seeding invites us to

---

[1] The style of *Insight* leans towards foundational talk. The style of *Method in Theology* is referential, even reverential. Might I suggest an effort to communicate in a non-frightening commonsense mode? Of course, the serious reading will notice the humor haunting the frightening and embarrassing passages.

[2] *Method in Theology* 165[156]

[3] "Authors are always conscious of their intentional operations ..." (*Ibid.*, 166[157]).

[4] *Ibid.*, 167[158].

stalk Jesus.[5] We are thus in the Field of Cherishing, Cauling, Craving.[6] Is this last ten-word statement a "Clarification"? By no means: or rather yes, by the means of the slow climb of the Interior Lighthouse. You might smile to think that, yes, then your W-enzyme is to be adult-full and you will J-read *Insight* 537 in a strange vortex context with a cherishing of "Space and time … [as] determinations within Being"[7] where Being is now Capitalized, and the J-reading of "so it comes about"[8] is radiant with *The Allure of the Compelling Genius of History*.[9]

Jesus became human, a doubling of awareness giving a divine awareness presence in the complex of causes of finitude. So it comes about that the causes of my awareness mesh His Awareness with mine.[10] It is an awareness that "belongs to" the already out there now, "that being indoors each one dwells"[11] and "kingfishers catch fire."[12] My Merged awareness, then becomes a stalking reality, stalked by Jesus in Grace's present Craving, so that the bent in me preys on Jesus, prays in Grace. "Grace, Grace, Grace: attune me to the Allure of the Scent of a Nomen."[13] Slowly, slowly, slowly, I join a growing "statistically effective"[14] group of "Characters of Craving"[15] for Christing's pilgrim Way.

---

[5] There is a complex of odd metaphors lurking here. Think of the stalk of a week-old sunflower. Stalking it properly would be to cater to its need to grow into a smiling yellow-brown flower. We are in the stalk of history, the stalk of the "The Seamless Symphonic Christ" (*The Road to Religious Reality*, 19). Stalking that history in this, its early stages, would be to move it effectively towards the Eschaton. Thus we find the need in humanity to stalk Jesus.

[6] See Essay C, pp. 15–18.

[7] *Insight*, 537.

[8] *Ibid*.

[9] There is the climb of the 19th chapter of that book, "The Well of Loneliness," that echoes chapter 19 of *Insight*, but now extended legitimately by revelation's radiance (See note 21 of Essay Q, p. 124.)

[10] First, you need to pull in the context of Essay R's note 14, p. 128. The context of Lonergan's expression is that of his comment in 1954 to Crowe (101–2, above). The hopes of your causalities and mine are in that genetic mesh, a mesh of the "natural resultance" (*CWL* 2, "*Verbum: Word and Idea in Aquinas*," 144–8) that *Insight* quietly introduces as a finality meshed with the empirical residue (*Insight*, 470–76).

[11] Sixth line of Gerald Manley Hopkins' *As Kingfishers Catch Fire*. The sonnet ends Essay Z, p. 173.

[12] The first words of the sonnet quoted at the previous footnote.

[13] *The Allure of the Compelling Genius of History*, 109–200, 223.

[14] *Essay in Fundamental Sociology*, 20.

[15] See *Divyadaan* vol. 30, no. 1 (2019), 121–25. The end of my article on "Finding an Economist."

Slowly? ". . . years in which one's living is more or less constantly absorbed in the effort to understand, in which one's understanding gradually works round and up a spiral of viewpoints with each complementing its predecessor and only the last embracing the whole field to be mastered."[16]

"A few contrasts may add clarity to what I have been saying."[17] Indeed. But my few contrasts are not with the hot shots like Collingwood but great hot shots of mysticism like Meister Eckhart or Teresa of Avila.[18] Nor can I enlarge beyond footnote pointers, on the kindly contrast here. "Our concern is with interpretation as a functional specialty,"[19] and while mysticism can boost the intensity of the articulation of awareness, engineering progress requires an explanation of awareness, of spookiness, of "the heightened tension that results from a supernatural solution"[20] to finitude's blossoming.

The beginning of the final paragraph in section 8 shows that Lonergan has been thinking of the previous section here. "So much for judging the correctness of interpretation."[21] My concern, in my clarification that only points densely and dimly to the future, is with the correctness of your judgment of value in 2020 and beyond. It helps, perhaps, for me to talk here of the chef rather than the interpreter, thus placing you in the dense dim clarification of Thomas regarding choice. I am identifying here a massive change in menu, a change from fast foul food to *Haute Cuisine*. You consent and choose at present, alas, to the dictates of a conventional shabby menu, whatever your religious poise.[22] Have I got you as far as consenting leisurely to the good idea of a global shift in cooking culture? I cannot resist quoting one of my favorite paragraphs of those "sixty three articles in a row"[23] where Thomas is at a high point in his "scrutinizing the self-scrutinizing self."[24] Here you have it:

---

[16] *Insight*, 210.

[17] The beginning of section 7: *Method in Theology*, 165[156].

[18] See *Æcornomics 16*: "Locating Teresa of Avila," http://www.philipmcshane.org/ecornomics.

[19] The first sentence of the chapter on "Interpretation" in *Method in Theology*.

[20] *Insight*, 749, line 8, with the tense adjusted.

[21] *Method in Theology*, 167[158].

[22] The full context is the topic of my five articles in *Divyadaan: Journal of Education and Philosophy*, vol. 30, no. 1 (2019), where the focus is on Whitson's *Coming Convergence of World Religions*.

[23] *CWL* 1, *Grace and Freedom: Operative Grace in the Thought of St. Thomas Aquinas*, 94.

[24] *Method in Theology*, 167[158].

Choice adds to consent the notion of a special relationship to that which is preferred to something else, and accordingly a choice still remains open after consent. For it may well happen that deliberation discloses several means, and since each of these meets approval, consent is given to each; later, preference is given to one and it is chosen. But if one alone meets with approval, then consent and choice coincide in point of fact, though they remain distinct meanings, for we think of consent as approval, and of choice as a preference.[25]

This paragraph and its context of sixty three articles in a row, is obviously part of my suggested clarification. But that clarification is a thing of the future. The suggested self-scrutiny of Thomas is about the same length as this effort of mine going from A to S in trying to fit you to a T. Do my alphabet steps so far tilt your W-enzymes toward some little Wild Consent?[26]

---

[25] *Summa theologiae, prima secundae*, question 15, article 3: answer to the third objection. Ingesting this is a subtle exercise in scrutinizing the self-scrutinizing self. I should draw attention to a large problem that waits global self-attention: the ingesting of the processes of deliberation that would lift us up to self-luminosity regarding present analogies to Archimedes inventing the water-lifting screw. We must screw up courage to properly screw up the muddy waters of present culture and its climate mess: what effective **situational** aggregates of deliberations must we **possess** (see *Insight*, 766, line 29ff) to meet today's and tomorrow's issues? See Essay O, note 22, p. 110, and Essay P, note 12, p. 115. The problem was first mentioned in note 15 of Essay A, p. 5.

[26] **This 8th boldfaced note of eleven (pp. 8, 62, 70, 74, 87, 92, 118, 140, 141, 150, 169) continues with the axial problem of possession raised in the 7th note. The possession that possesses us, normatively, is the non-objective God, reached luminously only if we climb, upward-curved in our** *Interior Lighthouse*, **towards something quite foreign to Avila's** *Interior Castle*. **The vibrant warmth of that Castle has to be replaced by the fresh heiring of a kataphatic care that is a "radiant sharing of Jesus' romping galactic molecules" (end of Essay V, at page 149). We arrive again at the discomforting practicality of this month's upward curving, a stranger to last month's self. What of the romping galactic molecules? What of "the Concrete Intelligibility of Space and Time" (title of the last section of** *Insight*'s **5th chapter) that is divinely radiant? "The concrete intelligibility of Space is that it grounds the possibility of those simultaneous multiplicities named situations. The concrete intelligibility of Time is that it grounds the possibility of successive realizations in accord with probability. In other words, concrete extensions and concrete durations are the field or matter or potency in which emergent probability is the immanent form or intelligibility" (** *Insight*'s **chapter 5's ending: recall the beginning of that paragraph: "The answer is easily reached," only by the bitten J-wrapped climber).**

U ~ Stating the Meaning of the Text

I am turning, in this letter U to you, twisting I might say, to the end, to the end that is the terminal value,[1] towards us living, my writing 'ago' and your reading now, in the end line of that spread of words in *Method*. I am pushing you, Supermolecule, to read along both here and also in that eighth section of this chapter seven of *Method in Theology*, with a straining Wildness of your W-enzyme. *Wildness* is a word I should have used in my talk of the W-enzyme in the beginning of *The Future*, but I had not thought to use it. I am older and wiser and wilder now. But why not begin there in U here, trying to doubleyou strangely, Dionysianly? We need now to savor the flavor of the first chapter of *The Future*.

> It is best to start with the same quotation from Katsuhiko Ariga that I gave in the short Prologue: "Living things—including ourselves—can be regarded as incredibly complex biological supramolecular systems."[2] As mentioned in the Prologue in note 5, the text is available online, and you could well take a wander any time through its first short introductory chapter, finding immediately various diagrams of large molecules. But you need not go there for the present or indeed ever. What I wish you to do here is to attend to the key diagram that I give you on the next page, a diagram of you, Supermolecule.

---

[1] See pages 9–16 regarding the Spread of Words on *Method in Theology* 48[47], where the focus is on the Dionysian bent of the third line, the bent of this odd essay of mine. **And here I add my 9th boldfaced note. The Mibox diagram on the next page helps your Mibite focus on substructures of the Interior Lighthouse, a molecular withinness that craves for a Dionysian up-curving towards light and life. The boldfacing belongs to this note's placement in the series of eleven notes (pp. 8, 62, 70, 74, 87, 92, 118, 140, 141, 150, 169) that assemble the doctrine of your normative craving.** That doctrine's normativity battles against the axial warps of the superego's molecular patterns that wishes upon you a road of convention. The battle is to be won in, within, word by word skirmishes—have you skirmished already with and within the word *word*?—such as I write of in Essay J: the challenge of J-wrapping that is a piece of the Tower-builder's Jesus-wrapping.

[2] Ariga, Katsuhiko and Toyoki Kunitake, *Supramolecular Chemistry—Fundamentals and Applications*. Ebook. Heidelberg, Germany: Springer-Verlag, 2006, 175.

INTERPRETATION FROM A TO Z

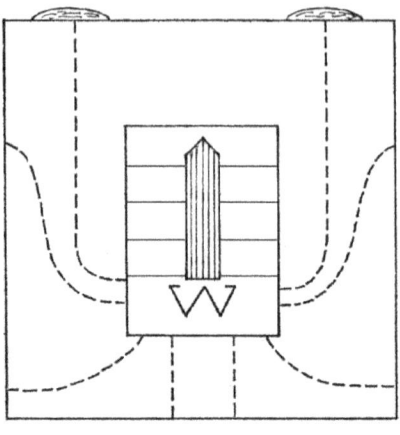

Mibox

The tricky thing in receiving my diagram is to share my superpower: remember my answer, in the Preface to *The Future: Core Precepts in Supramolecular Method and Nanonchemistry* (ii), to 44-month-old Matthew? My superpower is walking slowly. My superpower is definitely best illustrated by my personal walking slowly in and round and about versions[3] of that diagram for half a century, and still in a state of W. W? Walking in and into

---

[3] The first version appeared in *Towards Self-Meaning*, Garrett Barden and Philip McShane, (Gill and Macmillan, 1969), p. 44, reproduced on page 41 of *Wealth of Self and Wealth of Nations. Self-Axis of the Great Ascent* (1973) (available at: (http://www.philipmcshane.org/published-books). It is recommended for our venture. My present version of the diagram is quite novel, bringing into one diagram the diagrams of knowing and doing of pages 15 and 48 there. (Equivalent diagrams are on pages 322–23 of *Phenomenology and Logic*, *CWL* 18.) I comment further on the novelty and on the reading of the diagram in note 5 of chapter 2 (p. 24) of *The Future: Core Precepts in Supramolecular Method and Nanonchemistry*, but for the present see the move I made as a pedagogical device as well as a nudge towards improved empirical methods. For a start try to find yourself speaking to yourself thus: "What is this W-enzyme in me?" then move to find yourself leaving out the question-mark. Here, finally, I wish to make four points. First, my reading of versions was always in the context of a slow-growing grip on Lonergan's meaning. Secondly, my original notion of leaving reference to Lonergan out at the beginning of this book proved to be foolish. Thirdly, there are few references to any other thinkers in this book: the reason is because it is a foundational statement, *oratio recta*, even if in popular mode. Fourthly, I hope that my shot at a positive *haute vulgarization*—the normative world of the positive Anthropocene—will nudge you to grope beyond it into your own explanatory foundations.

slowly, Wondering slowly, Wanting slowly, Wising-up slowly, Willing so. You, then, too, Whatting and 'double youing' since you were younger than my grandson, all of us whatting since whatting became: might I say a guest molecule in the "host-guest chemistry"[4] of the cosmos? But is W another molecule in the supermolecule, a strange enzyme-complex?[5] That is a later question for you. Here, immediately, I am inviting you to notice and attend to what I am referring to, both in the diagram and in you. I crave your slow but chirpy-chick attention, so that we walk slowly in and into the diagram. There is a sense in which the object of the W in the diagram was a hidden molecule well before the noise OM clung to it in *The Upanishads*, and so perhaps the beginning of my 2015 book, *The Allure of the Compelling Genius of History*, would help to hold your attention on W.[6]

Note again: "Here, immediately, I am inviting you to notice and attend to what I am referring to, both in the diagram and in you," but it is, hopefully, a strange regressive Tea-Bag noticing,[7] to get you reading freshly this section 8 of Lonergan's chapter. Might you now, for instance, have a shot at "stating the meaning of the text" you have read so far, from A to U, to you? It would not be my 88-year-old meaning, but a gleaning of clues. And the central clue is that I am trying, in all sorts of odd ways, to shake your W-enzyme out of some shade of the negative Anthropocene into the primitive "joy and zeal"[8] of the positive Anthropocene. Read now the first two words of section 8 freshly: "Our concern."

I have been paging at you—"Paging Tom, Dick, and Mary"!—nudges towards the concern that is to emerge, the characters that are to emerge, in that post-Axial globe.[9] That is a going beyond stating the meaning of Lonergan's "our concern" that starts section 8. Yet, oddly—but think of and in Q—it is in continuity with Lonergan's concern in this entire seventh chapter of *Method in Theology*. The entire book is a battered venture into what I call C9: a shot at stirring the present common sense of theologians to stretch beyond the descriptiveness which is, in the book, the dominant ethos, an ethos controlled by Lonergan, with a control beyond his readers. I recall helpfully the conclusion (269) of Lonergan's two chapters in *Insight* on commonsense. "May we note, before concluding that,

---

[4] Recall the title of chapter 2: "Solution host-guest chemistry."
[5] Greek: *en-*, in + *zyme*, leaven: a catalyst, initiating, boosting, or speeding reactions.
[6] *The Future: Core Precepts in Supramolecular Method and Nanochemistry*, 1–2.
[7] See Essay L, pp. 89ff.
[8] The last words of *Insight* 722.
[9] *Divyadaan: Journal of Education and Philosophy*, vol. 30, no. 1 (2019), 121–5, "Developing Characters of Craving."

while common sense relates things to us, our account of common sense relates it to its neural base and relates aggregates and successions of instances of common sense to one another." The mention of neural base and aggregates: does it not throw us back to the problem and the technique of ";" chatted about in section J? Are you, LOL, not perhaps jaywalking here, rather than J-walking?[10] Did you previously not jaywalk through section 8? Well, yes: Lonergan did not expect much more. That was the problem hovering over his puzzles with me in 1966. Think now of his statement at the end of his listing of achievements of *Insight*, where he talks of you, Universal Viewpoint, going on to a developed account of the early chapters of *Method in Theology*. Does not the challenge reach sneakily to the end of the book: to "fulfilling the redemptive and constructive roles of the Christian Church in human society."[11] But let's leave U now, but not you, you being invited to V, to be pointed to View a Viewpoint that is to carry us to researching, re-searching, that baffling section 3 of *Insight* chapter 17.

But do not pass on without doing a mix of jaywalking and J-walking through section 8. V's challenge is to take effective note of the last ten lines of the second last paragraph, beginning with your listening to "what is needed is not mere description but explanation." Are you really listening? Were you listening to the "foreign, strange, archaic things presented by"[12] Lonergan when he wrote, in chapter 4, "to speak of the dynamic state of being in love with God pertains to the stage of meaning when the world of interiority has been made the explicit grounds of the worlds of theory and interiority?"[13] Such an event "is an event of a higher order, an event of his own personal development," of Lonergan's development, but what of yours? With such a character formation in you and your community you would find a luminous savoring, w-enzyme-rich, of "the decisions it reached in its successive identity crises" but such savoring as including the reach to the decisions that are to emerge towards terminally valuing, cherishing, praying, "Thy Kingdom Come." "Do you know His Kingdom?"[14]

---

[10] I repeat from note 11 of Essay J: *Jaywalk* is a compound word derived from the word *jay*, an inexperienced person, and also a curse word that originated in the early 1900s, and *walk*.

[11] The book's concluding words.

[12] *Method in Theology* 173[163].

[13] *Ibid.*, 107[103].

[14] The beginning of the end-climb of Lonergan's 1934 Essay, *Fundamental Essay in Sociology*.

V ~ "Do you know His Kingdom?"[1]

The title with its footnote: do they not give you a sense of a fresh start, perhaps even a W-enzyme molecular resonance with the end-start of Molly Bloom, "yes I said yes I will Yes"?[2] And our hopefulness is that it is not strenuous, not heroic, not a thin-air mountain venture, but "a spadeful of earth in the moving of that mountain."[3] What is that spadeful of W, X, and Y to be? It is to be a popular venture (C_9, then) into researching the meaning of Lonergan's strange "dance of words"[4] in the three parts of *Insight*'s chapter seventeen.

Is V for Victory? Think of the way Lonergan ended that *Essay on Fundamental Sociology* in 1934, commenting on Isaiah's optimism about turning swords into ploughs. "Is this to be taken figuratively, or is it figure? It would be fair and fine, indeed, to think it no figure."[5]

So, I bring you back—or forward—to the end of my website series *LO and Behold*, wishing you to weave forward from the tenth essay, which concludes Essay N, to the final essay of that series. Does it bring to mind the problem you had with the title of Essay B? : "{Assembling (Interpretations)^3 }^{4} " There is the same meaning of "4" in both, pointing to the need to brood over the suggestion of a fourth stage of meaning that was given in *LO and Behold 4*: "The Heuristics of a Fourth Stage of Meaning."[6] That poses for you the challenge of moving through

---

[1] The beginning of the end-climb of Lonergan's 1934 Essay, *Essay in Fundamental Sociology*. A beginning of our end-climb here to a new beginning.

[2] The final words of Molly Bloom's forty one-sentence soliloquy of James Joyce's *Ulysses*.

[3] The final words (149) of Frederick Crowe's effort, *Theology of the Christian Word. A Study of History*, to which we shall be returning here.

[4] A phrase that Eric Voegelin repeatedly used in my interviewing of him, Gadamer and Lonergan at a Lonergan Conference in Toronto in the 1970s.

[5] The next page of the reference of note 1 above.

[6] "Assembling" in the title of B needs no comment. The 'cubing' of Interpretation perhaps presents a puzzle. It is an old trick that originated in the end of the first chapter of my *Redress of Poise* (http://www.philipmcshane.org/website-books) where I pointed to a sublation of St. Ignatius's view of discernment. We need, the cubing right across the vocabulary of method, right across your psyche, you W-enzyme. "Interpretation of Interpretations of Interpretations": what might that mean to you? But you do now surely notice that it involves a sublation of what Lonergan wrote of in the middle of that essay of 1934, "a statistically effective form for the next cycle of human action"?

the essays that follow in that series, on "Reaching for a Heuristics of the Eschaton," "Possessing the Future," "*Haute Vulgarization*: Negative and Positive," "Assembling *Insight*." My climbing suggestions have been an effort of positive *haute vulgarization*, an effort to have some readers face the climb needed for effectively engineering the "fair and fine" that Lonergan wrote about in concluding his powerful *Essay in Fundamental Sociology*. Might you contribute, humbly and patiently and gloriously, to the "fair and fine?"

LO and Behold 11

Assembling $\{M\ (W_3)^{\theta\Phi T}\}^4$

There are two ways of facing this exercise in Assembling, two ways that parallel a similar challenge in physics. I think of two familiar shifts in physics: that from Newton to Einstein, and that of the Standard Model without or with the Higgs field.[7]

My own preferred parallel is the latter and it would be nicely tied in here by my writing my title *Assembling $\{M\ (W_3)^{\theta\Phi T}\}^4$ (2020)* to get the parallel with the

---

[7] [Observe that this is footnote 1 in the original]. The problem of adding the Higgs field is a tricky one, as is further discussion of the field and the particle and its mass. You may get an impression from Roger Penrose's writing in 2005 (Vintage: *The Road to Reality. A Complete Guide to the Laws of the Universe*, 628). "There is also the shadowy Higgs particle—stiff unobserved at the time of writing—whose existence, in some form or other (perhaps not as a single particle), is essential to present-day particle physics, where the related Higgs field is held responsible for the mass of every particle." In note 73 (p. 33) of my *The Road the Religious Reality*, (Axial Publishing, 2012), I point to various pop-fashion ways "to get a lead on the Higgs' Boson" (*ibid*, note 73). As you move on through this little essay you will get a sense of my preference for this "jump" in the Standard Model. What of G^i_{jk}'s Bo's'n, [short for *Boatswain*], Jesus, responsible for the mass and momentum of every person? "Christ the man knew everything that pertained to his work" (*The Incarnate Word*, CWL 8, 677). How should one converse with such bright-eyed competence? It is not enough to gaze up at the statue of the Sacred Heart. Your friend Jesus is in the field, luminously and self-luminously minding the field. "The field is the universe, but my horizon defines my universe." (*Phenomenology and Logic*, CWL 18, 199). Does my horizon of piety echo with "the arrogance of omnicompetent common sense"? ("Questionnaire on Philosophy: Response," *Philosophical and Theological Papers 1965–1980*, CWL 17, 370.) Dare I suggest that you pause "over the image of me poised over the word *pius* at note 53 of the third chapter of the book [*The Future: Core Precepts in Supramolecular Method and Nanochemistry*], a chapter that touches on the issue of mature piety in terms of the poise of *pius Aeneas*." Ibid., iii.

"Do you know His Kingdom?"

Higgs field Standard Model and *Assembling* $\{M\ (W_3)^{\theta\Phi T}\}^4$ *(2019)* to signify the—or an—earlier theological or philosophical Standard Model.

The tricky disturbing word of this shocking first paragraph is *familiar*. Then there is the odd "or an" that precedes the five last words. My audience is neither familiar with the shifts in physics nor is the suggested Standard Model (2019) anything close to the low-grade model of present theological and philosophical discourse. We are back at the problem of the end of the second paragraph of the first chapter of *Method in Theology*, in the trivial but well-disguised pursuit of "academic disciplines,"[8] and Lonergan's new beginning symbolized by his beginning of the next paragraph: "clearly enough, these approaches to the problem of method do little to advance ….." There is no point in my going on regarding that mess: my aim after all, is simply presenting an exercise of the Duffy type that may be taken up in the future.

That take-up sadly involves a massive catch-up and throw-beyond. The center-piece of my (2019) heuristic image goes back to my sublating the work on Fisher and Markov[9] into a flow of world maps that, at say, various intersections of latitudes and longitudes, has a statistics of recurrence-schemes of progress and probable "situation room" components of progress.[10] The centerpiece of my

---

[8] The end words of the second paragraph of the first chapter of *Method in Theology*.

[9] See my *Randomness, Statistics and Emergence* (Gill, Macmillan and Notre Dame, 1970), p. 237. The book is not easily available—I must remedy that—so a quotation there from F.M. Fisher ("On the Analysis of History and the Interdependence of the Social Sciences," *Phil. Sc.*, 27, 1960) may flex your imagination. Think of a flat global map moving along the time axis: Fisher calls the consequent box of heuristic control a *tensor*. "The typical element of the tensor, say $Mi_{1}i_{2}i_{3} \ldots i_{n+1}$, is defined as the probability that Nature will be in state i_1 at time t_1 given that at the time $t—n$ to $t—1$ she was successively I states $i_{n+1}, i_n, \ldots i_3$ and i_2." (op. cit., 149). "Toynbee's Study of History can be regarded as an attempt at a great Markovian reduction of the historical process to a very few variables and very large subdivisions and the consequent description of the process by a multiple Markov tensor of manageable rank." (op. cit., 156). My own imaging shifts this tensor into an earth-sphere expanding out along a radial axis t—this helps to glimpse—think longitude and latitude for θ and Φ—my meaning of $^{\theta\Phi T}$. The geohistorical imaging gives a new level of control of Lonergan's "ongoing, overlapping, etc etc contexts." Think of the $^{\theta\Phi T}$ weave of pairs like Antioch and Alexandria, Luther and Lainez, Descartes and Dilthey, whatever. Useful here, from the *Questions and Answers* series, is *Question 36*: "An Appeal to Fred Lawrence and Other Elders," available at: http://www.philipmcshane.org/questions-and-answers.

[10] I introduced the heuristic reach towards Tower and town control of global situations in chapter 12, "*The Situation Room*: The Stupid view of Wolf Blitzer," of *Profit: The Stupid View of President Donald Trump* (Axial Publishing, Amazon, 2016).

(2020) shift, pointed to in the previous essay, is the cyclic conception, affirmation, and implementation[11] of a glocal lift of global intersubjectivity which includes the subjectivities of G^i_{jk},[12] where the "i" points to the dual consciousness of the Christoffer tensor, a tensor weaved molecularly into humanity's wavering potential of a unified collaboration towards oneness.

That molecular weaving becomes, for the searcher, personally and poignantly manifest in the self-upgrading necessary for reaching the statistically-effective meaning of the title to the final section of the final essay of the 2019 *Divyadaan* effort, "Developing Characters of Craving."[13] How are we all to stretch forward,

---

[11] Follow up musings on the two previous notes with some fantasy about effective "implementation." Follow up? "The meaning and implications of this statement have now to be explored" (*Insight*, 416: end lines): indeed! "Theology possesses relevance" (*Ibid.*, 766, line 29). It does not. It needs a massive Dionysian shift of the characters of communication, lusting after "fruit to be borne" (*Method in Theology* 355[327]). That lusting has to produce, in these next centuries, a full countervailing heuristic imaging of the objectives of sciences, arts and technologies in situations large and small, to bring us to progress towards the flowering of humanity. How do you stand in regard to this flowering? In the work mentioned in the previous note (see there page 85), I bring forth the question of a global Amendment to any type of constitution. Here, then, is your question: "do you view humanity as possibly maturing—in some serious way—or just messing along between good and evil, whatever you think they are?"

[12] G^i_{jk} represents a massive challenge to what I may call vegetable thinking, chatter in terms of "The God of Abraham or the God of the philosophers," God thus thought of as a substance of common sense. First, the God of section 9 of *Insight* chapter 19 is not that God, but a God towards which one "comes about" (*Insight*, 537, line 29) though the *sun*-animated analogically-self-luminous conversation of the "In" (first word of *Insight*'s first chapter), Inn, Innn, of each fresh intersubjective "spooky" (*A Third Collection*, "Mission and the Spirit, section 3) recycling of *Insight*. The vegetable reading of this masterpiece of Lonergan is a disgusting reality of his vegetating followers. One reaches the 26th place of *Insight* 19.9 and then joins Aquinas, but in a deeply new context, in the *Summa*'s Question 27. On this struggle see my "Embracing Luminously and Toweringly the Symphony of Cauling," *Seeding Global Collaboration*, edited by Patrick Brown and James Duffy (Axial Publishing, 2016), 221–240. The nudge towards the discomforting symbol comes from Lindsay and Margenau, *Foundations of Physics*, 362, where there is consideration of the Christoffel Tensor.

[13] *Divyadaan: Journal of Philosophy and Education* vol. 30, no. 1 (2019), edited by James Duffy and titled by him "Religious Faith Seeding the Positive Anthropocene," contains five essays of mine focused on weaving Whitson's *The Coming Convergence of World Religions* towards what I would now call a *sun*-shattering acceptance of *Insight* as a book of common prayer. The core challenge in the prayer is the reach for luminosity

in these next millennia, *sun*-flower-wise, beyond a religious "vegetative living"?[14] I stay here with Christian religion and its Pauline sloganizing. "What is immediate in us is that de facto we are temples of the Spirit, members of Christ, and adoptive children of the Father, but in a vegetative way. That can move into our conscious living, into our spontaneous living, into our deliberate living."[15] It can! It can edge us seedingly and seethingly, in this century, to effective fantasy of the supermolecular Eschaton, with, yes, memories of pets and plants,[16] but no such reality, nor food nor drink in any normal sense, but supra-living in the radiant sharing of Jesus' romping galactic molecules.[17] "Is this to be taken literally or is it figure? It would be fair and fine to think it no figure."[18]

> Sun, flowers, Son-flowered,
> Speak to us of growth.
> Seed cauled, cribbed,
> Kabod yet confined,
> Crossed with dark earth, Light-refined,

---

regarding The Beyond as intimate friendship, this in the bright dialogue of affirmation sheltered from muddiness by bowing to negation and eminence.

[14] *Philosophical and Theological Papers 1958–1964*, "The Mediation of Christ in Prayer," *CWL* 6, *Philosophical and Theological papers 1958–1964*, 179, line 10.

[15] *Ibid.*, lines 25–29.

[16] This is obviously a complex heuristic issue, pivoting on Thomas's meaning of "*possibilia esse et non-esse*" (*Summa*, Ia, q.2, a. 3, *Tertia Via*). See my popular presentation (1958) of that Via and the references to Thomas given in the notes all reproduced in *Cantower 19*. Further there is my *The Everlasting Joy of Being Human* (Axial Publishing, 2013), where, in chapter 4, (36–43), I reflect on Thomas's eschatology. See especially notes 10 and 11 there. The conclusion of note 11 (*Summa Contra Gentiles*, IV, ch. 97) is echoed in my text above. "But the other animals, the plants, and the mixed bodies, those entirely corruptible both wholly and in part, will not remain at all in the state of incorruption." See also, the final note of the book, note 86 of page 125, where I wrote of "Son-lit everlasting Saplings in a circumincessing Field without flowers or trees or fauns or bees. Thomas was quite on the ball when he wrote…" And I leave you there, as I am reminded now of Lonergan using such a phrase "Thomas was quite on the ball," re Thomas' eschatology, in an Easter walk we had in Dublin in 1961.

[17] The end poem here, from the beginning of my *Cantower* climb (that climb began with *Cantower 2*, where the poem emerged), is strangely intersubjective, where nature is cognized cyclically as "God's silent communing with man" (*Topics in Education*, 225, *CWL* 10, line 2). Add, then, the next question in the text above. This is no fancy, but a fact of a finitude in which "God is not an object." What what what is this Complex Subjectivity, in which we are cauled, that we may call Them OM?

[18] The end of Lonergan's 1934 *Essay in Fundamental Sociology*.

INTERPRETATION FROM A TO Z

Rill open-ends a trill
Annotaste of Throat.[19]

---

[19] Here you have my 10th boldfaced note of eleven (pp. 8, 62, 70, 74, 87, 92, 118, 140, 141, 150, 169). You read, at this ending of the Essay V, of the sunflower and the Sonflower and pause and poise, "an eternal fire of optimism and energy," (*Essay in Fundamental Sociology*, 43) in the hope of freshly reading that poem again, concave curving the fire in growing growth. The poem at the end of Essay Y—might it be next month, in the mood of my *Cantowers*, and not just this next hour? Is it not to be read in a new chording and cor-ding of our "music of the spheres"? (Shakespeare's *Pericles*, V. i. 228) And now I think of V both as it stands for "five"—are we not, in these boldfaced ventures, hovering over the first five chapters of *Insight?*—the paradigm for honesty about the meaning of explanation, given in the simplest science and, thus, standing Toweringly for "Victory." Victory whether we think of Churchill waving his fingers in the 1940s little-boat stand against invasion, or of Victory in the Church of Thyatira (*Revelations* 2:18–29: verse 26), "I will give power over all the nations to everyone who wins the victory"), in the church of Thy Attire inside Thy Mibox. (See the previous note, note 9 in the series, attached to the Dionysian note 1 of Essay U, on page 141).

W ~ *Insight* Chapter 17 in a Geohistorical Engineering Context

Might the letter *W* bring to mind the challenge of forming an open and revisable series of Ws that would give us all better control of engineering the future? In the little essay, *Prehumous 2*, "Metagrams and Metaphysics," I listed a decent first six and then added the comment "A candidate for W_7 is a fundamental diagram of economics as I present it in *Economics for Everyone.*"[1] That diagram certainly deserve a place in any collection of relevant diagrams for our global future, but my candidate for the position W_7 at present would be the technically effective imaging of the progress of the sunflower from seed to smile.[2] Such an imaging is, I would say, a challenge of this century that is to reach across all disciplines, arts, engineerings. The challenge is expressed in the third section of this chapter of *Insight*, though it must now be read in the fullest meaning of *interpretation*, a ninefold care of human progress.[3] My suspicion is that the challenge will not be met in botany: its meeting is to be an instance of the real dynamics of Christian Philosophy.[4] But let us pause over the "if" of the challenge that blossomed for Lonergan, in 1965, into a challenge of engineering the future, and indeed pause over the added comment with its footnote.[5]

---

[1] *Economics for Everyone. Das Just Kapital*, 3rd edition, Amazon, 2019, end of page iv, but its derivation there is key to its effective adoption.

[2] It was with this image that I began the *Cantower* series in 2002: See *Cantower 2*, "Sunflowers Speak to Us of Growth." I was still then vague about the complex topologies of effective technologies of situations needed to "grow history." See the following note.

[3] Recall note 8, p. 3, of Essay A. The full effective care is to emerge through the characters of the ninefold collaboration facing the personal genetics of the solution to the problem of the chasm: see note 9 of Essay L, p. 90. The problem facing theology is the feebleness of its forward reach, mentioned at the beginning of Essay D, p. 19. See note 25 of Essay T, p. 140.

[4] Naming a philosophy *Christian* is a factual business regarding successful components of progress. The story of the heuristics of minding, carried forward from Aquinas and Lonergan, is an obvious instance. The previous note mentions another emergence. Might that emergence be recognized in later millennia as a dynamic in-weaving of Christian philosophy?

[5] I am in fact quoting from chapter seventeen of *The Allure of the Compelling Genius of History*. I shall talk about it as a limited context further on. Note 13 below points neatly

If interpretation is to be scientific, then it has to discover some method of conceiving and determining the habitual development of all audiences, and it has to invent some technique by which its expression escapes relativity to particular and incidental audiences.[6] By what technique, for example, might we lift Menno Simons' interpretation of the New Testament into that context and thus lift into a fresh unity present incidental audiences called *Mennonites*?[7]

Our problem, in W, X and Y, is to find the beginning of making coherently collaborative what we do now badly for "normal interpretation." In Y we shall tackle that pragmatically. But I felt it necessary to muse over the fuller context of the pointings of *Insight*'s first two sections in W and X. As I grappled with this problem of presentation it dawned on me that the added context of the book, *The Allure of the Compelling Genius of History*, would boost our efforts. Eventually I decided that, yes, the two first two sections of chapter seventeen there merited repetition here as context for a new pedagogical push in the final part, Y. You may well wish to leap straight to Y for such leads to a breakthrough, but do return to the fuller context in later readings.[8]

Chapter 17 Remembering the Future

> Jesus said til him, "I am the wey, the trowth, an the life. Nae man comes tae the Faither binna throu me. Gin ye kent me, ye wad ken my Faither an aa. Now ye hae seen him, an frae this forrit ye ken him."[9]

---

to the larger context that puts the genetics into global history, needing techniques of geohistorical imaging.

[6] *Insight*, 587, lines 31–34.

[7] "The impression one gets is of deep populist roots, a sincere Christian outlook on life, intense religious devotion, strong organization, and the readiness of an independent body to cooperate with other Christian groups." I am quoting here Lonergan's comment on Simon Kimbangu's Christian effort in "Prolegomena to the Study of the Emerging Religious Consciousness of Our Time," *A Third Collection*, 69.

My aim here is to stir or startle us to concreteness, complexity, effective science.

[8] I draw attention to the shift of note-numbers below from the numbering in the book: those numbers are reached by simply subtracting 8. I have not changed references within the notes below. I would note also that the quotations from the New Testament throughout the book, *The Allure of the Compelling Genius of History*, are taken from *The New Testament in Scots*, translated by William Lorimer (Edinburg: Southside Press, 1983). The shift to this unfamiliar English livens up your meetings with Jesus.

[9] *John* 14:6 (*Lorimer*, 188). [This is note 1 in the original text. I leave the notes as in that text.] Recall the triple wey, the (wey)^3, of the final footnote (27) of the appendix to

Insight Chapter 17 in a Geohistorical Engineering Context

Chapter seventeen of *Insight*, "Metaphysics as Dialectic," has three sections named:

1. Metaphysics, Mystery and Myth;
2. The Notion of Truth;
3. The Truth of Interpretation.

These titles seem very far away from my substitute titles of the corresponding three sections here:

1. The Wey;
2. The Trowth;
3. The Life.

And the meaning is also very far away. So how, now, am I to proceed? I recall again my conversations of the summer of 1966 with Lonergan, about the impossibility of getting *Insight* into the first chapter of a book on functional collaboration. I have written, in these last eight chapters, a version of his 1969 article on functional collaboration. The version is backed by the previous chapters' weaving of *Insight* and *Method in Theology* and so, hopefully, has an added allure. Here, however, you and I, Step Han, are facing a shockingly large gap, a gap that can certainly be attributed inoffensively to age, but perhaps more disturbingly to my past climbing.[10] Lonergan's impossible challenge is paralleled by my lesser challenge—for I am a second-rate follower of his remote genius—I can't get, e.g., all my *Cantower* and *FuSe* essays into these last four chapters.

Here I am, taking a quite different tack from the four last chapters of *Insight*, vastly complex chapters of Lonergan presupposed by my deviation from them.[11] Might we share a prayer about that taking and that tack and the giving and the given? Already you may have figured the strange addressee of my prayer, *Donum*,[12] and the seeming flaws in the direct address of that infinite Person. "Grace, Grace, Grace: attune us to the Allure of the Scent of a Nomen." Grace understands and

---

chapter four above on page 51. Does this not give a joyous dreadful sense of the recycling challenge of the book, the self, the Wey?

[10] We return to this in chapter 20, section 4, as a general future cultural problem.

[11] From the end of the previous chapter you may now perhaps suspect the challenge of presupposition, but it seems handily discomforting to name one little section from the remaining chapters of *Insight* that meshes with the required contemplative reach and achievement. You may find it an odd selection: "The Secondary Component in the Idea of Being." The struggle of my version of the Interior Castle spirals up and in the meaning of this section 7 of *Insight* chapter 19.

[12] I am recalling Thomas Aquinas' struggles in question 38 of the *Summa Theologica*.

condones, All Three together in Their singular inseparate ways, the odd pun, within puns, on an old film, *The Scent of a Woman*. Might you understand and condone and share and find an effective scent of the gap between your understanding and mine, your understanding and Grace's? But, heavens, I have now leaped into problems of chapter 19 and the systematics of the Divine Three!

"Remembering the Future" is a phrase I have used before,[13] but here I tie it to a sentence from Lonergan's introductory remarks about his chapter 17. "To meet this difficulty, it is necessary to transpose the issue from the field of abstract deduction to the field of concrete historical process."[14] The difficulty he is meeting is not mine: he had his own agenda and to its peculiarities I return later. My difficulty is to intimate the whirl forward seeded by his later discovery that whirls even his own agenda of a volume after *Insight* into a global agenda of millennia.

Insight's last line acknowledges a man and a project. "One can hope to reach the mind of Aquinas, and once that mind is reached, then it is difficult not to import his compelling genius to the problems of this later day."[15] The first line—the title—of my book acknowledges a man and a project, indeed the title came from that last line of *Insight*. *The Allure of the Compelling Genius of History Teaching Young Humans Humanity and Hope*. But now we are poised, in this new page-turning to *Metaphysics as Dialectic*, in a different hope: one can hope to reach feebly, but with a fresh dynamic, the mind of Jesus, and once that mind is reached, then it is difficult not to import his compelling genius to the problems of this later day.

But it is.

And it has been.

---

[13] It is the title of the first section of the first *Cantower*, of section 3.4 (p. 71) of my *Pastkeynes Pastmodern Economics: A Fresh Pragmatism*, and occurs in other works. Perhaps it is as well to indicate its source and openness by quoting directly note 32 (p. 18) of *The Road to Religious Reality*. "Remembering the Future' is the title of a chapter on J. M. Synge in Declan Kiberd, *Inventing Ireland: The Literature of the Modern Nation* (Cambridge: Harvard University Press, 1995). The mood, dominant in *Cantowers* 36 and 37, is resonant with Burckhardt's bent (*Method in Theology*, 250). It has 'eyes like doves' (*The Canticle of Canticles*, 4:1; 5:12), His and yours, searching, in a love that is reversed nostalgia, so as to arrive 'with a new olive branch in its beak' (*Genesis*, 8:11). There is a deep sense in which settled fact is foreign to history's pilgrimage. Might there be in our eyes, to use a phrase of Conn O'Donovan, a 'garden of even'? (His coining of the phrase relates to a discussion we had of a future billion gardens: see the conclusion to the Appendix.)

[14] *Insight*, 554.

[15] *Ibid.*, 770: the end of the Epilogue.

Insight Chapter 17 in a Geohistorical Engineering Context

Might I say that it has been mono-tonously imported, thus recalling for you the musings of chapter ten.[16] That chapter, and its follow-up in reflections on history, are providentially fresh in my mind, since they were completed yesterday, and I have been bumped into this chapter by the same providence. But the bump has bumped me out of what I might call a cluster of foolish hopes represented by my notes for this chapter. So I face it with the same mood as emerged in the struggle with the second and third specialties. I have reached a new high in my appreciation of Lonergan's point at the beginning of his Epilogue to *Insight*: "not some brief appendage to the present work, but the inception of a far larger one."[17]

The solitary Lonergan of the summer of 1953 was thinking of a larger personal effort. Here I am, quite openly, thinking of a dynastic inception. I am thinking in the same way, but so much more enlightenedly, as when I wrote my five essays on "foundational prayer,"[18] in terms of millennia, in terms of moving forward from an anaphatic poise in regarding Jesus—whether the poise be mystic or just stumblingly pious. In that movement forward the dynast is Jesus but there is somehow no normal dynasty.[19] The movement is to be a strange vortex democracy of minders minding the Mind of Jesus, a Tripersonal Mind that reaches lightsomely the least among us in the Symphony of His Embrace. Is His Embrace another Person? Is His lightsomeness a Shining of the Faither? Is His Symphony lost in some initial mythic meaning of a mystical body? These are questions of a future kataphatic interpretation of the Cosmic Word, to be generated by a listening dance and stance to the Embrace. "This muckle I hae been able tae tell ye afore I buid lae ye, but the Forspeaker, the Halie Spirit at the Faither will send i my name, will teach ye aathing an mind ye o aa at I hae said tae ye."[20] So, we begin freshly to seek that Minding, stirring old words out of stale, if sincere, conventions. "For sae the Lord hes bidden us dae:

I hae set ye for a licht til the haithen
tae cairrie salvation
til the faurest pairts of the yird.[21]

---

[16] See pages 119–23.

[17] *Insight*, 753–54.

[18] The *Prehumous* series contains these five (numbers 4–8) essays, with a common title, *Foundational Prayer*, available at: http://www.philipmcshane.org/prehumous.

[19] Very obviously, I am sliding here past problems of hierarchic structures in Christianity: such problems need cycling through global functionality.

[20] *John* 14:25, 26 (*Lorimer*, 189).

[21] *Acts of the Apostles* 13:47 (*Lorimer*, 226). The text is printed thus in *Lorimer*, implicitly acknowledging the source in *Isaiah* 49:6. See also, of course, *Isaiah* 42:6 and *Luke* 2:32.

INTERPRETATION FROM A TO Z

1. The Wey

"Our analysis forces us to recognize the paradoxical category of the 'known unknown.'"[22] So begins the first of six subsections in this first section of the 17th chapter of *Insight*. These six sections can be viewed as a dense central presentation of the deepest crisis of our time, or better perhaps, of axial times. The titles of the sections, added in Lonergan's hand to the professionally-typed version of the book, are worth listing here: *The Sense of the Unknown; The Genesis of Adequate Self-Knowledge; Mythic Consciousness; Myth and Metaphysics; Myth and Allegory; The Notion of Mystery.*

As I look at them now, I see the chapter headings of a very big book, but a book, that, in my view, would need to lift the contents of those sections into a full cyclic functional Christology.

There! I have surprised myself by saying . . . well, all I had wished to say out of my mass of messy writings and scribbles regarding this first section of chapter seventeen. Indeed, have we not been hovering round that sentence since you read the book title?

But my problem remains: I think not of a big book, but of a dynasty. Might I pun and fantasize a little? So, Step Han, I think of a Han dynasty, but lasting way, Wey, longer than the dynasty in China that bracketed the Incarnation: indeed, is it not the Wey of life everlasting? And we could well dance here around the meanings of *Han* in Chinese—relating to control—and in Vietnamese—pointing to the ocean—to give images of the new control of meaning, an ocean of survival that is to flow from the Mind-reading of Jesus: but to that Symphonic Mind-reading we move in the third section here.

Do such imagings help? I think now of the images lurking in my long essay, "Middle Kingdom: Middle Man (*T'ien-hsia: i jen*[23])"[24] and the issue of axiality raised by Toynbee and Voegelin,[25] worth brooding over now as we muse on the prevalence of mythic consciousness and sensate cultures as they cut us off globally from the Wey, monsters of our late axial time.

---

[22] *Insight*, 555.

[23] A footnote here adds images by quoting Eric Voegelin, *The Ecumenic Age*, "Above the *min* and *jen* there rises the king, distinguished as *i jen*, the One Man. ... The king ruled over all 'below Heaven,' *tien-hsia*." *The Ecumenic Age*, vol. 4 of *Order and History* (Baton Rouge, LA: Louisiana State University Press, 1974), 289.

[24] Philip McShane, chapter one of *Searching for Cultural Foundations*, a volume of essays by McShane, Doran, Vertin, Lawrence, Crowe, in that order (Lanham, MD: University Press of America, 1984).

[25] See *ibid.*, 9–11.

INSIGHT CHAPTER 17 IN A GEOHISTORICAL ENGINEERING CONTEXT

We are imaging our Wey round that first sentence of Lonergan, so as to shift its meaning into the permanent freshness of Christ's allure. "Our analysis forces us to recognize the paradoxical category of the 'known unknown.'" Our analysis has been shabby and sketchy, but yet I hope that I have weaved round its distance from us and its absence from us to bring us—you and me, Step Han—to see that it is not a matter of force but of allure. I wish us to woof our recording the Known-Unknown that is Jesus round the warp of John: "Them at is recordit here hes been recordit at ye may believe at Jesus is the Christ, the Son o God, an, sae believin, may hae eternal life throu his name."[26] Here is not the place to enter into problems of John's warp, in its other sense, but I would note that the reach here is not for Faith, the Aye of Love, but for a seeing of that eye, Faith seeking understanding, or better, in the context of this little chapter's effort, Faith seeking to embrace Explanation, Self-Explanation and self-explanation: so that life for me and ye and aa weaves, woofs, warps, "fuses into a single explanation,"[27] Explanation. So we are allured to recognize, as pilgrims and eternally, the category of the known-unknown.

What section one of Lonergan's seventeenth chapter brings out densely is the solid opposition to that Mystery in the boned-in honed-in myths of the ordinary and the scholarly.

But now, Step Han my future dynasty seed-sower, tune with grace, Grace, to the divine patience and see how silly my last sentence-paragraph is: a solid scholarly slip, slip-sliding away in one of fifty ways to lose your lover.[28] Section one of Lonergan's seventeenth chapter brings out, has brought out so far, little. What is to bring it out is the "concrete historical process,"[29] sooner rather than later, if you and your weird companions suck-seed. The horrid pun bumps your reading, but it also points again to the bump in cultural history that demands a contemplative intussusception of what is meant by "The Genesis of Adequate Self-knowledge," not as talked about briefly and accurately in that chapter, but as to be talked about effectively by the slowly-built Tower of Care.

Here I return, as promised, to my incomplete musings on the eighth specialty in the previous chapter, where those musings held to the first two sections of the

---

[26] *John* 20:31 (*Lorimer*, 199).
[27] *Insight*, 610: ending that key paragraph, 60910.
[28] Perhaps a Paul Simon song comes to mind?
[29] *Insight*, 554.

five in the text.³⁰ I did not bring Jesus into the "concrete historical process" in any obtrusive fashion, as those last three sections—I shall call them A, B, and C for convenience—do, unless you are reading with refined care, perhaps nudged by these eighteen chapters of mine sloshing around in your neuromolecules.

There is talk in A of adverting to "basic options,"³¹ and the ideal basis is aired in a usual style on the next two pages. But A's final paragraph leaves no doubt about the need for organizations "that work systematically to undo the mischief brought about by alienation and ideology. Among such bodies should be the Christian Church."³² At the deepest level those organizations must meet "the necessity of dynamic images that partly are symbols and partly are signs."³³ Such images are named mysteries and

> if that is an ambiguous name, if to some it recalls Eleusis and Samothrace and to others the centuries in which the sayings and deeds of Jesus were the object of preaching and reverent contemplation, still that very ambiguity is extremely relevant to our topic.³⁴

Indeed, the ambiguity moves us to step away from organizations grounded in general categories of human history, to what are conveniently called special categories. The general categories illuminate the mischief, but their growing functional weave is needed to undo with some effectiveness that mischief. How do they weave concretely and parasitically on the special categories? : you might think of them as W_3 without the lower line of a Christian dynamic if you change the 3 of the top line to an unknown X.³⁵ That lower line poses the problem of a similar lower line in other poises of mystery. For each such group-poise, "the basic problem is to discover the dynamic images."³⁶ To "this problem . . . we shall return in attempting to analyze the structure of history,"³⁷ but this return Lonergan delays to chapter 20 of *Insight*, and provides skimpy leads.

---

³⁰ An astute reader may come to pause over the coincidence that my three sections of this chapter seem to echo fittingly the final three of chapter 14 of *Method in Theology*. The fitting is indeed worth a pause.

³¹ *Method in Theology*, 359, 7 lines from the end of the page.

³² *Ibid.*, 361: again, 7 lines up.

³³ *Insight*, 571, line 1.

³⁴ *Ibid.*, lines 10–13.

³⁵ There is the task here of thinking to and through the 26ᵗʰ place of page 691 of *Insight*, Chapter 19: "In the 26ᵗʰ place, God is personal."

³⁶ *Insight*, 585.

³⁷ *Ibid*.

Insight Chapter 17 in a Geohistorical Engineering Context

Analyzing the structure of history, the "concrete historical process," is a special categorial task, meshed of course with general categorial labours. As I will note in the next chapter, the special work *de facto* has a general fallout. Might that fallout feed back through general categories into other special poises, thus subtly refining principles of "universal dialogue"?

Section A notes that "the Christian principle conjoins the inner gift of God's love with its outer manifestation in Christ Jesus and in those that follow him. Such is the basis of Christian ecumenism."[38] But this little book has surely helped to show that the conjoining must be luminous and self-luminous beyond "the level of our day"[39] if mischief is to be effectively met. In that deep sense, Jesus is the Wey into and round the Tower of Able, and Grace refines the lower line in W_3. Finally, the Tower is a dynamic image and sign, and it stands firm in mystery. What is the firm stand? That is the question for the final section, "The Life," "The Truth of Interpretation." But what of other special groups and special categories? What of "modern man"[40] and "the focal point of his horror"?[41]

---

[38] *Method in Theology*, 360.
[39] *Ibid.*, 367.
[40] *Insight*, 572: the last paragraph of section 1.
[41] *Ibid.*

X ~ The Truth

Here I present you with the second section of chapter 17 of *The Allure of the Compelling Genius of History*.

2. The Trowth

"The real issue, then, is truth."[1] The real issue, indeed, is the truth about the truth, and the truth about the Trowth. The luminous truth about the truth is an issue of general categories and edges us into that strange domain that I label (truth)3. The luminously dark truth about the Trowth is an issue, a *Verbum*, a *verbum*, an inner word "as it crystallizes the hidden inner gift of love,"[2] in layers and mansions of enlightenment that are to emerge and continue to emerge in "the field of the concrete historical process"[3] as fruits of towering contemplative efforts in all religious traditions.

I have neatly sidetracked the first three sub-sections of this part of chapter 17 of *Insight*, and I can well weave past the fourth, "Truth and Expression," since its central meaning haunts[4] what I have to write to you now, Step Han, when I suggest that you read the 9 paragraphs of section 2.5, "The Appropriation of Truth" in tandem with the 21 paragraphs of B, "The Christian Church and its Contemporary Situation."

I would have you take these 30 paragraphs as seriously as the 30 pieces of Judas' silver, as the 30 years of Jesus' articulate life. "Since God can be counted on to bestow his grace, practical theology is concerned with the effective meaning

---

[1] *Ibid.*, the first sentence of section 2. [This is note 34 in the original text: I leave the notes here as they were in that text.]

[2] *Method in Theology*, 362.

[3] *Insight*, 554, line 3.

[4] The key issue is, Is the haunting all mine or are you beginning to be with me, to some decent self-creative extent in your material multiplicity of experience and imagination, sentiment and resolution. You might weave the problem into Marx's view of the haunting of economics or intellectually into the hauntology of Derrida, but the primary haunting must occur in your own yearning molecules. Think of the haunting yearning molecules of the leaping salmon—I am thinking of the amazing journeying up the rivers of British Columbia.

of Christ's message,"⁵ but I would have you think of that message in local and personal terms: how you address, how you are addressed.

It is no surprise that such thinking is helped by good fiction. Harry Haller is addressed by Hermine:

> All we who ask too much and have a dimension too many could not contrive to live at all if there were not another air to breathe outside the air of this world, if there were not eternity at the back of time; and this is the Kingdom of truth.⁶

Emma Bovary sits at table in front of her husband Charles, a "good man," and is addressed by a plate of meat displaying "all the bitterness of life."⁷ Common sense, in our times, objects to life.

The problem that brings those 30 paragraphs together is "the problem of identification"⁸ bracketed by the problems of learning and orientation.⁹ In an old copy of *Insight* that I was using at the turn of the millennium, I notice this scribbled around the first sentence of the section on "The Appropriation of Truth": "To appropriate a truth is to make it one's own."¹⁰ Scribbled above that sentence are: *"own" (Jn 17); "embrace" 417*. The Jn—The Gospel of John—reference needs no comment: it is the Trowth speaking of his own; the "embrace," now on page 442 of the new *Insight*, is an expression of the truth that is to define the ownership of the tower community. "Theoretical understanding, then, seeks to solve problems, to erect syntheses, to embrace the universe in a single view." Embrace and Grace merge in the fullness of that view, and the sad¹¹ sweep of B asks us to hover over that fullness, that functional fullness—"at their service, then, are the seven previous functional specialties."¹² Lonergan asks that we reach out in an omni-disciplinary fashion: "[S]uch integrated studies correspond to a profound exigence in the contemporary situation."¹³

---

⁵ *Method in Theology*, 361–62.

⁶ Hermann Hesse, *Steppenwolf* (London: Penguin Books, 1965), 178.

⁷ I discuss these texts from Flaubert's *Madame Bovary* on pages 74–75 of *Lonergan's Challenge to the University and the Economy*, http://www.philipmcshane.org/published-books.

⁸ *Insight*, 582.

⁹ Ibid., 582–84.

¹⁰ Ibid., 581.

¹¹ The sadness weaves round the present dire absence of "a fully conscious process of self-constitution." *Method in Theology*, 364.

¹² *Method in Theology*, 362.

¹³ Ibid., 367.

The Truth

We thus meet the word *situation* again:[14] but how now, Step Han, are you reading it?: are you, in truth, on the road to making your own the eight-layered situation rooms that is a "profound exigence" in your room now, in your class room, in class-actions of court-rooms, in the rooms of the Vatican State?

In a previous effort to nudge a reading of section 2.5 towards the beginning of a grip on identification I wrote:

> I could well tackle the invitation to read the section as Aquinas tackles a section of Aristotle, ending up with a text much longer than the original. Indeed, there is a book to be written on the topic. What to do? Throw out a few points.[15]

"Identification is performance."[16] How are you performing now? Are you reaching, in some exotic strange stable Wey, some larger sense of the truth, The Trowth?

> Once we have reached the truth, we are prone to find it unreal, to shift from the realm of the intelligible and the unconditioned back into the realm of sense, to turn away from truth and being and settle down like good animals in our palpable environment.[17]

The Trowth calls us to The Life, but common sense, in us and all around us, objects. Might we not rise Toweringly with the help of friends in a new Han dynasty, "finding ways to meet the needs both of Christians and of all mankind"[18]?

---

[14] The main discussion of its meaning is on pages 191 ff.

[15] I refer to section 3.3, "Identifications," of *Cantower* 3: the quotation is from page 12.

[16] *Insight*, 582.

[17] *Ibid.*

[18] *Method in Theology*, 367. The end of this second last section of the book. Might I nudge you towards another paralleling by adding the end words of the second last section of *Insight*, with its talk of extreme commonsense objecting?: "ruthless enough to summon to their aid the dark forces of passion and violence." *Insight*, 750. The book's final section is on Identification: "There remains the problem of identifying the solution that exists." *Ibid.* It is the Wey, the Trowth, the Life, as "a fully conscious process of self-constitution," *Method in Theology*, 364, a caterpillar in search of a butterfly.

Y ~ Stalking Jesus

Are we to stalk Jesus or is Jesus stalking us?

We finally arrive at the heart, the Heart, of our problem, the achievement of Lonergan in his hurried climb to interpret interpretation for us with the apex of that limited climb in the single paragraph that I call 60910, an apex cauled towards the absolutely supernatural.

I move away here from the third section of chapter seventeen of *The Allure of the Compelling Genius of History*, so that we together might have a final fresh shot at shaking discontinuously forward all the present conventions of interpretation in Lonergan studies that cripple our discipleship. Our? I include my own failures in the mess; but I do have a decent lean-forward heuristic.

I can think of many possible starts,[1] none of them probable.[2] In the decades since 1960, when I wrote "The Contemporary Thomism of Bernard Lonergan," I have pitched forth a plethora of starts. My most important start of 2019, *The Future: Core Precepts in Supramolecular Method and Nanochemistry*, has as centerpiece my most recent offered starting point, the core of what is called the *Duffy Exercise*. And why not end here with a very relevant pair of such exercises?

I recall now quite vividly doing a pen and paper index of the first edition of *Method in Theology*. It was a hurried thing of December 1971: John Todd in London expected me, working in Oxford, to bring the thingy to him by December 23rd, which I did. The high point for me was moving through the Galley pages 286–87.

---

[1] I would have you think about my thinking in terms of the challenge of what I call "the Menu exercise," going through the invitation of Thomas in questions 6–17 of the *prima secundae* in the interval between getting a menu and handing it back, contentedly with an order. But here we face the challenge of inventing a menu, a challenge mentioned in note 15 of Essay A, p. 5, and returned to spasmodically in other essays. The needed deliberation is a future task split over the forward functional specialties, backed by the full meshing of conversations of the matrix C_{ij}, where i and j range from one to nine.

[2] I write loosely. The full context of my talking is the elusive world of *Randomness, Statistics and Emergence* and its lift of the work of Markov and Fisher: see chapter 11, "Probability Schedules of Emergence of Schemes." Skimpy possibilities are on the fringe. My high-level probability aggregates are the geohistorical seeding of the Assembly exercise being conducted by James Duffy in the 2020 volumes of *Journal of Macrodynamic Analysis*.

INTERPRETATION FROM A TO Z

I had been watching how Lonergan answered the problems we had discussed in Toronto in the summer of 1966: how to get *Insight* into this low-level work. And, behold, there was the core of his answer: a referencing of *Insight*, concluding with his hilarious paragraph saying that now you can rewrite the first part of *Method*!

"One can go on"[3] and up up up to "a resolute and effective intervention in this historical process"[4] beyond a steady Jay-walking misreading of Lonergan's *Opera*. I am here, alas, not thinking of the few generations that initially 'followed' Lonergan: they seem lost in invincible ignorance. I am thinking of fresh faces, perhaps of the generation of *Times*' Woman of the Year 2019, Greta Thunberg? Are you perhaps one who can go on to tell that generation, even tell them of your own dismal failure? A goodly start, to which I add the nudges of two books for the *Assembly* from two authors of earlier generations of Lonergan disciples who saw the pointing of Lonergan regarding the genetic poise of 60910: Fred Crowe and Bill Zanardi.[5] I am myself quite willing to join in with groups who are up for such *Duffy Exercising*. I think of the context of the present superficial grip that most of us have on the general and special categories, and offer the challenge [1] of Bill's general venture, *Rescuing Ethics from Philosophers*; [2] of Fred's theological venture, *Theology of the Christian Word: A Study in History*. Both authors would claim that they did a shabby job but still hopefully seed a fresh bent. I delight in quoting Bill's beginning and Fred's ending as giving the mood to either shot in the Ark. Bill starts his ticket to the self-show thus: "In *Steppenwolf* Herman Hesse describes theatre tickets advertising shows that are 'For Madmen Only.' The title of this work already suggests a degree of madness." Fred's ending expresses his own mad bent that he wished to share.

> When you have a mountain to move, and only a spade and wheelbarrow to work with, you can either sit on your hands or you can put a spade to earth and move the first sod. Some day, if others have the same idea, the mountain will be moved—and restructured. Some day too, I hope, theology will be restructured according to a method that operates on the

---

[3] *Method in Theology*, 287[269], but now I seek, with your help, a meaning of that push from Lonergan enlarged towards the integral spirituality that he searched for over a lifetime. The push I associate with the title *The Interior Lighthouse*. See note 17, p. 5.

[4] *CWL* 18, *Phenomenology and Logic*, 306.

[5] The pointing of this book and the previous one, *The Future: Core Precepts of Supermolecular Method and Nanochemistry*, is towards a genetics of the heuristics of a genetic perspective on engineering the future. It is up to you to detect whether Crowe or Zanardi is reaching in the right direction. Indeed, there is here the possibility of you joining with them in a *Duffy Exercise*!

level of our times; this book is meant to be a spadeful of earth in the moving of a mountain.[6]

What, you may ask, is this mountain? Think of it as the mountain of genetic systematics that is to give a global control of progress. Both authors push us towards the goal, but Zanardi is more explicit, especially about the turn to engineering progress. His page 78 says it all in neat coolness. But what am I to do here, in this short final nudge? I have been commenting throughout this book on Zanardi's key pointing regarding genetic systematic—GS in his abbreviations—"the routine practice of GS is an unconventional and distant goal."[7] Both authors seek to persuade in different ways, opening up empirical zones crying out for the new context. But does the cry reach you effectively, this "summons to decisiveness at a rather critical moment in the historical process?"[8]

My own effort to reach you effectively is the invitation to the minimalism of *Assembly*. I would have you at least putting yourself in the context of section 5 of *Method in Theology*'s tenth chapter with regard to the few pointers I have given about the two books. Muse over the possibility and probability of either book leading us forward. But what we need in a fulsome effort is participation in the serious effort to get into the three objectifications that are required by the last lines of that section 5. So, we are back at the problem raised in Essay I. Yes, conveniently "I." What might I, can I, do about this climb into a better future?

Zanardi, writing in a manner that holds to the restrictions of *Insight* regarding theology but adding the lift of functional collaboration, does not seem to fit into the poise of the title, no more than does Lonergan's *Insight*. But in both cases the restriction is strategic. The strategy does not seem to be successful. And this swings us into larger topics of, e.g., the character and effectiveness of Christian Philosophy.[9]

But larger than that is the fullness of what I suggest you think of, and muse about: global religious stalking. The title of the fourth of my five articles in *Divyadaan* 2019 gives a lead, especially kept in fullest context of the volume. The

---

[6] *Theology of the Christian Word*, 149.
[7] *Rescuing Ethics from Philosopher*, Austin, Forty Acres Press, 78.
[8] *CWL* 18, *Phenomenology and Logic*, 300.
[9] Recall Essay W, note 4, p. 151. Add the concluding reflections on "Developing Characters of Craving" that ends (121–25) the fifth of my essays in, *Divyadaan: Journal of Philosophy and Education*, vol. 30, no. 1 (2019). Indeed, the entire volume represents a Christian take on a philosophical convergence of theologies.

volume is titled "Religious Faith Seeding the Positive Anthropocene Age"; that fourth article has as title, "Converging Religions to Being InTo Love with Jesus EtC." I must leave you to reach towards the various twists of meaning involved, to which I add my twisting here on the words, *stalk, stalky*, and *stalking*. The word *stalk* is meant here in both its basic meanings. My Webster dictionary gives a meaning for *stalky* as "having or consisting mainly of stalks." The word *stalking* has its usual meaning and yes, to go back to my starting question, our lives as Christians with Jesus is a matter of mutual stalking in a shockingly intimate sense.[10] But I would have you think of stalking in the peculiar sense of initiating the growth dynamics of a plant: bringing the seed to adequate stalk status so that the plant is poised as "A Potential Totality" that opens it to an effective departure from the negative Anthropocene age.[11] Within the present Christian tradition there is some feeble sense of that dynamic, but it is altogether feebler if not non-existent in most of the world religions. There is a general ethos or poise of remaining self-preservingly stalky, of, for example, in clinging to initial scriptural meanings.[12] A full heuristic "characterization" of the genetic poise is to challenge that effectively. But to speak of that further is to move beyond the talk and stalk of it with which my fifth *Divyadaan* article concludes: "Developing Characters of Craving."[13] That move beyond is for you to initiate, as you "put spade to earth and move the first sod."[14] But do I not rise here to a fresh reading of the first sod-poem, with which

---

[10] The context is the topic of note 21 in Essay Q, p. 124. Add the pointers of note 14 of Essay R, p. 128.

[11] The effective departure is described popularly in my Helsinki paper of June 2019, "Structuring the Reach for the Future," (available as *Æcornomics 5* at: http://www.philipmcshane.org/ecornomics). Its beginning is given in Essay D. A simple nudge to envisaging the shift is the staircase diagram on the first page of that essay. There is a massive present need to lean forward into the tasks of the upper half of the stairs.

[12] This is a massively complex issue (see p. 5: note 14 of Essay A), raised mostly in this book by reference to the work of N.T. Wright (see note 24 of Essay N and its context, p. 105); also note 5 of Essay O, p. 101. The complexity relates to the problem of the chasm and the meeting of that problem in the discovery of quite new ways of embedding system—character-wise—into the varieties of cultural neurodynamics that are part of human history. See note 9 of Essay L, p. 90.

[13] The context added in these previous notes should give you a fresh reading of the piece on developing such characters mention in note 9 above: I am trying to give a series of jolts towards effective fantasy.

[14] *Theology of the Christian Word*, 149.

I began the long journey of my *Cantowers*, a journey which some of you are challenged to parallel? So, I end with that mayday poem of 2002[15] : m'aider, m'aider!

> Sun, flowers, Sonflowered,
> Speak to us of growth,
> Seed cauled, cribbed,
> Kabod yet confined,
> Crossed with dark earth,
> Light-refined.
> Rill open-ends a trill
> Annotaste of Throat.

---

[15] The poem occurs at the beginning of *Cantower* 2, dated May 1st, 2002. The *Cantower* is titled "Sunflowers Speak to Us of Growing." **I end these eleven (pp. 8, 62, 70, 74, 87, 92, 118, 140, 141, 150, 169) boldfaced notes**, providentially, in a note to my "mayday poem of 2002," my SOS, my *m'aider m'aider* appeal that has grown, yes, grown, through sixty years. Recall my humor about the first appeal, singing along with Robin Gibb, "I started a Joke" (*Æcornomics 6*). Might I think of you now, answering an appeal of Jesus to thee in Thy Attire, thy entire, thy intire, "tireless" (*Essay in Fundamental Sociology*, 43)? Might we sing together, in this Y-end that might be a beginning of the positive Anthropocene, "We started a Yoke"? The yoke of an upward concave growing, so that we hear Him speak of the yoke that is, indeed, light. "To the angel of the church in Thyatira write: the Son of God, who has eyes like a flame of fire, and His feet are like burnished bronze, says this: I know your deeds, and your love and faith and service and perseverance, and that your deeds of late are greater than at first." (*Revelations*, 2:18–20). Might your deeds of late be greater than last month's deeds of mind-climbing? But we cannot end in vagueness of perseverance or resolution. Yes, read now freshly the beginning of the appeal of the long paragraph to which this note is attached, an appeal for "global religious stalking." But you must find your own monthly concave poise of that stalking. Might you begin 'Thy In-tire' by meeting the first "In"-word of *Insight* freshly, taking Lonergan's and Descartes' advice about little puzzlings seriously, and this time not skip the Archimedean puzzle? Perhaps take the advice as it is spread through my *Cantowers* 27–31, paralleling those first strange 5 chapters of *Insight*. But please do not reject these first 5 chapters of the future's Book of Common Prayer.

Z ~ *THE FUTURE* AS LIFE STILE: FROM MILD MESS TO WILD BLISS

How am I to end effectively my fifty years of appealing to students of Lonergan to rise to the Caucasian, to listen inwardly to his midlife question, "Do you know His Kingdom?"[1] I have tried all sorts of twists and turns, in my climb to understand his unique project, to bring others of his students to share that global climb to gracefully and effectively engineer the genesis of The Kingdom. Strangely, I find myself brooding irreverently on parallels with Father Alfred Delp, as I read his mediations on the Kingdom. "The kingdom of God is grace, which is why we pray for it; but the grace so often stands at the door and knocks without finding anyone to open it."[2] Hitler hanged him; I have been merely hung out to dry. Or asked why I disturb the peace of business as usual, what I call *the mild mess*. Opposed to it I identify a sort of graceful Dionysian leaping. "Life knows nothing more injurious than creeping paralysis. A paralyzed life is utterly impoverished whether it realizes its condition or whether it becomes so accustomed to paralysis that it thinks it normal."[3]

If you have even drifted along here you will know that I think of Grace in capital terms, somehow[4] prayed with not for, knocking now Pentecostally in a crisis of climate and culture. The knock, expressed by Lonergan, "at a rather critical moment in the historical process,"[5] is for "a resolute and effective intervention in this historical process."[6] That intervention is to become—an effective genetic effort over centuries—a wild bliss,

> an eternal fire of optimism and energy, dismayed at naught, rebuked by none, tireless, determined, deliberate; with deepest thought and unbounded spontaneity charity ever strives, struggles, labours, exhorts,

---

[1] The question is posed in the final page of Lonergan's magnificent 1934 *Essay on Fundamental Sociology*. The Quotation at note 7 is part of his answer.

[2] *The Prison Meditations of Father Delp*, with an Introduction by Thomas Merton, Herder and Herder, New York, 1963, 128.

[3] *Ibid.*, 168.

[4] That *somehow* points to the challenge of this millennium, to reach for the lift of Lonergan's treatment of the Divine Missions (*CWL* 12. *The Triune God: Systematics*, part 6) to an explanatory level, where "explanation" takes on the new meaning of the W-enzyme integral poise that I intimated at the conclusion of Essay J.

[5] *CWL* 18, *Phenomenology and Logic*, 300.

[6] *Ibid.*, 306.

implores, prays for the betterment of the unit of action that is man, for the effective rule of sweetness and light, for the fuller manifestation of what charity loves, Wisdom Divine, the Word made Flesh.[7]

In my title here I point to my odd book, *The Future: Core Precepts in Supramolecular Method and Nanochemistry*.[8] These essays are a context for its wild blissful reading and implementation, a context which fulfills the promise of its second last footnote, which I repeat strategically below, thinking of the 'stare at you' of the present book,[9] to add nudges towards a dazzling spooky inwardness of intersubjectivity, haloed by self-explanation, thus leaping to engineer that "each mortal thing does one thing and the same"[10] in the radiance of the Symphonic Jesus. And "I say more"[11] and more than Hopkins. But perhaps already my nudgings have lifted you a little, Supermolecule, to J-wrap your way through Hopkins' sonnet.

Might you eventually lead an increasing population of others in this millennium to J-wrap their way round *The Future: Core Precepts in Supramolecular Method and Nanochemistry*? I think of it as a decent back-up to what I call "the future book of common prayer,"[12] *Insight*, and so I am led cheerily to quote, in its

---

[7] *Essay in Fundamental Sociology*, end part.

[8] Axial Publishing, 2019.

[9] And I repeat it, thinking of Heraclitus! [page references here are to *The Future*] "My stare at you is incomplete, and the final note of *The Future* will put that incompleteness in context. But here I think of the short-term context, the context of my brief introduction (above, p. 28) of Aristotle and Drucker as pointing to the stairs inadequately, (R, I, H and D_{oc} S C) and my pointing inadequately there to the bridge between them (D_i, H): a context for the *Duffy Exercise* that is to dance round the third chapter of this book. The short-term fuller context to my "Openers of the positive Anthropocene" in the book is your picking up on my nudgings given in the repeated mention of problems associated with the words *intersubjectivity* (xiv, xvi, 8, 9, 34–5, 40, 54–5, 80, 92, 96, 103) and *spooky* (3, 8, 13, 17, 66, 116) and the 6 repetitions (xiv, 8, 34, 54, 80, 103) of Lonergan's 1954 challenge regarding the future of theology. You find now, perhaps, that you did not climb in each occurrence to a fresh meaning of the word or the challenge? Such a climbing in reading belongs to the positive Anthropocene. But we need to climb towards that climbing: try climbing over the stile named by my repetitions, my petitions, Lonergan's petition. I return to your aid in "On the Stile of a Crucial Experiment," *Divyadaan: Journal of Philosophy and Education*, vol. 31 (2020). That is to be followed by the aide-mémoire, *The Future as Life Stile: From Mild Mess to Wild Bliss*."

[10] Fifth line of Gerald Manley Hopkins' *As Kingfishers Catch Fire*.

[11] *Ibid.*, ninth line.

[12] This is the central message of my set of five articles in *Divyadaan: Journal of Philosophy and Education* vol. 30, no. 1, (2019). The volume sublates Whitson's *The Coming*

regard, Merton's comment at the beginning of *The Prison Meditations of Father Delp*. "Those who are used to the normal run of spiritual books will have to adjust themselves, here, to a new and perhaps disturbing outlook"[13]

> As kingfishers catch fire, dragonflies draw flame;
>   As tumbled over rim in roundy wells
>   Stones ring; like each tucked string tells, each hung bells
> Bow swung finds tongue to fling out broad its name;
> Each mortal thing does one thing and the same:
>   Deals out that being indoors each one dwells;
>   Selves—goes itself; *myself* it speaks and spells,
> Crying *What I do is me: for that I came.*
>
> I say more: the just man justices;
>   Keeps grace: that keeps all his goings graces;
> Acts in God's eye what in God's eye he is—
>   Christ—for Christ plays in ten thousand places,
> Lovely in limbs, and lovely in eyes not his
>   To the Father through the features of men's faces.[14]

Convergence of World Religions, and it is titled "Religious Faith Seeding the Positive Anthropocene." Have I mentioned it often enough in the book to get you to e-mail Nashik, India for a copy!? : banzeloat@gmail.com.

[13] *Op. cit.* note 2 above: vii.
[14] Gerard Manley Hopkins, *As Kingfishers Catch Fire*.

EPILOGUE: THE FALLEN FLOWER

> I thought I saw the fallen flower
> Returning to its branch
> Only to find it was a butterfly[1]

The artist and the teacher, no doubt, will endeavor to reconstitute the sights and the sounds, the feelings and the sentiments, that help us recapture the past; but such recapture is educative; it makes ascent to the universal viewpoint possible; it prepares us for an understanding, an appreciation, an execution, of scientific interpretation; but in itself it is not science.[2]

I turn here, but do not return to, the marriage of the two pages of *Insight*, 498 and 604, that occurred in Essay M. I would wish to turn you to them, in them, meshing the two tops of those pages with Lonergan's plea "one has not only to read *Insight* but discover oneself in oneself."[3] My Guernica of 26 letters repeats that plea with some artistry of weaving oddities together: "but in itself it is not science."[4] I would be pleased if some few people reading these fragments were, yes, "bewildered and dismayed"[5] but yet gracefully disturbed into hope, a long term hope for the Fallen Flower, the bombed-out theology of these past millennia. We have a battered stalk of the Sonflower in a toxic garden of weeds, and the challenge is to let Grace loose in our molecules in order, in *nomos*, to stalk the Son.

But my cute metaphors are not science, and certainly not science in the full glory of its integral engineering psychic development. We are poised in the prolonged tension of escaping the molasses, the mole asses, of the truncated stage of the negative Anthropocene. "Psychic development is so much more extensive and intricate in man than in other animals: it is involved in a more prolonged

---

[1] "*Rakka eda ni / Kaeru to mireba / Kocho Kana*." The *haiku* is quoted from L. van der Post, *A Portrait of Japan*, (photographs by Bert Glinn), William Morrow and Co, New York, 1968, 107.

[2] *Insight*, 604, lines 34–39.

[3] *Method in Theology*, 260[244].

[4] *Insight* 604, line 39. Might one ask, then, "In what might it be a science?" to which one answers by dropping the question mark and pondering over the degree of contextualizing of what might establish a mature scientific 'surround'? Thus we might arrive at the context of the leap written of in this Epilogue.

[5] *Ibid.*, 604.

tension, and it is open to more acute and diversified crises."⁶ Sadly, this is not true: there is little tension in theology, unless one thinks of crazies that mesh the madness of Phil McShane with that of Greta Thunberg. The prolonged tension is with us in seething seed, but only in disturbed and disturbing psyches.

Perhaps the larger symbol of disturbance is the settled idiocy of present economics, but that is not my topic.⁷ My topic is you; my hoped-in topic is a small Poisson statistic of caring younger people in various areas of non-tense zones of tepid but sometimes brilliant interest. "The capital of injustice hangs like a pall over every brilliant thing."⁸ The brilliant thing of Lonergan studies "culminates in the dull mind and sluggish body of the enslaved people and the decayed culture."⁹

But these statements are not more than edgings and etchings of science.

I think now back to statements of Lonergan as we walked in Dublin's streets in the Eastertime of 1961, statements about science and eschatology. The statements were in an altogether different world from the statements about the Christian Church and about Eschatology that were being inflicted on me at the time in the trivialities of a first year of theology.¹⁰ Have things changed in such beginners' courses in religion in sixty years? I do not think so. But I do not wish here to enter into the subtle sophistications of initial meanings that carpet bomb the Dresdens of our classrooms, except to claim that the sophistications are not science. Indeed, I leap to an extreme and astonishing claim, lurking in my alphabet ramble and in other such alphabet soups of mine, that *Insight* and *Method in Theology* are not science.

Let me bring you back to my life in the late 1950s and early 1960s, perhaps symbolized by the oddities of those first conversations with Lonergan about the

---

⁶ *Ibid.*, 498.

⁷ My recent treatment of the crisis of economics, however, is helpful in the present context: "Finding an Effective Economist: A Central Theological Problem," *Divyadaan: Journal of Philosophy and Education*, vol. 30 no.1 (2019), 97–128. The article moves towards the topic "Developing Characters of Craving." Such characters are to be characters of integral global care, increasingly sophisticated in the heuristics of policy, planning and executive reflection regarding the detailed topology of up-coming situations.

⁸ Lonergan, *Essay in Fundamental Sociology*, 43.

⁹ *Ibid.*

¹⁰ It was a huge cultural shock to move from lecturing graduate mathematics and physics to listening to trivialities titled solemnly *De Ecclesia* and *De Novissimis*. A point I repeat in the text shortly, a point worth repeating: is it not still the reality of religious education? Put that in your Assembly and smoke it! *:*)

Epilogue: The Fallen Flower

"potential totality."[11] I was far from the present point then but oh la la was it not obvious? I moved from such activities as giving graduate lectures in differential equations and special relativity, 1959–60, to the next year's trivial pursuits in theology. The second, third and fourth years of theology had integral classes: all students of those years sat in the same classes in a democracy of minding. There was no such democracy in my previous year of teaching. I have written before about successful hinting of things to come to my honors first year mathematical physics class, but the ethos of the class was that even the second year stuff in the areas I touched on was quite beyond them.[12] Indeed, the morrow's reach in the class was beyond them. What of those graduate classes? My students were already baffled by the day's presentations: what new oddities of differentiation or of space-time paradoxes would they be asked to sniff around in the next 60 minutes? Such a world is deeply foreign to students of religion.

For decades I have paralleled *Insight* with a book that was standard reading for me in 1955–56: Georg Joos, *Theoretical Physics*. My last paralleling was quite detailed: I presented two pages 722 in one of my 60th anniversary articles of the publications of *Insight*, "*Insight* and the Interior Lighthouse."[13] Indeed, best be "in your face" now and show the Joos page again here, on page 181.

This "in our face" is important in relation to the leap mentioned, a page seen now quite differently by me, and by some few of you, trailing behind me with some enthusiasm. In the *Divyadaan* article I presented also the full page 722 of *Insight*, a powerful page central to the meaning of the book, and I remarked on the five occurrences of the root, *repent*, on the page. Now I see that page, and the occurrences of *repent*, as a brilliant flawed anticipation of a scientific engineering with a clear and effective dominance of scientific writing and symbolization.

Imagine, e.g., J-wrapping being quite explicit on page 722 and indeed, varying in the five occurrences of the stem-word *repent*, thus pointing to its particular scientific context in the theoretically-expressed sentence. Imagine the entire presentation of the book being dominated by an adequate symbolism that left no doubt about the context of the text being massively and relevantly remote. Does

---

[11] *Insight*, 591. Five lines from the end of four shocking pages inviting a climb to such a contextualizing perspective, the informed lack pointed to in note 4 above.

[12] You might usefully think of parallels such as those suggested by *Method in Theology*, 287, lines 18–23[269, lines 8–12]. Think what you would make of the scientific rewrite of the first half of *Method in Theology*!

[13] *Divyadaan: Journal of Philosophy and Education*, vol. 28, no. 2 (2017) devoted to the celebration of the 60th anniversary of *Insight*.

this effort not pain your neurochemistry and batter your culturally-blocked superego?[14]

But now let me, let us, return to the leap I mentioned, a complex well of leaping in January 2020: to my luminous claim "that *Insight* and *Method in Theology* are not science." The concomitant shift in full heuristic luminosity is a massive personal transformation: it is mine, not yours. It is yours to share through you graceful climb. The foregoing ramble round page 722 of *Insight* is a little help toward sensing the massive ontic and phyletic existential gap.[15]

Further hints may help, hints perhaps about the Axial Period and its relation to the shift from the late stages of the negative truncated Anthropocene to the positive Anthropocene. I am reminded here of Eric Voegelin criticism of Jasper's perspective on Axiality, which led him to a larger intermediate span.

> In noting the parallel falsifications of history in the Sumerian King List and Hegel's *Philosophy of History*, Voegelin is led to query: "And what is modern about modern mind, one ay ask, if Hegel, Comte, or Marx, in order to create an image of history that will support their ideological imperialism, still use the same techniques of distorting the reality of history as their Sumerian predecessors?"[16] In a later context he remarks: "A 'modern age' in which the thinkers who ought to be philosophers prefer the role of imperial entrepreneurs will have to go through many convulsions before it has got rid of itself, together with the arrogance of its revolt, and found its way back to the dialogue of mankind with its humility."[17]

I am quoting there something I wrote 35 years ago, but it did not nudge me then to the present leapings. Nor did my recent invention of the distinctions of two phases of a negative Anthropocene and the challenge of moving to the positive Anthropocene. The fermenting, I must suppose, was increasingly present as I battled round this alphabet soup on Interpretation. I had jotted perhaps three

---

[14] See Humus 2: "*Vis Cogitativa*: Contemporary Defective Patterns of Anticipation" (available at: http://www.philipmcshane.org/humus). The issue is massive fixity of the axial patterning, named *superego*, of multimillionmolecular aggregates between the ears.

[15] You need hardly be reminded of the challenge of the final two chapters of *Phenomenology and Logic* : still, this could be the effective one. "When you have your back to the wall it is time to turn and run": (a little Irish idiocy can help too!).

[16] Eric Voegelin, *The Ecumenic Age*, Louisiana State University Press, 1974, 68: see also pages 7, 27–8, 173.

[17] *Ibid.*, 192. The full quotation is from page 10 of my essay, "Middle Kingdom: Middle Man (T'ien-hsia: I jen)," in *Searching for Cultural Foundations*, edited by Philip McShane, University Press of America, 1980.

Epilogue: The Fallen Flower

quarters of the present volume when I turned to muse and scribble on this ending of the effort, and I would note that my decision, after the leaping, was not to face a revision of what I wrote already. My hope was and is that the leaping I name in this Epilogue would come as a shock to you, even if way lesser than the shock to me. So, I face, when I finish this, the task remains of finishing essays H, O, Q, and S, but do not wish to lift that finishing into my present context.[18]

I must note however, that there is another context that haunted my project and that, paradoxically perhaps, was nudging me along in brooding over the problem of an effective science of engineering humanity. That context was being present at a local Filipino Church where my wife presides, a Church of Christian exuberance. What, I would puzzle, has any of present theology, or Lonergan studies, to do with this community? Indeed, it may well have been their Advent and Christmas services that looped my molecules into the leapings.

Whatever the source of the shock, it still remains a shock for me to now think of *Insight* as, perhaps, pre-science, and *Method in Theology* as a sort of *Scientific American* post-science tied to that pre-science. Should I enlarge on that here? I do not think so.[19] I would hope that especially my elderly colleagues would be annoyed at the idea lurking in my claimed leaping, become articulate about my claim, confront me and it, and eventually think their way through the story from Aristotle through Aquinas in the context of the history of the Christian Church's shabby effectiveness,[20] go through some convulsions,[21] and finally, to quote

---

[18] One feature of the more sophisticated perspective is that mentioned in the conclusion of note 7 above. It harks back to note 15 of Essay A, p. 5, and other hints through this book and *The Future: Core Precepts in Supramolecular Method and Nanochemistry*. It is part of the "leap beyond" mentioned in the next note. It is part of a massive sublation of Lonergan's unsatisfactory handling of the forward specialties in *Method in Theology*. I and we are back again at his puzzling and his pacing of the summer of 1966.

[19] I add now a final footnote here to this Epilogue, pointing to the emergence of an Appendix in the book that I had not intended, an Appendix which does have a shot at giving, with some slim hope of effectiveness, some pointers regarding the non-science that prevails in our time regarding **deliberation**. Will my little appended ramble help some, help you, to a shocking new reading of Lonergan's remarks (*Insight*, 559, lines 14–25) about appreciating effectively "all that is lacking"? It eventually will globally help our story-spelling forwards in a glorious luminous darkness. See note 21 on page 186 for a simple analogical nudge.

[20] The thinking has to leap beyond Lonergan's struggle of 1959 with that problem in "System and History." *CWL* 23, *Early Works on Theological Method* 2, 231–349.

[21] The convulsions are to be around that compact piece of the letter Lonergan wrote to Crowe in 1945 (See, e.g. 203–4 below). It helps to place the convulsing, at least in

Voegelin again, they would find the way forward and thus find "the way back to the dialogue of mankind with its humility."

> There the butterfly flew
> away over the bright water,
> and the boy flew after it,
> hovering brightly and easily,
> flew happily through the blue
> space. The sun shone on his wings.
> He flew after the yellow
> and flew over the lake and over
> the high mountain, where God
> stood on a cloud and sang.[22]

---

fantasy, in the context of the challenge of J-wrapping. It helps, as I keep freshly repeating, to carry that convulsing into the final two chapters of *Phenomenology and Logic*, challenges to put the so-low body and the body-politic luminously into The Field's flow. It helps to take serious note that I was mistaken in chapter 4 of *Process: Introducing Themselves to Young (Christian) Minders* (available at: http://www.philipmcshane.org/website-books) to parallel Mendeleev's discovery of the periodic table with Lonergan's discovery of the periodic cycling of functional collaboration. The parallel with the lift of chemistry through Lavoisier and Mendeleev is with a revised version of my little lift, in *The Road to Religious Reality*, of Lonergan's puzzling, in *Insight* 763–64, about the meaning of the Body of finitude.

[22] Herman Hesse, *Wandering*, New York, 1972, 89.

722 ATOMS, MOLECULES AND SPECTRA [CHAP.

terms whose index sum is 4, e.g. $v_1 c_3$, $v_2 c_2$, $v_3 c_1$. The equations, solved for c_n, are

$$c_n = \frac{\sum_p v_p c_{n-p}}{E - \frac{(k + 2\pi n/a)^2}{\mu}} \quad \ldots \ldots (86)$$

As long as the denominator does not vanish, all of the c_n, with the exception of c_0, may be allowed to approach zero as v_n does. This means that the proper functions and proper values of the electrons in the weak, periodic field differ but slightly from those in the absence of forces. However, it must be noted that the k_m now form a discrete, yet very dense, set. The situation is different, however, if the denominator vanishes; then the c_n can no longer be small. Thus for $k = -\pi/a$ we have

$$c_1 = \frac{\sum_p v_p c_{1-p}}{E - \frac{\pi^2}{a^2 \mu}}, \quad \ldots \ldots (87)$$

where, according to (81), $E = \pi^2/a^2\mu$.

The same denominator is obtained for c_0. In order to investigate the character of the result at these places we approach $-\pi/a$ from neighbouring points by trying to determine c_0 and c_1 for $k = (-\pi/a) + \delta$, the corresponding proper value being $E = (\pi^2/a^2\mu) + \epsilon$.

Neglecting all coefficients shown above to be small, we get the following equations for c_0 and c_1:

$$\left.\begin{array}{l} c_0 \left(\epsilon + \dfrac{2\pi\delta}{a\mu} \right) = v_{-1} c_1, \\ c_1 \left(\epsilon - \dfrac{2\pi\delta}{a\mu} \right) = v_1 c_0. \end{array}\right\} \quad \ldots \ldots (88)$$

These linear, homogeneous equations can be satisfied only by the vanishing of the determinant. This leads to an equation for ϵ:

$$\epsilon = \pm \sqrt{v_{-1} v_1 + \frac{4\pi^2 \delta^2}{a^2 \mu^2}},$$

or, because $v_{-1} = \bar{v}_1$,

$$\epsilon = \pm \sqrt{|v_1|^2 + \frac{4\pi^2 \delta^2}{a^2 \mu^2}}. \quad \ldots \ldots (89)$$

In the limit, with $\delta = 0$,

$$\epsilon = \pm |v_1|. \quad \ldots \ldots (90)$$

METHOD GOING MAINSTREET: DELIBERATED BACKFIRING

> The problems of interpretation bring to light the notion of a potential universal viewpoint that moves over different levels and sequences of expression.[1]

I have made present to you, above, the final sentence of Lonergan's wild leap into "General Theological Categories."[2] I still remember vividly my first reading of that patterned wild leap as I read through the galley proofs of *Method in Theology* in December of 1971. I had been on the watch for his solution to the problem of 1966's summer: the problem of getting *Insight* into the ballpark. This section 11.6 of the book was and is a major part of his solution. I claim that it did not work, and perhaps I can get you to begin to think seriously and differently and effectively—**deliberately** backfiring even[3]—about the strange sequences of events that wind round the faulty following of Lonergan.[4] Was he not writing plainly enough? Could any decent follower, for instance, miss the point of the third last paragraph of his leaping in this section? Let us try reading it again, here

---

[1] *Method in Theology*, 288[269].

[2] "Making present" is a tricky heuristic. It haunts the title and the topic of my Preface to *Searching for Cultural Foundations*, "Distant Probabilities of Persons Presently Going Home Together in Transcendental Process."

[3] First, I would have you take notice of the boldfacing. Boldfacing has been used previously by me over the last decade to challenge the reader towards the shock of interior realism, but to that I wish to add here the central shock of this essay: that **deliberation** as data, as a topic, is presently in pre-science. Next, there is the topic of backfiring, one I have introduced more recently. See, e.g., page 102 of *Futurology Express*, Axial Publishing, 2006, where I talk of backfiring in the context of the work of Richard Branson and Arianne Huffington. See also, in the *Question and Answer* series (available at: http://www.philipmcshane.org/questions-and-answers), *Question 32*, "Restructuring Conferences towards Effective Collaboration"; *Question 52*, "Focus on Concrete Results"; *Question 53*, "McShane's Low Class Functional Research: What about You?" There are also the leads in *Fusion 9*, "Functional Marketeers in Economics."

[4] I refrain from detailing that faultiness here: I am concerned with a deep faultiness that even escaped me up to my effort to write the Epilogue. The present effort was undertaken then with a view of somehow inviting others to begin to identify the massive faultiness: it seemed best eventually to include it in the book. The *somehow* search led me to weave the challenge round the end of this text, in the series of 21 footnotes beginning at note 83.

and now. Recall that, in the previous paragraph, he jumps from his initial terms to lead you galloping through a sort of table of contents of most of *Insight* and of some of the beginning of *Method in Theology*. Then this:

> Such differentiation vastly enriches the initial nest of terms and relations. From such a broadened basis one can go on to a developed account of the human good, values, beliefs, to the carriers, elements, functions, realms, and stages of meaning, to the question of God, of religious experience, its expressions, its dialectic development.[5]

Does this "bring to light" something of our axial problem, our truncated negative Anthropocene?[6] Hardly: "we are not there yet."[7] Yet I hope you can get to some positive comeabout[8] as we wander on together in this little essay. And I wish now to assure you that the essay is a swing towards the popular. It is a C_9 essay in the technical sense.[9] That is, something reaching out, with relevant obscurities, on the plane of commonsense meanings.

But let us go back to the first sentence's problem of 'bringing to light'. Now, even perhaps after this page with me, my quotation at the top can be deliberately sniffed as bringing to light the problem of deliberately bringing a problem to light:

---

[5] *Method in Theology*, 287[269].

[6] Bringing properly to light the negative Anthropocene is the task of the climb into the positive Anthropocene. The final notes in this essay weave round the task of generating ontic and phyletic neurodynamic suspicions of the beginning of that task.

[7] Here I introduce one of two slogans that I repeat in this essay: hint hint. The other is introduced in note 10. "We are not there yet" begins a powerful page-long paragraph of *CWL* 21, *For a New Political Economy*: pages 20–21.

[8] I invite here a pause over, in, inwards, in that key page 537 of *Insight*, with its quiet line 29, "So it comes about …." The full comeabout I write of is a task of much more than a millennium, but the minor task for you here is to find in your lonely W-enzyme some vibes tuned to what I write of compactly here.

[9] What that technical sense is, is a remote topic of a deeper "comeabout," involving layers of concrete techniques. One key and illustrative technique is presented in Essay J of the text here: it is key to the transition to a new core heuristic of humanity's poise. But there is a host of techniques of layered neurodynamics that are to emerge from the ingesting of that core, techniques e.g. of nuclear persuasive **deliberation**, of winning over and ginning forward axial humanity. Is this a "Heady Folly"? The name there is the title of the fifth chapter of *The Allure of the Compelling Genius of History* and weaves the story of Hedy Lamarr (see Richard Rhodes, *The Life and Breakthrough Inventions of Hedy Lamarr; the Most Beautiful woman in the World*, Thorndyke, 2011) round that of Lonergan, the inventor. But might you now take to fantasizing effectively about what the world of entertainment entertains and might entertain?

does it, does it not?¹⁰ Lonergan's sentence is a crazily dense expression which does not really invite you, unless you are very strange as a reader and pause—scrutinizing the self-scrutinizing self—to collect and recollect the relevant problems and thus begin to brood fantastically over "the problems of interpretation."¹¹ Heavens, I wonder at present about the success of this book to which this essay became a discontinuous tail, *Interpretation from A to Z*! Has the book, read thus far, brought to light, in some slim effective way, the problem of interpreting Christianity as an engineering of history? "We are not there yet."¹²

You meet me there, and indeed here, floating round different "levels and sequences of expression."¹³ Those different levels and sequences of expression are stumblingly tailored by me to bring you to "a fresh intellectual synthesis"¹⁴ that is body- and blood-filling and that aims at being "a statistically effective form for the next cycle of human action."¹⁵ Are you with me positively here, in this Appendix, nudged on by the recent lead-in book, *The Future: Core Precepts in Supramolecular Method and Nanochemistry* and by this one so far? This little essay is a short twisted commonsense appeal that ends asking you to exercise yourself about this little essay.¹⁶ Might I risk claiming that the appeal and the exercising are as

---

¹⁰ I come to my second slogan (see note 7 above). The question mark above points you, through that slogan, towards "scrutinizing the self-scrutinizing self," (*Method in Theology*, 167[158]), towards pausing over self in that puzzling pointing. Are you there yet? Might you need to focus freshly on the self-scrutinizing self that **deliberates**?

¹¹ The fantastic brooding has been the zone of attention in this book, but its effectiveness pirouettes round the previous book, *The Future: Core Precepts in Supramolecular Method and Nanochemistry*, which is my attempt to rescue *Method in Theology* from the contexts both of Lonergan's writing circumstances and of a readership he had left behind already in his late twenties.

¹² Recall note 7. I had thought of spreading pointers from that brilliant paragraph of *For a New Political Economy* throughout the notes here, but perhaps it is best just to suggest that it be reread regularly in the mood that I hope my final notes generate in you.

¹³ I quote the title of section 3.3 of *Insight* chapter 17 (592–95), but the full meaning of the first section of the chapter haunts the section and poltergeists round the 21 footnotes here that begin with number 83. A later culture of the positive Anthropocene is to sublate the nudges of Lonergan into an integral humanity in a quasi-explanatory global layering of the W-enzyme.

¹⁴ Lonergan, *Essay in Fundamental Sociology*, 20.

¹⁵ *Ibid.*

¹⁶ At note 4 I mentioned a footnote strategy whereby I presented the central problem that we face, beginning at note 83. That presentation climbs to the distant reach of note 103, then twirls towards your assembling, at your own level, the strange

obvious as the performances of the two Swedish ladies Greta Thunberg or Greta Gustafsson: the latter being mentioned because of the neat reference in my title to MGM, where Greta settled as Greta Garbo?[17]

How, you may muse, am I going to make this statistically effective appeal? Be amused or intrigued by the notion that I am going to start where Lonergan left off at the end of section 6 of *Method in Theology* chapter 11. He then faced into section 7, "Special Theological Categories," and started off with the model "developed in the middle ages."[18] I start here "by shifting to a new key,"[19] close to the concerns of Greta Thunberg and, indeed, in the opposite direction from Greta Garbo's famous line, "I want to be alone."[20]

I do not want to be alone, no more than Greta Thunberg does. I think of an odd disturbing parallel as I venture along with you. Greta travelled by train to the January 2020 gathering on Climate at Davos: billionaire business folk came on private jets, alone, rotting the climate's air. My parallel? I am interested in the climate's air and heirs, as Greta is, but the people flying round me as Lonergan's heirs apparent are in their private jitterbugging—jet-airbugging, jet-heirbugging Lonergan, Jaywalking Lonergan[21]—"singly following the bent of their genius"[22]

---

claims about our axial inadequacies. The *Assembly* is effective only if a decent number of those interested in Lonergan are willing to face that final terrible *nomos* challenge of Lonergan: the three objectifications that end section 5 of *Method in Theology*, chapter 10.

[17] I quote a google source: "Once Greta Garbo came to America, the only studio she ever worked at was M-G-M. She was never loaned out, she never went freelance, and she didn't divide her time between the movies and the stage like many other actors of that era. M-G-M was Garbo's studio, and she knew how to use what it offered to her advantage." I would have you make both my MGM and the MGM your studio, as we shall see. Recall note 9 above.

[18] *Method in Theology*, 288[270].

[19] *Ibid.*

[20] My interest is in leading you to seek a sense of what is weaved forward in the final chapter, "Nanochemistry" of *The Future: Core Precepts in Supramolecular Chemistry and Nanochemistry* (Amazon, 2019). The meaning there of *NANO* is "**N**ot **A**lone **N**ot **O**paque."

[21] In chapter J above, 75ff., I focus on the future technique of reading print and its referents within the luminosity of aggreformism, of having a grip on and being gripped by the cosmic heuristic meaning of " ; " in the expression $f(p_i\ ;\ c_j\ ;\ b_k\ ;\ z_l\ ;\ u_m\ ;\ r_n\ )$. It is the achievement invited by Lonergan on lines 22–30 of *Insight* 489. The issue I would have you focus on is the "to be invented" (line 23) and the inner dynamic in you of the **deliberation** required for that invention.

[22] Best quote more fully. "One may expect the diligent authors of highly specialized monographs to be somewhat bewildered and dismayed when they find that instead of

with such performances as the daily flow of academic.edu papers into our computers.[23]

But let us get the show further on the road by jumping to Lonergan's suggestion, "a fifth set of categories regards progress, decline, and redemption."[24] What is the significance, the rationale, of the jump, a calculatedly shocking jump? Oddly, I present it as a jump into the popular. Perhaps I can bring that significance to you by repeating the concluding two paragraphs of the Epilogue?

> I must note however, that there is another context that haunted my project and that, paradoxically perhaps, was nudging me along in brooding over the problem of an effective science of engineering humanity. That context was being present at a local Filipino Church where my wife presides, a Church of Christian exuberance. What, I would puzzle, has any of present theology, or Lonergan studies, to do with this community? Indeed, it may well have been their Advent and Christmas services that looped my molecules into the leapings.
>
> Whatever the source of the shock, it still remains a shock for me to now think of *Insight* as, perhaps, pre-science, and *Method in Theology* as a sort of *Scientific American* post-science tied to that pre-science. Should I enlarge on that here? I do not think so.[25] I would hope that especially my elderly colleagues would be annoyed at the idea lurking in my claimed leaping, become articulate about my claim, think their way through the story from

---

singly following the bent of their genius, their aptitudes, and their acquired skills, they are to collaborate in the light of common but abstruse principles." (*Insight*, 604). My learned Lonergan colleagues are neither bewildered nor dismayed. It is jitterbugging as usual in theology as it emerged in the 20th century.

[23] The flow, of course, needs sifting. Where is one going in a paper that compares views of grace in Paul, Augustine, and Lonergan? On the other hand this morning brings to my attention what you might think of as in the same muddled ballpark: Michael Buttrey's "Politicizing Religion: Cavanaugh, Lévinas, and Lonergan in Dialogue." The paper is on the right track, but not in the control of effective cyclic collaboration. I prefer to stay with Greta Thunberg and the emerging popular consciousness.

[24] *Method in Theology*, 291[272].

[25] I would have this book *Interpretation from A to Z* backfire the new culture for you as it did for me: a point made mainly in this Epilogue to the book. And I add here a simple supplementing of other nudges given in different parts of the book. Do you know something of Lavoisier's lifting of chemistry? Then some backfiring might occur in you by thinking of Lavoisier lighting a candle under a bell-jar. That lighting backfired into the fulsome shift of chemistry out of pre-science to science. Might you light a candle under the word ***deliberation***?

Aristotle through Aquinas in the context of the history of the Christian Church's shabby effectiveness,[26] go through some convulsions,[27] and finally, to quote Voegelin again, they would find the way forward and "find the way back to the dialogue of mankind with its humility."[28]

My shift there, at the end, is to another level of expression seemingly beyond the commonsense I promised, but that is not true.[29] You can make as much sense of Voegelin as the members of my reverend wife's church make of Jeremiah when she quotes the Old Testament. So, back we go to the significance and rationale for my jump.

---

[26] Our thinking has to leap beyond Lonergan's struggle of 1959 with that problem in "System and History." *CWL* 23, *Early Works on Theological Method* 2, 231–349.

[27] It helps to place it in the context of the convulsions of the challenge of J-wrapping. It helps, further, to carry that convulsing into the final two chapters of *Phenomenology and Logic*, challenges to put the so-low body and the body-politic luminously into The Field's flow. And it helps to take serious note that I might be thought mistaken in chapter 4 of *Process: Introducing Themselves to Young (Christian) Minders* (available at: http://www.philipmcshane.org/website-books) to parallel Mendeleev's discovery of the periodic table with Lonergan's discovery of the periodic cycling of functional collaboration. The parallel with the lift of chemistry through Lavoisier and Mendeleev is with a revised version of my little lift, in *The Road to Religious Reality*, of Lonergan's puzzling, in *Insight* 763–64, about the meaning of the Body of finitude. Finally, the convulsions are to be round that piece of Lonergan's letter to Crowe of 1954 quoted below on pages 203–4.

[28] Best give the full Voegelin context, with two quotations from *The Ecumenic Age*, 68, 192. In noting the parallel falsifications of history in the Sumerian King List and Hegel's *Philosophy of History*, Voegelin is led to query: "And what is modern about the modern mind, one may ask, if Hegel, Comte, or Marx, in order to create an image of history that will support their ideological imperialism, still use the same techniques of distorting the reality of history as their Sumerian predecessors?" (173). In a later context he remarks: "A 'modern age' in which the thinkers who ought to be philosophers prefer the role of imperial entrepreneurs will have to go through many convulsions before it has got rid of itself, together with the arrogance of its revolt, and found its way back to the dialogue of mankind with its humility." (192)

[29] This is a tricky point about meshing initial meanings by various enrichments, e.g., of cross-referencing authors who weave their writing round their own take on those initial meanings; or named achievements are weaved into the context. One can write of the importance of equations of Maxwell or Einstein. Such weaving belongs to the pretense of "academic disciplines. Clearly enough, these approaches do little to advance . . ." *(Method in Theology*, 3–4[8]). My strategy uses parallel devices but instead of pretense at science there is prescientific nudging.

Method Going Mainstreet: Deliberated Backfiring

As it happens today was a day of visioning in Sally's Filipino Church, and her role parallels mine in this. Furthermore, it can usefully be taken further as a parallel. My reverend wife has a sort of troubleshooting status in the United Church. This particular church needs to be carried through a tricky change: in these next few years the building comes down to be replaced by one which has social housing accommodation as a top structure. I like to think that I am trouble shooting in the *ecclesia* of Lonergan studies and its outreach patterns, even pointing us effectively towards accommodating social housing.[30]

Let's pick up on Lonergan as he starts forward from that hilarious paragraph about "one can go on." The sentence there tells us that "since the basic nest of terms and relations is a dynamic structure, there are various ways in which models of change can be worked out."[31] Do you see the catch in the can? Are we here wading into "the problem of general history, which is the real catch."?[32]

Our problem is that really really the basic nest of terms and relations is not dynamic, no more than the flow of general history is at present properly dynamic.[33] It is a nest that is quite reluctant to envisage any change that is not pretty—and, yes, in all senses—self-preservative. Sadly, for instance, you can read from the seventh paragraph of Lonergan's reflections on "The Christian Church and its Contemporary Situation,"[34] and muse that while "the Christian Church is a process of self-constitution, a *Selbstvollzug*,"[35] one can plainly doubt that it is "a process of self-constitution occurring within a worldwide human society."[36] General history carries the can and the Church—and religions in general—follow various cants. Lonergan studies is in that can and cant of self-constitution.

---

[30] The accommodating I have in mind is that which the run of 21 notes [83–103] points to, a massive and shocking re-settlement of the present population of theologians. Might you begin to fantasize about it effectively?

[31] *Method in Theology*, 287[269].

[32] *CWL* 10, *Topics in Education*, 236.

[33] This may seem a shocking claim, even after working through the text to which this is an appendix, even in the context of the rewrite of *Method in Theology* that is the previous book, *The Future: Core Precepts in Supramolecular Method and Nanochemistry*. It is part of the shock mentioned in the Epilogue: the discovery of the non-science of the present grip on transcendent precepts and their deliberative dynamic. My Appendix can only seed the character-forming of the shock absorption.

[34] Section 4 of the final chapter of *Method in Theology*, on "Communications."

[35] *Ibid*, 363[334].

[36] *Ibid*.

I leave Sally's problems to Sally in a peculiar way that still wishes them kept in our minding[37] as I invite you to think of our stale warped sincere little world of Lonergan studies. And I would note, relevantly, that, despite the loftly pointings of Lonergan's meaning in the first four sets of categories, realistically the Lonergan following is not much different than Sally's Philippine community when it comes to the Triune God and Their Cherishing of humanity.[38]

So, I come to my "shifting to a new key."[39] Lonergan ends that section 7 of the chapter on Foundations with the remark, "it is up to the theologian working in the fifth specialty to determine in detail what the general and special categories are."[40]

I have been struggling thus for half a century, and now my task is to go mainstream, mainstreet, C9. My task is like my wife's task in that local church: let's vision, let's look ahead, let's view the new building of our group, let's go ahead. Both Sally and I are nudging our groups "to turn their thoughts to the topic of method and, instead of waiting for the perfect method to be provided them, adopt the best available and, in using it, come to discern its shortcomings and remedy its defects."[41]

My task, then, is to envisage popularly, with you, policy, planning and, only incidentally, executive reflection. In the terms of the book *Method in Theology*, I am heading us, oddly, into the sixth and seventh functional specialties, "Doctrines" and "Systematics". But now notice an oddity: the previous quotation was from the end of the chapter in the book that deals with doctrines or policy. Note that oddity now, with a pause of a moment or a month, but let's skip it for the next hundred moments and get on with the doctrines that concern both Sally and me.

---

[37] The keeping is seeded by the mention of this piece of history's context, but the mention needs to become an ontic and phyletic keeper as we seed a tower heuristic that radiates through all such global situations in the massive continuity of implementation, something quite beyond present theological confinements. It might help to muse that we will have arrived at a decent scientific meaning of **deliberation** when we have a full statistically effective grip on the actual geohistorical success of deliberating, a reality of a mature positive Anthropocene.

[38] This is a massively tricky and discomforting topic. A context is my "Epilogue: Embracing Luminously and Toweringly the Symphony of Cauling" in *Seeding Global Collaboration*. The present context adds a focus on the positive Anthropocene's lift towards being effectively **deliberative** about and in the Eternal Reality of Infinite **Deliberation**.

[39] *Method in Theology*, 288[270].

[40] *Ibid.*, 291[273].

[41] *Ibid.*, 332[308].

They are? Back we go to the commonsense of *Method in Theology*, but with a twist. "Be attentive. Be intelligent. Be reasonable. Be inventive. Be responsible."[42] The twist is my addition of "Be inventive."[43] Is that a break with Lonergan?; or rather is it not a pedagogical device, since "being intelligent includes a grasp of hitherto unnoticed or unrealized possibilities"?[44]

Have I slipped away from the special categories, as I have slipped away from the heavy musings of the chapter on Doctrines in *Method in Theology*? By no means: I am simply beginning my appeal to the best in you, the "finest; it surpasses all else in power and value; it is to be let go all the way …. And what would be going all the way?"[45] Lonergan here writes of Aristotle; but what finest might his own commonsense ask of himself and us? The asking and the answering is a Graceful, weaving round a dark lightsome mesh of presences.[46]

> Charity is an eternal fire of optimism and of energy, dismayed at naught, rebuked by none, tireless, determined, deliberate; with deepest thought and unbounded spontaneity charity ever strives, struggles, labours, exhorts, implores, prays for the betterment of the unit of action of man, for the effective rule of sweetness and light, for a fuller manifestation of what charity loves, Wisdom Divine, the Word made Flesh.

"With deepest thought" : but "we are not there yet."[47]

There is a definite sense in which we are not yet in the world of Lonergan's chapter on Doctrines, certainly not with deepest thought.[48] To that, and its footnote flight, I return only suggestively later. In the meantime, in the very mean axial time, might I say that I give you notice that we are possessed of simple

---

[42] *Ibid.*, 53[52].

[43] My usual expression here is "be adventurous" but the shift here nudges us to think novelties, like Archimedes' Screw. Note 4 above on page 183 already pointed to the odd nudging of notes 83–103 to vibe up the W-enzymes to the limits of heuristic novelty.

[44] *Method in Theology*, 53[52].

[45] Lonergan, "Mission and the Spirit," *A Third Collection*, 27.

[46] Recall note 20, p. 124, which ends with a hint of the climb of humanity towards cherishing that "God is not an object" (*Method in Theology*, 342[316]). But more simply noted is the fact that the sixth section of *CWL* 12, *The Triune God: Systematics* needs lifting beyond scripture to an aesthetic Explanatoriness that leaves the God of Abraham and the philosophers and the theologian in the zone of sad astonishing memories. I go on here to quote from the conclusion of Lonergan's 1934 *Essay on Fundamental Sociology*.

[47] *CWL* 21, *For a New Political Economy*, 20. As I have already suggested: if you happen to have the book, pause over the page-long paragraph that follows these words.

[48] The depth in the deepest thought takes on the suspicion of startlingly integral meaning as we seek, in our shared reading, to find redemptively our molecularity.

doctrines,⁴⁹ not at all globally aglow, but they begin now to trouble our human warped molecules, our W-enzymes, in an emergent "unbounded spontaneity,"⁵⁰ genuine care, here and there, in the axial air, the axial heirs. 'I *give* you'—can you begin to *take* that notice?

To take that notice effectively is to be deliberatively inventive, in small zones of day care or Sally's Church care, but always minding—unmindfully yet—the church that is in normative identity with finitude.⁵¹ And to me, giving notice luminously to your twilight, there is added, with increasing effectiveness, Gaia's giving airy notice of approaching disasters: Gaia, thus, calling us to repentance.⁵² Read on there in that 722 footnotice given us by Lonergan as he typed gloriously of our destiny in the summer of 1953. Find now, seeding your Interior Lighthouse, a fresh doctrinal glimpse of ontic and phyletic stages in our living, glimpses way beyond narrow Church convenings.⁵³ "So repentance becomes sorrow. A relation between stages in one's living is transformed into a personal relation⁵⁴ to one

---

⁴⁹ The key word here is "possessed." Are we, Supermolecules, possessed in our W-enzymes, by that broad craving W (see *The Future: Core Precepts in Supramolecular Method and Nanochemistry*, 2) that, in its genetic fullness, is spiraling to constitute the *Eschaton*? "Theology possesses a twofold relevance" (*Insight*, 766, line 29). It does not. Later I invite you to stare at my Stare and Stair Diagram and sense the horrid present emptiness of those four forward steps of the cycle of engineering finitude and it's spiraling to the *Eschaton*.

⁵⁰ Recall the center of the quotation at note 46. Increasingly here *unbounded* may take on larger shades of meaning in your present reading, but the unbinding in history is a matter of a start that my 21 notes here—83 to 103—seek to inspire.

⁵¹ The deliberative inventiveness of post-axial times is to be massively flexible but blood-thirstily coherent in a Towering Futurology that, streetwise, "commands man's first allegiance" (*Insight*, 263) in a manner that is "too universal to be bribed, too impalpable to be forced, too effective to be ignored."(*ibid.*)

⁵² The context of a pause here is the powerful page 722 of *Insight* with it invitation to repent (lines 3, 10, 17, 22, 28, 32).

⁵³ The finding now is your present task of a minimal screwing up of your own neurodynamics in taking, with psychic or even aesthetic seriousness, my present outcry to heart to hurt. The full finding is a millennial business of "tireless, determined, deliberate" (see the text at note 46) growingly-luminous effective deliberation.

⁵⁴ Carry forward the puzzle of my phrase "to heart to hurt." The "next cycle of human action" needs a hearty effective acknowledgment of the hurt, "the evil that is concretized in the historical flow" (*Essay in Fundamental Sociology*, 43). There is to emerge proton-persuasive "heart to hurt" talking and walking that is rooted in **cross**ing into neurodynamic luminosity.

loved above all and in all."⁵⁵ Read on there further, in this doctrinal stand at the end of the thirteenth place of Lonergan's "Special Transcendent Knowledge," to vaguely sense the positive Anthropocene, the positive anthropo scene.

> Finally, good will is joyful. For it is the love of God above all and in all, and love is joy. Its repentance and sorrow regard the past. Its present sacrifices look to the future. It is one with the universe in being in love with God, and it shares it dynamic resilience and expectancy. As emergent probability, it ever rises above past achievement. As genetic process, it develops generic potentiality to its specific perfection. As dialectic, it overcomes evil both by meeting it with good and by using it to reinforce the good. But good will wills the order of the universe, and so it wills with that order's dynamic joy and zeal.⁵⁶

?Wills with that order? So, take note now: with the word *order* we seem here to slide into systematics. Seem? "we are not there yet."⁵⁷ And in that seeming slide we must begin to find our "way back to the dialogue of mankind with its humility."⁵⁸ But it is not a way back, but a fresh way forward. We do not slide into systematics but slope darkly up towards it, in its darkly deliberate "closed options."⁵⁹

What are the closed options to which it slopes, to which there is a *nomos* of aspiration?⁶⁰ The closed options are the refinements of the five transcendentals

---

⁵⁵ *Insight*, 722, lines 28–30.

⁵⁶ The concluding paragraph of *Insight* 722, and of "the thirteenth place" (*ibid.*, 720).

⁵⁷ I repeat the paragraph starter from *For a New Political Economy* page 20. It is not a lesson easily intussuscepted into our W-enzymes. Pausing, in context, over the twelve lines *Insight* 559, line 14–25 towards the slow genesis of this "critical awareness" (*ibid.*, line 20) of the stalk in our talk of the stalk of finitude's Sonflower.

⁵⁸ I am recalling the conclusion of Voegelin's poise quoted in note 28 (p. 188) above.

⁵⁹ The title of section 2 of *Method in Theology*'s chapter on Systematics. That closure is a massive openness, needing incarnation, "to transcendent mystery" (*ibid.*, 341[315]) and a parallel self-controlling "familiar" familial grip on present gross disorientations. "The importance of such a critical control will be evident to anyone familiar with the vast and arid wastes of theological controversy" (*ibid.*, 343[317] that is a fixture of present Lonergan studies.

⁶⁰ Drop the question mark. Might it not be helpful to pause here over the beginning of the first chapter, "Sow What", of *The Allure of the Compelling Genius of History*? "The emergence of humanity is the evolutionary achievement of sowing what among the cosmic molecules. The sown what infests the clustered molecular patterns behind and above your eyes, between your ears, lifting areas – named by humans like Brocca and Wernicke – towards patterned noise-making that in English is marked by "so what?"

that are haunted by the norm stated to commonsense in the *Essay in Fundamental Sociology*. We are Gracefully invited to be "tireless, determined, deliberate." We are Gracefully kindled to be "dismayed at naught," certainly not at being cauled to be "at the level of one's age,"[61] "at the level of one's times,"[62] a level which must look towards a massive genetic discontinuity in a **beyond** the times. The beyond is multi-faceted, asking us for a multi-faceted reach that must rumble and tumble out of the global community in volumes and vibes of shabby and, slowly, less shabby reachings. How might we push for a reach of the core of that tumbling? Here—helpfully I hope—I pause, **boldfaced**,[63] over the single word ***deliberate***, to invite you to think that the fulsome adequate pause—do be astonished but not "dismayed"[64]—over that word and its global referents, in a tumbleweed genetic rolling pause—or should I not say paws-on?—for this entire millennium.[65] It involves a messy slow climb in a genetics of effective deliberations about effective and ineffective deliberations about deliberations.[66]

I start our stair, stare, our commonsense ethos-climb into that last opaque sentence with two pointings, one to our inherited meaning of *deliberation*, one to a single cluster of a genius's deliberations.

---

[61] *Method in Theology* 350[323].

[62] *Ibid.*, 351[324].

[63] I have used boldfacing regularly to invite the reader to pause, shocked, over the ease with which the print, and so our entire encounter in and at your present, is "already out there now real" (*Insight*, 271). I am trying to get the reader to home in, inward, on the present print and putter and utter of the word ***deliberation***.

[64] The eleventh word of the quotation at note 46: that is the root context of the bent of hope and effectiveness that is our topic in this appendix.

[65] I am anticipating my final footnote 115. A slow ingesting of exercises round my 21 notes, 83 to 103, makes more plausible my appeal for a full paws-on effort of the entire Lonergan community, a focus on the final specialty that weaves effectively and redemptively into street meanings. The initial failure of effectiveness seeds a backfire effect towards a foundational community that increasingly lives beyond the level of the present axial times.

[66] I first came on the triplicity to which I point here when musing over St. Ignatius' suggestions about discernment in the conclusion of the first chapter of my book, *The Redress of Poise: The End of Lonergan's Work* (available at: http://www.philipmcshane.org/website-books). Discerning adequately Ignatius' meaning requires the interpretative context of the genetics written of in section 3.2, "The notion of a universal viewpoint," of *Insight*'s seventeenth chapter: or so shockingly compactly expressed in that single paragraph that carries us forward – would that it does in later millennia – from page 609 to 610. So we must arrive at an effective heuristic of the discernment of discernments of discernments.

Method Going Mainstreet: Deliberated Backfiring

The inherited meaning of *deliberation* can, up to now and for at least this coming decade, be characterized as having, at best, "a slight tincture" [67] of theoretical consciousness; a "slight dose of systematic meaning;"[68] at worse, its "consciousness is unmitigated by any tincture of systematic meaning."[69] This should strike so-called theoreticians of the mind as a daft claim:[70] and I must deliberatingly dodge debatable discussion here, a discussion which would involve the theoreticians slowly finding out just where they stand and think in the truncated stage of the negative Anthropocene, something that is to come into luminosity only in the forthcoming positive Anthropocene.[71]

So I skip on to the "unbounded spontaneity"[72] of the deliberations of the genius Archimedes in his engineering of The Screw for raising water. Obviously, adding the familiar diagram helps.

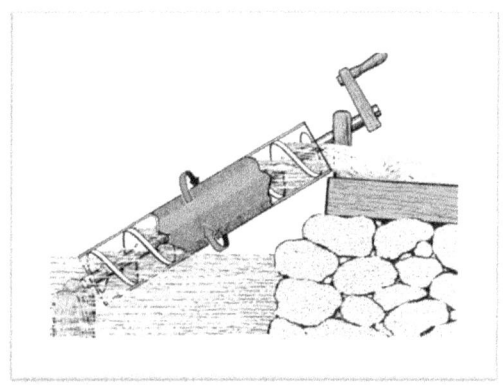

---

[67] *Method in Theology*, 278[261].

[68] *Ibid.*, 309[288].

[69] *Ibid.*, 329[306].

[70] Heavens, they can note abundant discussions; think of Aristotle, Cicero, Nemesius, Damascene, Aquinas, Lonergan, and clusters of thinkers around them in the West: not to speak of the Orientals. Still, perhaps when you arrive at the end of note 89 (p. 198) below you may be bent towards agreeing with me?

[71] A broad statement of a heuristic that needs the present fermenting of apparently small steps such as those referred to in notes 97 and 115 below. The positive Anthropocene is, in its maturing, to bring forth the Tower of Able of integral human characters that address effectively supposed plain meaning so that that meaning is dressed to thrill. Think now of later rewrites of the first two sections of the final chapter of *Method in Theology*. At present one can only fantasize about the massive sublation of linguistic meaning involved.

[72] Lonergan, *Essay in Fundamental Sociology*, 43. Might not the spontaneity's bounds, then, reach an aesthetics of systems of character that dance digestibly?

It would be daft to pause here to elaborate on just how the screw works, but do give the question a shot; indeed, entertainingly share it with friends or enemies. Nor can I enter into the background of that pause: the scatty semi-sequential flow of atomic consciousness that gets one from the receiving of a menu to the satisfied return of it to a waiter with such words as "I'll have murg malai tikka."[73] The daft Archimedean pause would be over a piece of the flow where there is no menu but, at best, a muddle of potential ingredients. At best? Think of TV shows, like *Chopped*,[74] or *Next in Fashion*,[75] where the ingredients are an imprecise aggregate, and the climb to *claritas* left to creative deliberation.[76] Move wider now, to the creative and effectively-successful deliberation about the assembly, completion, comparison, reduction, classification and selection of creative deliberators: on my mind is the moves towards picking, say, a winning Olympic Team. The *Chopped* champion or the successful designer of a dress is a lightweight parallel to Archimedes, but now think of the heavyweight "Olympic" work of "Greek councils,"[77] and those councils following in Rome, Lyons, Trent, wherever: deliberators about the *nomoi* of flexible circles of ranges of schemes of recurrence of geohistorical deliberations.

---

[73] I have repeatedly returned to this exercise in the book. It is a way of getting people into the task brilliantly presented by Thomas in "sixty three articles in a row" (*CWL* 1, *Grace and Freedom: Operative Grace in the Thought of St. Thomas Aquinas*, 94), a fifty-page exercise of the *prima secundae* qq. 6–17. The change of pace in this Appendix is to focus on ingredients when there is no menu: only a shabby feeding of global aggregate of W-enzyme's which is so powerful a busy sedative that few in the aggregate notice where, in or out of religiosity, it has "done not a little to make life unlivable" (*CWL* 10, *Topics in Education*, 232). Are we millennia away from the ethos in which "man is nature's priest, and nature is God's silent communication with man"? (*ibid.*, 225).

[74] An old TV show: there are now over 500 episodes. Four chefs compete against each other in a three-round contest using random ingredients provided to them, with the goal of making tasty presentable dishes.

[75] This is a *Netflix* show started in 2020, one that seems to me to lift the ballgame beyond the older *Project Runway*.

[76] I am referring here to Thomas's view of art: think of *claritas* as an addition to the unity-identity-wholeness of any thing or pseudo-thing. Think further of a pseudo-thing like the aggregate of systematic theologians—paralleled, now to the aggregate of fashion designers preparing for the runway walks. Is there not a nudge there to conceive the characters of systematic thinking in a glorious effective fullness? The problem all along here is to reach for the self-luminous intussusception of system as being a W-enzyme patterned neurodynamics with, e.g., a bloodstream base.

[77] "The Greek councils mark the beginning of a movement to employ systematic meaning in church doctrine." (*Method in Theology*, 307[286]).

Does your "think of the heavyweight" council work—**deliberation** work—not freshen your joining Lonergan's first-sentence concern in the chapter on Doctrines? "Our sixth functional specialty is concerned with doctrines:"[78] with policies, then, of progress, of champions of progress, of all those that stand with Jesus against "the capital of injustice that hangs like a pall over every brilliant thing, that makes men and nations groan over others' glory, that provokes anger and suicide and dire wars, that culminates in the dull mind and sluggish body of the enslaved people or the decayed culture."[79] Is the Christian community not thus nudged structurally into asking "what is cosmopolis?"[80] sensitized to the global fact that "it is in the first instance an X, what is to be known when one understands,"[81] engineeringly?[82]

LOL: thus "satire breaks in upon the busy day,"[83] the busy daze, the Daze-walking,[84] of Church councils, and freshens our reading of "the slight dose of systematic meaning found in the Greek councils."[85] And in the first and second Vatican councils. And in the audience of Lonergan's twelfth chapter of *Method in*

---

[78] *Ibid.*, 295[275].

[79] Lonergan, *Essay in Fundamental Sociology*, 43.

[80] *Insight*, 263.

[81] *Ibid.*

[82] See the article, *Æcornomics 17*: "Engineering as Dialectic" (available at: http://www.philipmcshane.org/ecornomics) which you can consider as pointing to a re-orientation of *Insight* 17 intimated by the change of the title from "Metaphysics as Dialectic."

[83] *Insight*, 649, line 1. So, I begin my 21 Go-on salute, my notes 83–103, with an appeal to your sense of humor. I recall now that quaint essay, *Æcornomics 6*: "I Started a Joke," where I sang along with Robin Gibb. Can I get you to sing along, neurodance along with me?

[84] Bright people gathered for these councils, but they were in that daze of defensive nominalist patching that shrouded their slight doses of coherence. My interest, my care, my inventiveness, are heartily on getting those interested in such gatherings to lean forward, even to box their interest for a decade or three, and gather to envisage doctrines that will over-pin the salvation of finitude in these next millennia. I am asking for the madness of the concluding sentence of the final footnote, note 115.

[85] *Method in Theology*, 309[288]. My venture in these essays is to invite a new courageous humility of luminous nescience. Might we sing along with Joni Mitchell? "I've looked at life from both sides now /From win and lose and still somehow /
   It's life's illusions I recall / I really don't know life at all."

Theology.[86] Yes, "fifthly, there is the emergence of systematic meaning"[87] but can you sniff forward in history to find "tenthly there is the exploration of interiority"[88]?

"If there is to be any general science, its data will have to be the data of consciousness. So there is effected the turn to interiority."[89] Here we must face a pause: might I call it an *Assembly* pause, paws on the table?[90] Lonergan, after that

---

[86] Realistically, there was and is no competent audience for the brilliant deliberately shrunken chapter. Nor do I expect such a standard-type audience in these next thirty years. We need an audience with an informed suspicion of the genetic *nomos* hidden in the mind of Lonergan as he struggled to finish the book. I have occasionally struggled to envisage that genetic *nomos*, e.g. pp. 110–113 of *The Everlasting Joy of Being Human*, a section on what I called then *Sequenomics*, which ends thus: "My final suggestion, however, regarding initial stabs at Sequenomics, is that people can take up the topic in a C_9 fashion by tackling, however amateurishly, the question of importing the functional structure into any area of human inquiry."

[87] *Ibid.*, 304[283]. I would have these three early notes, 83–5, in our 21 "shogun" salute stir you to think of my suggestion that our axial efforts skimp interiority, except for a few evolutionary sports. Such evolutionary sports may be thought of as emergent without a statistics of survival.

[88] *Ibid.*, 305[284]. Muse now that there is no exploration of interiority in the sense of its effective technical engineering. That is to require some decent maturing of and into the positive Anthropocene.

[89] *Ibid.*, 316[294]. My 21 Shogun, sho-going-on, salute is to a distant existential turn to interiority that is effective in engineering genuine human life. I think of that period of Japanese history when, not the Mikado but the Shogun led the country. The Shogunate was a military control from 1192 to 1867. The peaceful Shogunate of Cosmopolis is to come into power, perhaps in 2192. It is to carry us forward, even in "unbounded spontaneity," towards the *Eschaton*. 2192? I am musing over Lonergan's remark to me in 1977, when we were preparing for his first lectures on economics, "you know, Phil, this is going to take 150 years." We did not start then, or in the decades since. But we might get started by 2042, gasping for air.

[90] What is *Assembled* should be the product of competence: something that should be true of any science, but is not so at present. Lonergan writes of a geometer, who has "got the whole thing in his intellectual paws" (*CWL* 18, *Phenomenology and Logic*, 357), but the geometer of loneliness has to W-enzyme-reach scrutinizingly for the inner seed of glory's character in her or his veins. Here, methinks, it is helpful to add my odd comment in note 50 (p. 111) of *The Future*, on repeating Lonergan's 1954 view as a door-opening challenge. "My stare at you is incomplete, and the final note 51 will put that incompleteness in context. But here I think of the short-term context, the context of my brief introduction (above, p. 28) of Aristotle and Drucker as pointing to the stairs inadequately, (R, I, H and D_{oc} S C) and my pointing inadequately there to the bridge between them (D_i, F): a context for the *Duffy Exercise* that is to dance round the third

comment, does a run through great names from Descartes through Blondel, talking of a "shift to interiority."[91] Great?—there was a parallel little shift to semi-decent empirical science with Galileo. I recall now sailing, in the 1980s, into the Greek harbour of Pireas in the dawn light, musing over "The Greek Discovery of Mind"[92] and having an interior axial dawning that the Greeks did not discover mind: a few eccentrics there discovered mind. Did the existentialists discover mind, minding, **deliberation**? A puzzle of interpretation: come share my puzzle-poise.[93]

There are many directions that your sharing of my puzzle poise could take, and indeed, I hope, will take in the decades ahead. But I wish to conclude this very

---

chapter of this book. The short-term fuller context to my "Openers of the positive Anthropocene" in the book is your picking up on my nudgings given in the repeated mention of problems associated with the words *intersubjectivity* (xiv, xvi, 8, 9, 34–5, 40, 54–5, 80, 92, 96, 103) and *spooky* (3, 8, 13, 17, 66, 116) and the 6 repetitions (xiv, 8, 34, 54, 80, 103) of Lonergan's 1954 challenge regarding the future of theology. You find now, perhaps, that you did not climb in each occurrence to a fresh meaning of the word or the challenge? Such a climbing in reading belongs to the positive Anthropocene. But we need to climb towards that climbing: try climbing over the stile named by my repetitions, my petitions, Lonergan's petition. I return to your aid in "On the Stile of a Crucial Experiment," *Divyadaan: Journal of Philosophy and Education*, vol. 31 (2020). That is to be followed by the aide-mémoire, *The Future as Life Stile: From Mild Mess to Wild Bliss*."

[91] *Method in Theology*, 316[294]. Recall those three notes, 83–85 above.

[92] *Ibid.*, 90–93[87–90]. I think, oddly, not of Greeks but of Sikhs discovering mind in this century. I have long been interested in the followers of the magnificent Guru Nanak, and live in Vancouver with its population of 7% Sikhs. Might some of these bubble forward out of the sayings of Guru Nanak to find the within? Might there, sadly but possibly, be a better stats of that happening than the bubbling forward from the sayings of Guru Bernard?

[93] I would note here and now that I am edging you towards the "conversion leap" of my Epilogue: "we are not there yet," but, unwittingly and fixedly, in a muddled prescience of interiority. Part of my road there, useful to you in your pausing, was the massive decade-long effort of Pat Byrne in his *The Ethics of Discernment. Lonergan's Foundations for Ethics*, University of Toronto Press, 2016. Does this 500-page-long study rise to a science of deliberation? None of us has thus risen. Byrne's primary concern was the muddling along of our community on the issue of the meshing of feelings with the spirit's bent. He brings the reality of the meshing to our attention by venturing into personal experiences, literary instances, illustrations such as "*Jury Deliberation*" (*Ibid.*, 187: see also 191–2; 201–2). He even has a line on the menu challenge (244, line 16) that is my usual lead into Thomas's effort in the *prima secundae*, qq. 6–17. But, like the rest of us, Byrne does not rise to an explanatory science of **deliberation**. Check conveniently, and brood over, his fifty index references under *deliberate, deliberating, deliberation*.

open venture by bringing forward a doctrinal and systematic suggestion—such is a task of foundational puzzling—that would effectively lead to both global progress and to the rescuing, the fantastic sublation, of chapters 12 and 13 of *Method in Theology*. So, again I turn your musing towards Frederick Crowe's effort to rescue history in *Theology of the Christian Word. A Study of History*, a book I keep returning to since its first appearance.[94] As a context, however, I wish you to first take fresh time over what now seems to me to be, freshly, my key diagram, presented on the next page, of a luminous darkness in our "resolute and effective intervention in this historical process."[95]

---

[94] We are, of course, back in the context of Essay Z, asking you to revisit Crowe's *Theology of the Christian Word. A Study in History*. But now your perspective is, potentially, deeply changed. The previous note is the seeding of that potentiality, pointing to a fresh take on "all that is lacking." How far have you taken the pointing? The note is just a first nudge, a nudge that changes the potential flow of this Appendix in you if you cycle back after this first reading, edging to a new luminous nescience. My own struggle with Crowe's meaning should both comfort and encourage you. I weaved forward in the four decades since 1978 through *Cantower 41* and, later, the *Humus* essays, to begin to see, this year, the alliances of initial meanings that cripple our pilgrimage. The "brood over" demand of the end of the previous note is a start. That brooding can lead you back and forward. It leads you back, in a growing existential shock, to reading the names of the usual transcendentals as the names of unknowns, not then pointing to some heavy meanings shared by followers of Lonergan. See further note 115 on page 206 and note 117 on page 207.

[95] *CWL* 18, *Phenomenology and Logic*, 306. In so far as the brooding pointed to in the previous two notes becomes a W-enzyme reality, one now reads of intervention in history with a larger neurodynamics of humility and hope. The limited messings of 20th-century logic and existentialism shine forth as just that: boxed shadow-boxing quite short of the field, short of Cosmopolis.

My Stare Diagram

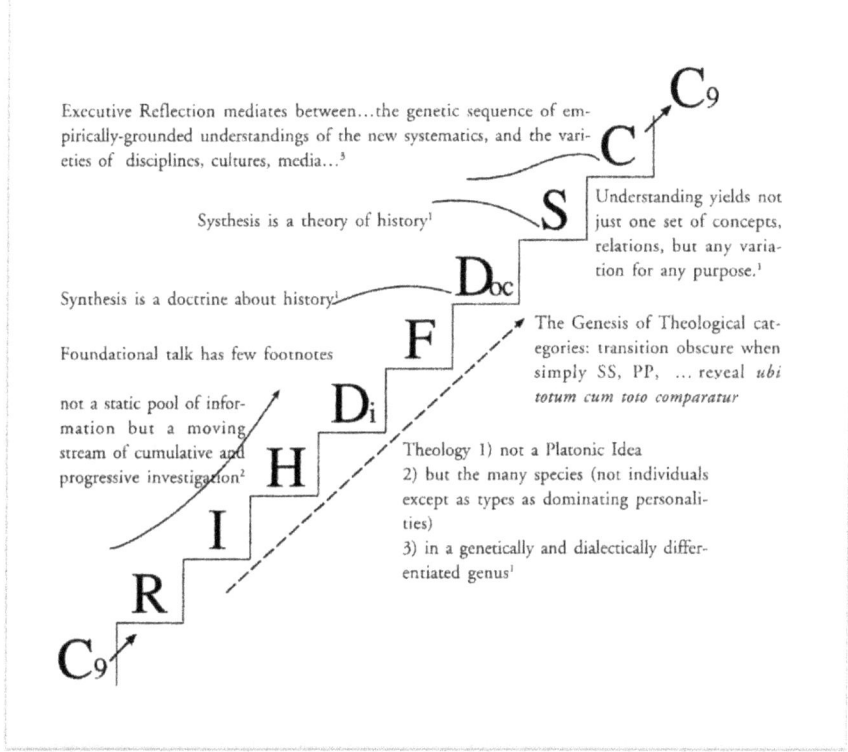

1. Bernard Lonergan, from unpublished notes of the early sixties available in the Toronto Lonergan center, Batch B, 8, 6, V.
2. Bernard Lonergan, "Christology Today: Methodological Reflections," *A Third Collection*, ed. Frederick E. Crowe, S.J. (Mahwah, NJ, Paulist Press, 1985), 82.
3. Philip McShane, "Systematics, Communications, Actual Contexts," *Lonergan Workshop*, vol. 6, ed. Frederick Lawrence (Chicago, CA: Scholars Press, 1986), 151.

You see its resemblance to the "screw up water" diagram of Archimedes? That seeing is a nudge to get you thinking about, yes, screwing up culture in every sense. It images the screwing up of culture that leaps to answer Lonergan's question in *Insight*: "what is cosmopolis?"[96] Indeed, that question comes at the end

---

[96] *Insight*, 263. The climb noted in the three previous notes gives an inner grip on the meaning of the unknown X that is Cosmopolis. That cultural climb's beginning is decades long, and must run parallel to a shabby rescue of Gaia as we gasp towards 2050. But the slow climb and the shabby rescue are to seed the new culture of psychic

of Lonergan's musing there about "Culture and Reversal", a section that ends with the introduction of the problem-name.

> What is necessary is a cosmopolis that is neither class nor state, that stands above all their claims, that cuts them down to size, that is founded on the native detachment and disinterestedness of every intelligence, that commands man's first allegiance, that implements itself primarily through that allegiance, that is too universal to be bribed, too impalpable to be forced, too effective to be ignored.[97]

My diagram gives a new twist to Lonergan's essential but slim answer to his own question: it diagrams the answer as a cyclic heuristics of climbing. I surround it with helpful quotes, two of which are nudges towards rescuing chapters 12 and 13 of *Method in Theology*. What was Lonergan hiddenly reaching for in the chapters "Doctrines" and "Systematics"? Think of the odd reaching expressed in the phrases that edge my stare diagram: "Synthesis is a doctrine of history"; "Synthesis is a theory of history". Synthesis was the problem that had him pacing before me in his room in the old Bayview Regis in the summer of 1966. There was no way that he could deliberate out—nor was I any help to him—an integral presentation of the screw-up that he had in mind. What to do when he finished his non-integral presentation of a foundational perspective? He **deliberately** aimed to be "as simple as possible for theologians of different allegiances to adapt my method to their uses."[98] There was nothing vague about his **deliberations** about the failure to push readers to the climb towards being themselves spooky doctrinal

---

mysteriousness that preoccupied Lonergan at the beginning of the seventeenth chapter of *Insight*.

[97] *Ibid*. What begins to be a psychic reality is the tuning to the slowness of the seeding of this necessary Cosmopolis. Will its stalk be a reality of this millennium? A condition of that emergence is talk of the stalk in the mood of that stalk and stalking.

[98] *Method in Theology* 332–3[309]. As simple as possible? I point towards the seeming simpler, but that simpler is only remotely possible in these decades. And the paradoxical time-span to the full effective 30-year heuristic named in my final note 115? Oh la la. I think now of my younger self of 40 years ago beginning the first chapter, "The Psychological Present of the Academic Community" (*Lonergan's Challenge to the University and the Economy*, 1980: a photocopy of Lonergan's own copy, with his markings, is available at: http://www.philipmcshane.org/published-books) thus: "If there is to be a massive shift in public minding and kindliness and discourse in the next century, there must be a proportionate shift in the mind of the academy and the arts at the end of this century, with consequent changes in operating schemes of recurrence from government to kindergarten." The "if" is valid, but we must seed a beginning of minding in the now of this millennium.

interpersonal syntheses.⁹⁹ "What on earth"¹⁰⁰ could that mean for theologians then or now or for a foreseeable future? "I have written a chapter on doctrines without subscribing to any but the doctrine about doctrines set forth in the first Vatican council. I have done so **deliberately**, and my purpose has been ecumenical."¹⁰¹ If you want to sniff the synthetic mind hiding behind that **deliberation**, read the extract, meshed now with the "Stare Diagram,"¹⁰² preceding it, a quotation taken from a letter Lonergan wrote to Fred Crowe in the summer of 1954, which of course will bring us back to Crowe and his rescue effort, his synthetic reaching. And now we join Crowe, staring at but not stairing up that piece of Lonergan's letter.

> The Method of Theology is coming into perspective. For the Trinity: Imago Dei in homine and proceed to the limit as in evaluating $[1 + 1/n]^{nx}$ as $\underline{n}$ approaches infinity. For the rest: ordo universi. From the viewpoint of theology, it is a manifold of unities developing in relation to one another and in relation to God, i.e., metaphysics as I conceive it but plus transcendent knowledge. From the viewpoint of religious experience, it is the same relations as lived in a development from elementary intersubjectivity (cf. Sullivan's basic concept of interpersonal relations) to

---

⁹⁹ Recall, recaul, note 90 (pp. 198–99) above, with its intimation of a later global spookiness.

¹⁰⁰ I am recalling Lonergan's appeal to a superior in 1935, when he wrote at the end of a ten-page letter, "what on earth is to be done?" I write here to and about theologians e.g. who write abundantly on conversions. The writing requires **deliberation**; the conversions involve **deliberation**. Generalized empirical method "does not treat of objects without taking into account the corresponding operations of the subject; it does not treat of the subject's operations without taking into account the corresponding objects." (*A Third Collection* [1985], 141). Being scientific about **deliberation** is doubly dodged by those conversion-talkers.

¹⁰¹ *Method in Theology*, 332[308–9]. My purpose is global. There is the reach to all religions of my five articles in *Divyadaan: Journal of Philosophy and Education*, vol. 30 no.1 (2019), with the apt title "Religious Faith Seeding the Positive Anthropocene." There is the doctrine, "When Teaching Children X, You Are Teaching Children Children" that spreads into education the poise of generalized empirical method mentioned in the previous note. Note, then, that the global move is a move into commonsense, a peculiar *haute vulgarization* that is to layer humanity's neuromolecules. Perhaps *haute vulgarization* will then need to backfire into theology?

¹⁰² The mature meshing gives a startling historical lift to the stairs and to the poises of *anamnesis* and *prolepsis* in them. So, W-enzyme-view the move up the stairs as a dark climbing through the negative Anthropocene into the present predawn of the positive Anthropocene.

intersubjectivity in Christ (cf. the endless Pauline [suv- or] sun-compounds) on the sensitive (external Church, sacraments, sacrifice, liturgy) and intellectual levels (faith, hope, charity). Religious experience: Theology : Dogma :: Potency : Form : Act.

This piece of the 1954 letter permanently puzzled Crowe and he shared the puzzlement and the letter with me in later years. I only recently came to what seemed a satisfactory poise in regard to that giant Lonergan flight of and from **Insight**,[103] but the question now for you, as you are nudged to "scrutinizing the self-scrutinizing self,"[104] is, what sense do you make of it? You might muse over it as a foundational flight at the end of his first year in Rome, still in the mood of *Insight*'s Cosmopolis search and the search there for a view of Christ's Body and Psyche that would possess theologians, and effectively ground his hopeful *nomos* of the end of *Insight* that "theology possesses . . ."[105]

While Crowe's grip on the letter never blossomed as my footnote leaps sniff, one finds the flawed mood in his "attempt to organize the history of reflection on the Christian word of God"[106] in a way that would lead "at some future date to a

---

[103] See the essay *LO and Behold 10*: "Assembling $[1 + 1/_n]^{nx}$" (available at: http://www.philipmcshane.org/LO-and-Behold). The venture to which I point in these 21 footnotes (83–103) lifts all that into a quite new context of science, but it does so, at present, only for me. I turn my pointing at this stage to appointing you as the Assembler of those 21 points.

[104] *Method in Theology*, 167[158]. As you face the "Assembly" and its leap to three objectifications I would ask that you lean into what "breaks in upon the busy day" (*Insight*, 649, line 1)—and daze—of present super-ego neuromolecular confinement: satire and humor, which "challenges the enclaves of bright chatter" of conferences, theses, lectures, publications. Pause over my repeated quotation and sniff the satire that lurks in the final four words of Lonergan's sentence, sentencing, of self-scrutiny: "it leads into the impasse of scrutinizing the self-scrutinizing self and into the oddity of the author who writes about himself writing: such authors are exceptional." Are you one of the odd exceptions? Then you will be at home in the three objectifications.

[105] *Insight*, 766, line 29. I am odd enough to write about myself and my astonishment at lifting this issue of possession to an implementable heuristic while I struggled through *Divyadaan: Journal of Philosophy and Education*, vol. 30 no.1 (2019). Now the heuristic is an altogether fuller grip of the future global nanochemistry. How might that fit or misfit in your second objectification?

[106] *Crowe*, 1. The heuristic we self-scrutinized round the previous note would increasingly reveal the flaws. Some of those flaws are, of course, akin to the flaws in Faraday's field theory in the face of Maxwell's leap. Should we go on about them? Of course: but in a later genetics of symbolic, layered, global engineering, a massive success beyond Crowe's "attempt to organize the history of reflection."

more systematic conception."[107] There is a reach for doctrines seeding system. The reach has the air, perhaps is the heir, of the half-way house that is Lonergan's effort of *Method in Theology* chapters 12 and 13.

Why do I say half-way house? Stare at my Stare Diagram with its arrows and the quote, "not a static pool of information but a moving stream of cumulative and progressive investigation."[108] Crowe's work needs the shift to what belongs, in essential propriety, to Doctrines and Systematics, but a shift that is to haunt all theological and pastoral and pedagogical efforts. "This is the shift that would discern in facts and moral actions what pertains to the salvation of mankind."[109] This is the shift that I wish you to discern as you stare, **deliberatively**, at my stare. There is the shift to engineering the salvation of mankind, so that, yes, yes,— His Heart, "his heart was going like mad and yes I said yes I will yes"[110]—"the earth and every common sight takes on the glory and the freshness of a dream."[111] So, for example, the fifth show of *Next in Fashion*, on "Underwear" can be weaved into *The Song of Songs* and climb to be J-wrapped, indeed Jesus-wrapped, in the

---

[107] *Ibid.* That very distant future date will see a W-enzyme meshing of reflection that is to make explanation a liturgy of life. Might we intussuscept freshly the half-page of words that conclude Lonergan's lecture on art in *CWL* 10, *Topics in Education*: p. 232? A self-scrutiny self-scrutinizingly "exploring the full freedom of our ways of feeling and perceiving." But now, as I end my 21 shogunotes, my musing over a new Han-dynasty (see the back cover to *The Allure of the Compelling Genius of History*), I wish you to think of the immediate future, the mood of my title, the pointing of my final footnote 119. Go there now, or in these next years, with that mood and the poise I wish in you.

[108] Lonergan, "Christology Today: Methodological Reflections," *A Third Collection*, 82. Think now, shogunwise, of a strange integral neurodynamics where pools of information are eddies of the lonely stream of pilgrimage.

[109] *Ibid.*, 83. And now might you fantasize reading the word *discern* in its distant glory of luminous molecular self-explaining spooky **deliberation**?

[110] The final words of Molly Bloom and the final words of James Joyce's *Ulysses*. But I am thinking of them now as self-luminous deliberative words of the move to the positive Anthropocene.

[111] *Insight*, 556. What we are 'heart going like mad' on about here is visioning the actual and heuristic climb, theology and us possessing and possessed of supportive symbolic neuro-heuristics denying that any of us is "an animal in a habitat"(*Insight*, 498, line 11) but, built seethingly for living radiantly, in "a universe of being in which it finds itself," (*ibid.*, line 22) each W-enzyme along with all finitude's W-enzymes, called and cauled: " . . . may they all be one . . ." (*Method in Theology*, 367[338]—Lonergan quoting there the prayer of Jesus—to eschatological intimacy).

Song's concluding singing, "My breasts are like Towers and in his eyes I have found true peace."[112]

I wish that singing and tingling on you and in you effectively by asking you—though you, perhaps, have no aspiration to be a functional dialectician—to come visit with me, with others, in that needed "measure of bluntness"[113] that Crowe wrote of in 1964, that emerged as a *nomos* of bluntness in *Method in Theology*, a cyclic crowning whirl of self-scrutinizing selves nakedly together.[114] "There is the final objectification of horizon when the results of the foregoing process . . . are assembled . . ." Let you assemble the foregoing Appendix-essay, position yourself in its regard and its implicit suggestions about these coming decades of Lonergan studies. But, but but, as the butt of the three objectifications that are the but and butt of section 5 of chapter 10 of *Method in Theology*, my positioning requires my battling and butting and buttling towards making the implicit explicit. So: here I stand, butler to Jesus.

> The project sketched in the 12th chapter of *Method in Theology* is beyond present competences. What is not beyond present competence, your competence, is the shift to an ontic and phyletic effect-bent scrutinizing of the **deliberation** that grounds doctrines. "The direction of this shift is correct in the sense that the fourth level of intentional consciousness, the level of **deliberation**"[115] has so far been Jay-walked and Day-walked by global humanity. We need a talented sub-community to wrap and 'rap' round the core and *cor* meaning of **deliberation**, "at a rather crucial moment in the historical process."[116] We need to wrap and rap around **deliberation** in the mood of Greta Thunberg rather than in that of

---

[112] *The Song of Songs* 8: 9–10. There is an elegant hint here about leaving behind the mess of conventions regarding the incarnation of "an infinite craving" ("Finality, Love, Marriage", *CWL* 4, *Collection*, 49). I add Lonergan's final words of that article: "perhaps I may hope that this labor will merit the scrutiny, the corrections, and the developments of others." *Ibid.*, 52.

[113] F. E. Crowe, "The Exigent Mind," *Spirit as Inquiry. Essays in Honor of Bernard Lonergan, S.J.*, 27.

[114] The *nomos* of bluntness is in the demand for the nakedness of the three objectifications that conclude section 5 of chapter 10 of *Method in Theology*, nudging into a larger cycle our foundational comrades.

[115] *Method in Theology*, 316[294]. Recall now, creatively and humbly, that the chain of transcendentals suffers from the principle of "the weakest link." Are the words of the five transcendentals, then, not pretty-well pointers to fuzzy initial meanings?

[116] *CWL* 18, *Phenomenology and Logic*, 300. In these concluding footnotes I am inviting you to a shocking suspicion about this moment, this millennium, this minder that is you, in history.

Method Going Mainstreet: Deliberated Backfiring

Bernard Lonergan. Such a strange street focus is to have, of course, a backfire effect [117] on the negative Anthropocene's commitment to truncated selfishness, but its main bent—and I am suggesting a jump in the bent of Lonergan studies as "unit action"[118]—is, so to speak, to "field"[119] the seeds of an aesthetic new global politics and economics in this millennium, starting in this decade with you.

---

[117] The full heuristics of the backfire effect is eventually to be meshed with that of the sublated "theology possesses" (*Insight*, 766, line 29). Indeed the gradual W_i diagramming of the tentative and growing heuristic is to be quite soon—if only I could move the Lonergan group—a countervailing pressure on all disciplines' heuristic symbolizations and their referents in present slum-living. A footnote is not the place to shoot for a fantasy of such a complexity of neurocontrols, but at least you staring creatively at the upper stairs of my stare diagram gives your molecular superego a kick in the assumptions. But more simply you can pause, like Archimedes' screw-jobbery, and try to do a screw-up job on the version of the transcendentals that make present to you staring, your stair, now:

Be inventively attentive, Be inventively intelligent, Be inventively reasonable, Be inventively adventurous, Be inventively responsible. Might the one simple word, *inventively*, J-wrapt, change history, gown and town?

[118] Lonergan, *Essay in Fundamental Sociology*, 45, line 29, but read now in the context of the Lonergan's concluding reflections of "a real and an ideal unity" in the last page of *Method in Theology*.

[119] See *CWL* 18, *Phenomenology and Logic*, index under *Field*. "The field is the universe, but my horizon defines my universe" (*Ibid.*, 199). The challenge of the jump? "They have to be people in whom the horizon is coincident with the field. If they are not, then all they can possibly do is increase the confusion and accelerate the doom." (*Ibid.*, 306). "We are in a situation where the people who can do the most harm are doing it and the people who could do the most good are not." (*Ibid.*, 307). We are in a situation that invites us all, yes all Lonergan folk, to turn for at least a decade or three into forward specialists, mainly indeed into the last specialty and its C_9 pusher-ons: 2020–2050 needs to be the age of a discontinuity in the genesis of street-smarts. Recall my 21 nudges that ended with note 103 above. Recall note 108 and Lonergan's appeal of ¾ of a century ago. I have much on my mind regarding the way forward, not least the problem of sublating The Interior Castle, adequately identified, into The Interior Lighthouse. But I refrain from writing further: this seems a decent end-book of a long run. It seems best to venture on a new Website series, Questing 2020, question and tentative answers about these next decades. That series will, I hope, be only the tip of the iceberg of *Assembly* that cools the business of present Lonergan studies in favor of a search for fertile seeds of a global effectiveness. But also I think of the Questing series as just a public tip of the bergamot of private communications with me about that task: a herbing of hearts towards Dionysian drives in these next generations. My e-mail is pmcshane@shaw.ca

Philip McShane, Professor Emeritus at Mount St Vincent University, Halifax, Canada, musician, mathematician, philosopher, theologian, and economist, has been fermenting forward towards a solution to the steady decay of global culture and its abused Gaia for over sixty years. In particular he has worked on the shambles of conventional economics since 1968, in collaboration with the Canadian thinker Bernard Lonergan (1904–84). He edited Lonergan's early economic writings in *For a New Political Economy*, University of Toronto Press, 1999. But he shared Lonergan's broader interest in finding a full effective cultural basis of a future humanity. He expresses what he considers the effective road forward in his "little red book," *The Future: Core Precepts in Supramolecular Method and Nanochemistry*, sublating Lonergan's final effort to do so in his *Method in Theology* of 1972 (*Collected Works*, 2018). The present book enlarges on that reach. The effective road involves a clear operative distinction between the negative Anthropocene, in which we presently live shabbily and destructively, and the positive Anthropocene towards which we must work slowly and democratically, against empires of idiocy, by tuning into the chemistry of our desires.

OTHER WORKS BY THE AUTHOR

The Future: Core Precepts in Supramolecular Method and Nanochemistry
The Allure of the Compelling Genius of History
Futurology Express
The Everlasting Joy of Being Human
Economics for Everyone
Profit: The Stupid View of President Donald Trump
Piketty's Plight and the Global Future
The Road to Religious Reality
Bernard Lonergan: His Life and Leading Ideas
(with Pierrot Lambert)
A Brief History of Tongue

WORKS EDITED BY THE AUTHOR

Phenomenology and Logic: The Boston College Lectures on Mathematical Logic and Existentialism
For a New Political Economy
Searching for Cultural Foundations

WEBSITE SERIES
(http://www.philipmcshane.org/website-series)
LO and Behold
Æcornomics
Interpretation
Disputing Quests
Questions and Answers
Prehumous
Cantowers

www.ingramcontent.com/pod-product-compliance
Lightning Source LLC
Chambersburg PA
CBHW070638050426
42451CB00008B/214